19th-Century Patterns for the Modern Body

19th-Century Patterns for the Modern Body

A Step-by-Step Guide

M. Elaine MacKay

BLOOMSBURY VISUAL ARTS
LONDON • NEW YORK • OXFORD • NEW DELHI • SYDNEY

BLOOMSBURY VISUAL ARTS

Bloomsbury Publishing Plc, 50 Bedford Square, London, WC1B 3DP, UK
Bloomsbury Publishing Inc, 1359 Broadway, New York, NY 10018, USA
Bloomsbury Publishing Ireland, 29 Earlsfort Terrace, Dublin 2, D02 AY28, Ireland

BLOOMSBURY, BLOOMSBURY VISUAL ARTS and the Diana logo are
trademarks of Bloomsbury Publishing Plc

First published in Great Britain 2026

Copyright © M. Elaine MacKay, 2026

M. Elaine MacKay has asserted her right under the Copyright,
Designs and Patents Act, 1988, to be identified as Author of this work.

For legal purposes the Acknowledgements on p. xi constitute an
extension of this copyright page.

Cover design by Holly Capper
Cover image: Unknown Maker, Day Dress, 1869, silk, satin, boning, and cotton.
Agnes Etherington Art Centre, Queen's University, Kingston. Gift of the estate of
Wilhelmina Gordon, 1968 (C68-590.14a-e). Photo: Bernard Clark.

Frontispiece: Half-scale mock-up of an 1870s dress using the instructions in
Chapter 8 created by M. Elaine MacKay. Opposite: Side front view of the primary dress
mock-up in Chapter 6, created by M. Elaine MacKay.

All rights reserved. No part of this publication may be: i) reproduced or transmitted in any form, electronic or mechanical, including photocopying, recording or by means of any information storage or retrieval system without prior permission in writing from the publishers; or ii) used or reproduced in any way for the training, development or operation of artificial intelligence (AI) technologies, including generative AI technologies. The rights holders expressly reserve this publication from the text and data mining exception as per Article 4(3) of the Digital Single Market Directive (EU) 2019/790.

Bloomsbury Publishing Plc does not have any control over, or responsibility for,
any third-party websites referred to or in this book. All internet addresses given in
this book were correct at the time of going to press. The author and publisher regret
any inconvenience caused if addresses have changed or sites have ceased to exist,
but can accept no responsibility for any such changes.

A catalogue record for this book is available from the British Library.

Library of Congress Cataloging-in-Publication Data
Names: MacKay, M. Elaine, author.
Title: 19th century patterns for the modern body : a step-by-step guide / M. Elaine MacKay.
Other titles: Nineteenth century patterns for the modern body
Description: London : Bloomsbury Visual Arts, 2025. | Includes bibliographical references and index. | Summary: "Whether you're adapting a Regency, American Civil War, or Late Victorian pattern, 19th Century Patterns for the Modern Body will help you to produce a perfectly fitted, historically accurate gown. Illustrated with clear diagrams of bodice, skirt, and sleeve blocks, each technique demonstrates how to transform the modern block into an historical one. Enhanced with sketches and photographs, each chapter follows the tried-and-tested methods M. Elaine MacKay has used to create period garments over a 35-year career drafting and fitting historical patterns for theatre, film, and museums"– Provided by publisher.
Identifiers: LCCN 2024031734 (print) | LCCN 2024031735 (ebook) | ISBN 9781350339712 (paperback) | ISBN 9781350339705 (pdf) | ISBN 9781350339736 (ebook)
Subjects: LCSH: Dressmaking–Pattern design.
Classification: LCC TT520 .M187 2025 (print) | LCC TT520 (ebook) | DDC 646.4/0709034–dc23/eng/20241128
LC record available at https://lccn.loc.gov/2024031734
LC ebook record available at https://lccn.loc.gov/2024031735

ISBN: PB: 978-1-3503-3971-2
       ePDF: 978-1-3503-3970-5
      eBook: 978-1-3503-3973-6

Typeset by Integra Software Services Pvt. Ltd.
Printed and bound in India

Online resources to accompany this book are available at bloomsbury.pub/
19th-c-patterns. If you experience any problems, please contact
Bloomsbury at: onlineresources@bloomsbury.com

For product safety related questions contact productsafety@bloomsbury.com

To find out more about our authors and books visit www.bloomsbury.com and sign up for our newsletters.

CONTENTS

Preface viii
Acknowledgements xi

1 Foundation 1
   Modern Basic Bodice Block 6
   Modern Basic Bodice Block Instructions 9
   Modern One-piece Sleeve Block 17
   Modern One-piece Sleeve Block
      Instructions 19
   Modern Two-piece Sleeve Block 22
   Modern Two-piece Sleeve Block
      Instructions 24
   Introduction to Historical Sleeves 27
   Historical One-piece Sleeve Block 27
   Historical One-piece Sleeve Block
      Instructions 28
   Historical Two-piece Sleeve Block
      Instructions 31
   Skirt 33
   Straight Skirt Block 34
   Straight Skirt Draft Instructions 36
   Standard Skirt Block 39

2 First Steps 41
   Reading an Image 42

3 Development of Period Patterns, 1800–15 47
   Period Dress in Historical Context 47
   Primary Step-by-Step Drafting
      Instructions 50
   Alternative Regency Gown Drafting
      Instructions 56

4 Development of Period Patterns, 1820–35 63
   Period Dress in Historical Context 63
   Primary Step-by-Step Drafting
      Instructions 67
   Alternative Day Dress Draft Adaptations 76

5 Development of Period Patterns, 1840–49 83
   Period Dress in Historical Context 83
   Primary Step-by-Step Drafting
      Instructions 86
   Alternative Day Dress Draft Adaptations 95

6 Development of Period Patterns, 1850–59 101
   Period Dress in Historical Context 101
   Primary Step-by-Step Drafting
      Instructions 104
   Alternative Day Dress Draft
      Adaptations 114

7 Development of Period Patterns, 1860–69 119
   Period Dress in Historical Context 119
   Primary Step-by-Step Drafting
      Instructions 123
   Detailed Instructions for an Elliptical
      Hoop Skirt 134

8 Development of Period Patterns, 1870–79 139
   Period Dress in Historical Context 139
   Primary Step-by-Step Drafting
      Instructions 141
   Alternative Day Dress Draft
      Adaptations 153

9 Development of Period Patterns, 1880–89 159
   Period Dress in Historical Context 159
   Primary Step-by-Step Drafting
      Instructions 163
   Alternative Day Dress Draft
      Adaptations 176

10 Development of Period Patterns, 1890–1900 183
   Period Dress in Historical Context 183
   Primary Step-by-Step Drafting
      Instructions 186
   Alternative Period Sleeve Draft
      Adaptations 196

Reflections 200
Measurement Sheet 206
Bibliography 207
Index 209
List of Figure Credits 212

PREFACE

19th-Century Patterns for the Modern Body: A Step-By-Step Guide is intended to be a resource for teachers and students of fashion pattern drafting and dress history. It provides a comprehensive, systematic guide to creating historical gowns from modern fashion blocks. Re-enactors, students of historical fashion, teachers of dress design and professional builders alike will find this book an invaluable text for practical and successful bespoke re-creations. Modern fashion makers will find the bodice, skirt and sleeve blocks and their variations are excellent foundations for contemporary fashion design. This book is very personal, as it is my next step in a thirty-five-year career that has taken me across Canada making historical dress patterns for theatre, film and museums. My story is reflected in the garments chosen for study, as they are all from Canadian museums, and most are from collections I have handled.

Chapter 1 gives drafting instructions for all the basic fashion blocks, which are the basis for further pattern development. Chapter 2 discusses ways to identify specific elements found in images of historical dress and ways in which the following patterns accommodate them. Chapters 3–10 focus on a particular nineteenth-century look, and manipulate the modern blocks into historical versions of that look. The step-by-step format demystifies the process by breaking it down into manageable tasks. It is systematic, reliable and repeatable. It describes how to achieve the photographed garment found at the beginning of each chapter, and then shows alternative shapes that can be achieved with further manipulations. The last chapter concludes with a sampling of half-scale mock-ups made from the actual patterns in the book. This book provides the student with concrete techniques to use in the re-creation of a multitude of period garments. It does not, however, describe how to take patterns directly from a historical garment. Rather, *19th-Century Patterns for the Modern Body: A Step-By-Step Guide* takes a modern pattern that has been fitted on a modern body and modifies it with historical details.

Ideally, the pattern maker will have some access to the actual garment. Those lucky enough to have the haptic experience of handling a historical garment will find it extraordinarily informative. Ingrid Mida and Alexandra Kim provide a step-by-step guide to reading the physicality and meaning of a garment with a series of questions in their publication *The Dress Detective: A Practicle Guide to Object-Based Research in Fashion*. This type of analysis can answer a myriad of questions about the fabric, cut, construction and the meaning of the garment as a historical object. This is an area that is becoming increasingly important as historians see dress as central to understanding the essence of an individual and the interconnected aspects of a community. One of the great strengths of this book is the three-step, systematic approach that Mida and Kim advocate for analysing clothing; observation, reflection and interpretation. As the dress historian and the dressmaker are different branches of the same tree, much can be learned from Mida's and Kim's approach.

Many twentieth-century dress historians were concerned with reading dress in terms of its physicality. Janet Arnold is a pioneer in translating historical clothing into accurate patterns. Arnold published three iconic pattern books during her lifetime, and left enough research material for many more. *Patterns of Fashion 1 and 2* are particularly helpful for nineteenth-century research. Arnold's research is accurate and detailed. Her sketches are lovely hand-drawn depictions of garments as they would have looked when worn. Each pattern is an exact replica of the garment scaled down to a publishable book size. Like Arnold, Nora Waugh provides patterns for specific garments in *The Cut of Women's Clothes*. Waugh's book contextualizes the garment using extracts from many historical documents with comments about the fashions of the day. Nancy Bradfield's *Costume in Detail 1730–1930* breaks down historical garments through dynamic drawings. There are no patterns, but the renderings beautifully convey the textile's drape, weight and texture. Jean Hunnisett wrote five volumes of *Period Costume for Stage & Screen*. Her focus was in making period reproductions for theatre costuming. Hunnisett's books use period illustrations and theatrical designs as the basis for her patterns. They include many construction suggestions that are used in theatre wardrobes. The patterns included are also to scale, so in theory they could be enlarged to a full size. These texts are invaluable for understanding period shapes. They answer many questions, including dart placement, volume of fabric used, and the grain of the fabric. All of these sources were consulted during the process of making the patterns in this book. The part they are all missing, which is provided in *19th-Century Patterns for the Modern Body: A Step-by-Step Guide*, is the further translation of drafting a historically inspired garment to a modern body.

There is always a challenge in re-creating garments from the past. In the nineteenth century, clothing that was intended for public gaze was worn over layers of undergarments, including wire shapers, petticoats and a corseted body. By its nature, clothing without some kind of armature is fabric without form. Two-dimensional images, such as photographs or artistic renderings, are sometimes problematic and often show only one side of a garment, but they are often the only way we can see how a garment conforms to the body.

Whether they are to provide an appropriate backdrop for a historical presentation, to re-create accurate representations of an historical individual, or to clothe oneself in an homage to the past, *19th-Century Patterns for the Modern Body: A Step-by-Step Guide* will provide the tools to draft your patterns. But remember, your hand is on the pencil. The outcome is completely controlled by your choices. You can decide to mimic specific details, or to modify them. You draw the necklines and hemlines. You can shift darts beyond the indicated placement, and you can exaggerate the sleeves as much as you want. What's more, I encourage you to do so. In so doing, you will learn to control the pencil to follow your every whim. Ultimately, you will make a connection with the historical collective aesthetic, and make it completely modern and personal.

ACKNOWLEDGEMENTS

This book would not have been possible without the support and contribution of many people. First, I'd like to thank the Bloomsbury staff involved in every aspect of its production and publication, especially Georgia Kennedy whose support was invaluable.

I'd also like to acknowledge the museum administrators who provided photographs of the primary dresses; Alicia Boutilier at the Agnes Etherington Art Centre, Leslie Cook from Black Creek Pioneer Village, and Jonathan Walford of the Fashion History Museum. Alicia Boutilier deserves a special thanks for allowing me unrestricted access to the Collection of Canadian Dress and providing the majority of dress images.

For their technical advice, I want to thank Dr. Lynn Sorge for her insight into shaping cage crinolines and Kat Penner for her excellent pleating technique. I am also grateful to my colleague Karyn McCallum for supporting the idea of this book and to my former students who offered kind support throughout the writing of it. Special thanks go to Jenny Mulligan, Cassandra Maloney, and Rachelle Bunbury who gave much needed reviews of individual chapters.

Thanks also go to Jessie Redmond for the beautiful photographs of my mock-up dresses.

Most of all, I want to thank Heike Wenaus. Heike not only supported me from the initial idea, but reviewed it with eagle-eyed attention to every detail. She always reminded me of the student's perspective and managed to do so with smiles and laughter.

And finally, my sincere thanks to Brad Allen who has taken me on so many adventures.

1
Foundation

This first chapter has step-by-step instructions for creating basic body blocks. Sometimes called 'slopers', these Basic Blocks are the foundations for all patterns for women's clothing, whether they are modern or historical. By altering the blocks with mathematical, or sometimes visual adjustments, we can develop patterns for any design. Subsequent chapters describe specific adjustments to create a pattern for the chosen historical garments.

We can envelop any shaped body with a cylinder of fabric as long as the material is large enough to comfortably go around the widest area of the body. Various cultures and dress designers have used this method of clothing design throughout the centuries. If, however, we want the fabric to follow the contours of the female body, we must think about how to create a three-dimensional shape from a flat surface.

I often start pattern-drafting classes with an investigation of simple, geometric shapes. The development of a cone from a circle can be especially informative. As children, many of us learn how to make a cone from a circle of paper by folding out one section. We discover that the severity of the cone shape is directly proportional to the depth of the foldout. The greater the depth of fold, the pointier the cone (Figure 1.2).

In pattern-drafting terms, the folded-out triangle is called a 'dart'. Darts are used whenever fabric needs to be eliminated for a closer fit. In the modern bodice pattern, front darts usually originate from the shoulder, the waist, or the underarm,

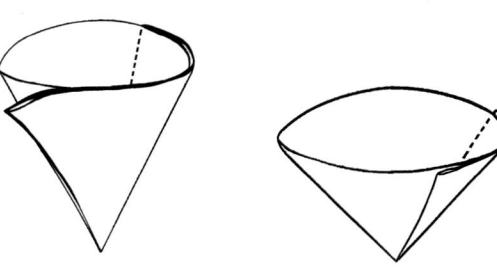

Figure 1.2 Pointed cones showing two different fold-out triangles resulting in two cone shapes.

Figure 1.1 Rack of dresses.

but always end at the fullest part of the bust, which is often the nipple.[1] The purpose of these darts is threefold: they eliminate excess fabric around the breast, they create a cup for the breast, and they stylistically emphasize the breast by pointing to its fullest part. While 'apex' is the technical term for the sharp point of a triangle, in pattern drafting this term is reserved for the point at which the waist, shoulder or underarm darts converge on the bodice front pattern (Figure 1.3).

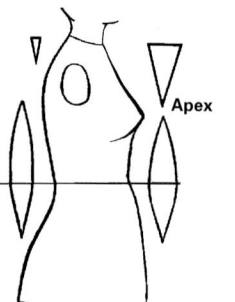
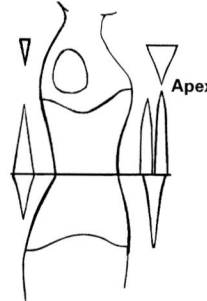

Figure 1.3 On the left, typical dart positions for a modern bodice. On the right, dart positions for a nineteenth-century corseted bodice. The historical bodice has a flatter and elevated bust position, a more defined waist and a more rounded seat.

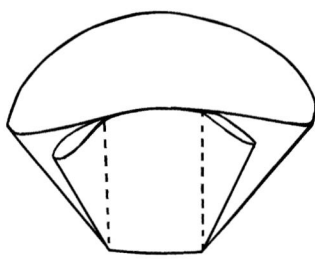

Figure 1.4 Flattened cone with two fold-out triangles.

The Basic Block drafts in this chapter will produce patterns that fit a modern body with small adjustments taken in a fitting. However, the modern aesthetic has not been the ideal silhouette throughout the history of dress. During most of the nineteenth century, the ideal bust shape was much flatter, higher and broader than it is in modern dress. If we return to the cone experiment and use two folded-out triangles rather than one, we find the shape becomes a shallow cup instead of a pointed cone (Figure 1.4). This is much closer to the bust shaping seen in the historical patterns in this book. It may explain why historical bodices often have two or even three bust darts. They extend from the front waist towards the armhole, rather than towards the nipple. While it is true that corsets were mainly responsible for the nineteenth-century bodice shape, bodice darts also reinforced and enhanced this popular silhouette. The following chapters each concentrate on one popular nineteenth-century silhouette. Adaptations to the Modern Basic Blocks in each chapter are designed to bring the silhouette and fit closer to the nineteenth-century one. Figure 1.3 shows how darts are situated for both modern and historical bodices.

Successful blocks often depend on the accuracy of the body measurements taken. It can be helpful to have an assistant record the measurements while you hold the measuring tape. Because an assistant is looking at the body from a different view point, they can also help ensure that horizontal measurements are taken parallel to the floor. Hold the tape firmly around the body part without pulling too tightly. Make sure that you can place one finger between the body and the tape. In small areas, like the neck or wrist, measurements are taken without placing a finger between the tape and the body. If you are in doubt about a measurement, intentionally pull the tape a little tighter. While still holding the tape in place, release the tension. The tape will adjust to the correct measurement. The client should be wearing light clothing, and should be standing comfortably and relaxed. Make sure the client isn't pulling in their tummy or flexing their muscles. I always take measurements in metric. While few people can visualize 91.44 cm, for example, most people have a preconceived concept of what 36" is and may react to it by either pulling in, or puffing out, their body on hearing that measurement.

It is always a good idea to ask the clients to wear the same undergarments they plan to wear with the finished garment. This is also true if they plan to wear a corset. There will be fewer adjustments to the pattern following a fitting if the measurements correctly reflect the body.

TERMINOLOGY

Basque: This is usually a short section that is added to the bottom of bodice or sleeve. It is sometimes fuller than the item it is added onto. Basque also refers to a tightly fitted bodice. See **Peplum**.

Blending: The process of joining disconnected lines that occur during cutting and spreading. Often the smooth and continuous new line is a happy medium between the two original lines.

Cartridge pleat: Sometimes called 'organ pleats', these are used in historical garments, especially skirts where there is a large amount of fabric gathered into a small area. See Chapter 5 for instructions on creating a sample for cartridge pleating and Figure 5.18 for a diagram.

Cutting and spreading: Often referred to as 'slashing and spreading', this is a method of adding volume to a pattern by cutting the pattern into a number of panels and distributing them with space between the panels. Any garment pattern can be divided into sections. These sections are then spread out to add as much volume to the pattern as is needed for the design. It is important to always be aware of the relationship between the sections. When spreading sections equally, place the sections along a grid line so that they keep the same horizontal axis. If more fullness is needed in one area than in another, the sections will be spread to reflect the difference, but neighbouring sections need to be spread along the same axis.

Cut and spread is often used to add stylistic detail. Gathers or tucks developed by the cut and spread method will always follow the direction of the divisions. If the sections are drawn vertically, the gathers or tucks will appear vertical as well. If drawn on an angle, they will appear in the direction of the sections. When using this technique, add a small amount of height. This helps ensure that the fullness is not flat, but has movement.

Dart: A wedge-shaped fold of a specific width that tapers to nothing at one or both ends. Darts convert flat fabric to a three-dimensional shape to follow the contours of the body.

Dart transfer: The process of moving a dart from one position to another. If we return to the concept of the cone, it is evident that the foldout can be placed in any position to achieve the same result. Darts are similar. In pattern drafting, the process of closing a dart in one position opens a new dart in a different position.

Draft: A pattern block developed from applying measurements according to a regulated procedure. It is the basis on which all other styles and shapes are developed.

Flared skirt: A flared skirt is wider at the knee than at the hip. An 'A-line' skirt has moderate flare. A fully flared skirt is a 'circle skirt'.

Gather: A technique for controlling volume of fabric and reducing into a smaller area. Often gathers are used for styling. Typically, the width of ungathered fabric is one and one-half to three times the gathered width.

Grain: Straight-of-grain is parallel to the fabric's selvage. Cross-grain is perpendicular to the selvage. Bias is found on a 45° angle to the selvage.

Master pattern: These patterns have no seam allowance, no extensions and no facings. The drafts in this book are master patterns.

Mock-up (Toile): This is a garment made out of inexpensive fabric and is made to test the accuracy and fit of a pattern.

Notches: Notches are cross marks on the seam line that help a stitcher line up garment pieces prior to stitching. They are also used to denote specific pattern points. For example, the SP (Shoulder Point) on a sleeve is notched, and is meant to match the notched SP on the bodice. They are used in the process of truing up a pattern. Traditionally, notches increase in number from front to back. For example, on a panel skirt, there is one notch between panel 1 and 2; two notches between panel 2 and 3; three notches between panels 3 and 4; and 4 notches on the Centre Back. Notches on a sleeve and the armhole are often called 'balance points'.

Panel skirt: A straight or standard skirt divided by seams into a number of equal panels.

Pattern: A completed draft. It may include stylistic details that are absent in a basic block.

Peplum: Usually a short section that is added to the bottom of bodice or sleeve. It is sometimes fuller than the item it is added on to. See **Basque**.

Pivoting: The rotating of a dart from one position to another without engaging the physical step of closing one dart and opening another at the pattern-making stage.

Pleats: Distinctive and regulated folds that reduce a width of fabric.

Sloper: In the fashion industry, every company has its own set of slopers that reflect that company's preferred shape. Slopers are usually cut from heavy card for longevity. See **Master pattern**.

Selvage: The edge of the manufactured fabric. It is usually more tightly woven than the rest of the fabric.

Sleeve cap: The area from the underarm line to the top of the sleeve patterns.

Sleeve head: The outer line of the sleeve cap.

Straight of grain: Straight-of-grain is parallel to the fabric's selvage.

Toile (mock-up): This is a garment made out of inexpensive fabric and is made to test the accuracy and fit of a pattern.

Tracing: The process of transferring a pattern onto another sheet of paper, or onto fabric using a tracing wheel. Also the process of outlining a photo or illustration to understand the garment's cut.

Truing up: The process of checking for accuracy of dart lines and seam lines.

Waist reduction: The shaping technique of reducing the waist or bodice with seams and darts to make it fit smoothly around the waist.

ABBREVIATIONS

Centre Back	CB
Centre Front	CF
Nape	N
Neck Point	NP
Shoulder	S
Shoulder Point	SP
Side Back	SB
Side Seam	SS
Side Side Back	SSB
Waist	W

The measurements used for all the following blocks are for a size 12 and are taken from a British Standard Size Chart.[2]

Table 1.1 Block Pattern Measurements

Bust	88 cm (34⅝")
Waist	68 cm (26¾")
Hips	94 cm (37")
Back Width	36 cm (14⅛")
Front Chest Width	33.5 cm (13¼")
Bust Point to Bust Point	19.2 cm (7½")
Shoulder	13 cm (5⅛")
Neck	37.5 cm (14¾")
Bicep	28 cm (11")
Elbow	25 cm (9⅞")
Nape to Waist	41 cm (16⅛")
Waist to Hp	20 cm (8")
Waist to Knee	60 cm (23½")

Modern Basic Bodice Block

These are the measurements required to draft the Bodice Block:

1. Nape to Waist (back)
2. Total Chest measurement
3. Back Width (across-back; X back)
4. Shoulder
5. Front Chest Width (across-front; X front)
6. Waist measurement
7. Neck circumference
8. Bust Point to Bust Point – useful, but optional
9. Hip measurement
10. Nape to Hip

A garment made to a person's exact measurements would be extremely uncomfortable unless the fabric has stretch. Pattern makers add extra to the body measurements to make the garment more comfortable. This extra is called 'ease'. The amount of ease differs depending on what type of garment is being considered. This Modern Basic Bodice Block draft includes a moderate amount of ease for a fitted, yet comfortable bodice. The Chest has 10 cm (4") ease and the Waist has 4 cm (1⅝") ease included. Some other measurements also have ease added.

Because people are almost symmetrical, patterns usually map only half of the body from the middle of the back to the middle of the front. **Therefore, all the horizontal body measurements are divided in half. Vertical measurements are not halved.** None of the drafts in this book include seam allowances.

Table 1.2 Modern Basic Bodice Block Measurement Chart

	BODY MEASUREMENT + EASE	PATTERN MEASUREMENT
1. **Nape to Waist** No ease is added.	41cm (16⅛")	41 cm (16⅛")
2. **Total Chest** The chest circumference plus 10 cm (4") ease allowance.	98 cm (38½")	49 cm (19⅜")
3. **Back width** The back width (X back) plus 1.5 cm (⅝") ease.	37.5 cm (14¾")	18.75 cm (7⅜")
4. **Shoulder**	14 cm (5½")	14 cm (5½")
5. **Front Chest width** The chest width plus 0.5 cm (³⁄₁₆") ease.	34 cm (13⅜")	17 cm (6⅜")
6. **Waist measurement** The waist circumference plus 4 cm (1⅝") ease.	72 cm (28⅜")	36 cm (14⅛")
7. **Neck** Measured at the base of the neck. No ease is added at the drafting stage. Standard measurements are used. Refinement takes place after the draft is complete.	35 cm (13¾")	17.5 cm (6⅞")
8. **Bust Point to Bust Point** No ease is added.	19.2 cm (7½")	9.6 cm (3¾")
9. **Hip** The hip measurement plus 5 cm (2") ease.	99 cm (39")	49.5 cm (19½")
10. **Nape to Hip** That is, nape to waist plus a standard 20 cm (8").	6.1 cm (24")	6.1 cm (24")

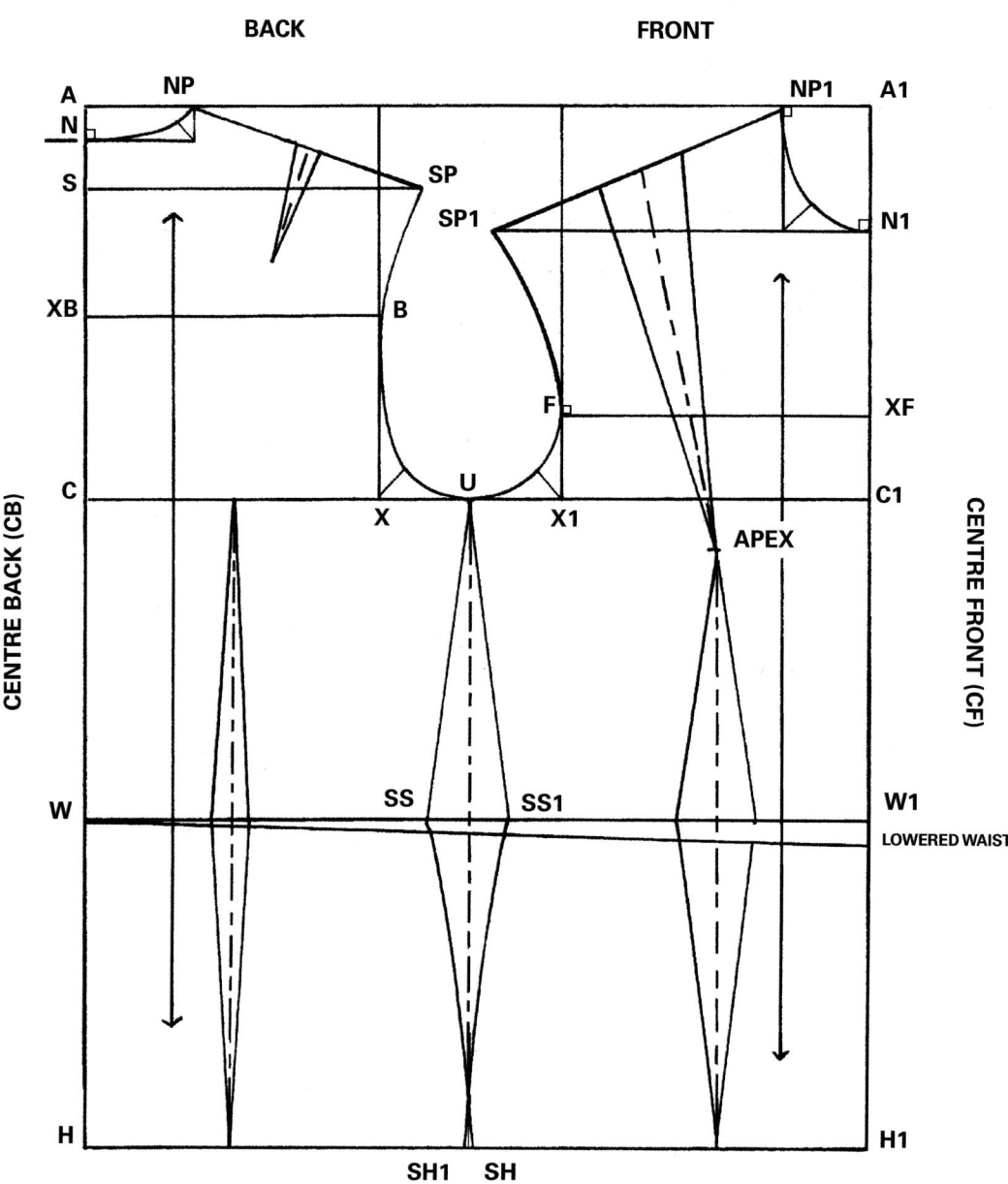

Figure 1.5 Modern Basic Bodice Block.

Modern Basic Bodice Block Instructions

Draft Frame

Figure 1.6

1. Take a piece of paper approximately 60 cm × 70 cm (23⅝" × 27½").
2. Draw a line about 5 cm (2") from the left edge. Call this line the **CB** (Centre Back line). The edges of paper can be damaged, so drafts are always started about 5 cm (2") from the edge.
3. Mark point **A** on this line about 5 cm (2") from the top of the paper.
4. Square a line across from **A**. This is the top of the draft.
5. **A–A1** = Chest pattern measurement. Refer to Table 1.2 for this measurement.
6. Square down from **A1** to form the **CF** (Centre Front line) on the right-hand side of the paper.
7. **A–H** = Full Length plus 2 cm (¾"). Extend a line from **H** to **CF**. Call this **H1**.

This completes the outside parameters of the draft. If stitched up in a cylinder, it would envelope the body. Shaping darts and side seams create dimensions to fit the body.

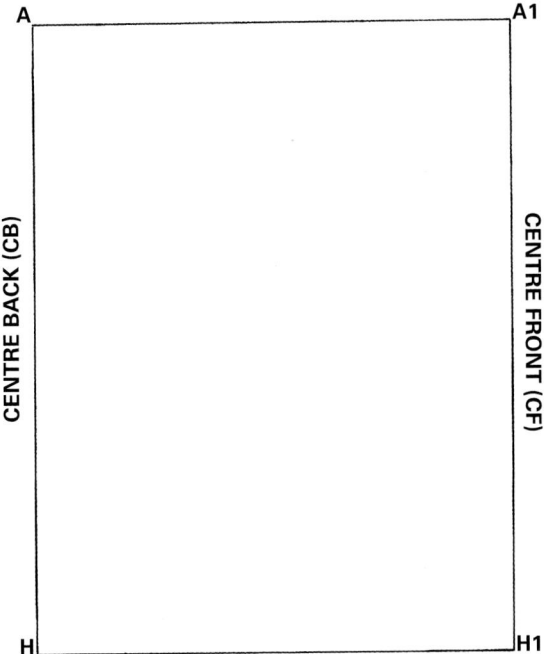

Figure 1.6 Modern Basic Bodice Block frame.

Back Horizontal Lines

Figure 1.7

Along the **CB** line, mark the following:

1. **A–N** = 2 cm (¾"), which is standard. Square across a line about 8 cm (3⅛"). **N** is the nape of the neck. It is very important because all other back lengths are measured from this point. Underlining **N** may help pinpoint your focus to this point.
2. **N–S** = 3 cm (1⅛"), which is standard. **S** represents the shoulder position. Square across a line about 20 cm (8").
3. **N–W** = Nape to Waist measurement = 41 cm (16⅛").
4. **N–C** = half of **N–W**, plus 1 cm (⅜") towards waist, 41 cm ÷ 2 + 1 cm = 21.5 cm (16⅛" ÷ 2 + ⅜" = 8½").
5. Extend **C–C1** on the Centre Front (**CF**). This is the underarm line, and is another important line on the draft.
6. **XB** is half of **N–C**. Square a line approximately half way across the draft.
7. Extend **W–W1** on the **CF** for the provisional waistline.

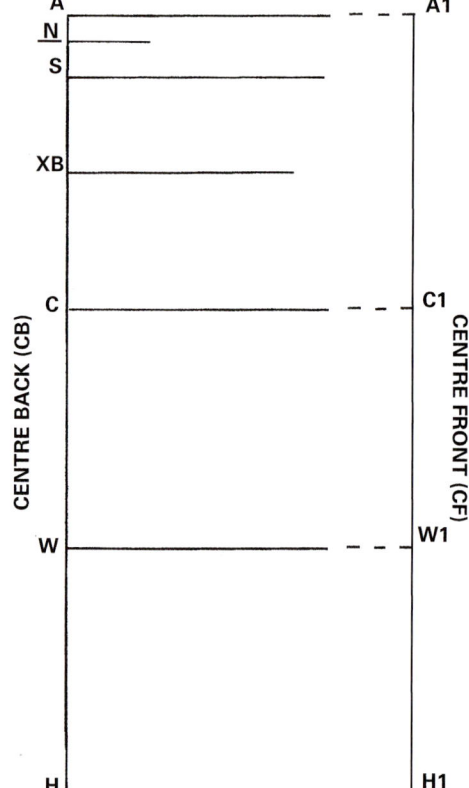

Figure 1.7 Back horizontal breakdown.

Back Body

Figure 1.8

1. Along the top line of the draft, **A–NP** (Nape Point) = 7 cm (2¾"), which is standard. Square down to the line drawn out from **N**.
2. Curve the neckline from **N** to **NP** going through a point 1.5 cm (⅝") diagonally from the corner. The neckline should meet the **CB** with a 90° angle for at least 0.5 cm (³⁄₁₆").
3. **XB–B** = back width from Back Width pattern measurement = 18.75 cm (7⅜"). From **B**, square a line to the top of the draft. Square down to the line **C–C1**. Call this point **X**.
4. **NP–SP** (Shoulder Point) is the shoulder measurement applied from **NP** to the line squared out from **S**.
5. For very close-fitting garments, a shoulder dart may be created. In that case, **NP–SP** = shoulder + 1.5 cm (⅝"). The added amount is for the dart. Mark the midpoint of this line. From this point, square down a line 7 cm (3") long. Create a small dart by marking 0.75 cm (¼") on either side of the midpoint and connect to the end of this line. Many of the drafts in this book include the back shoulder dart as it helps to shape the basic bodice block over the shoulder blades.
6. **Waist Dart**: Find the midpoint between **C** and **X**. Square down with a dotted line through the waist to the hip line. This will be the centre of the back dart. For a standard size 12, mark 1.25 cm (½") on either side of the dotted line drawn out from **W**, and connect up to the point where the dotted line meets the line drawn out from **C**, and continue down to the point where the dotted line meets **H–H1**. Calculations for depth of darts for other sizes immediately follow this draft.

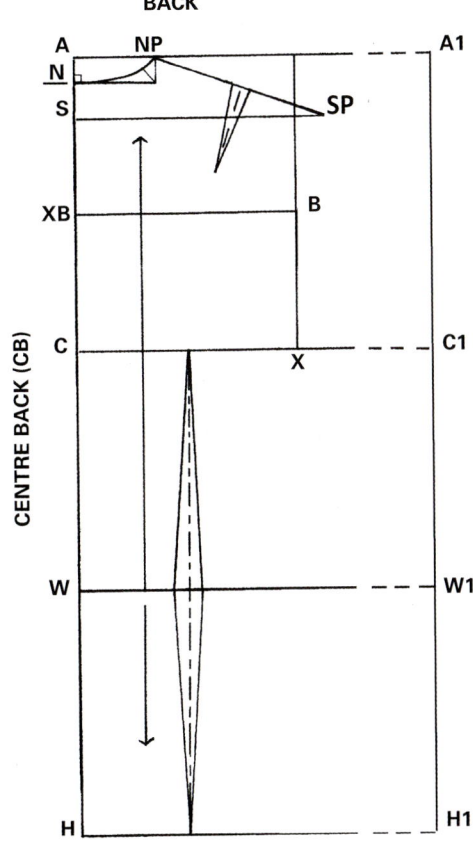

Figure 1.8 Back body.

Front Body

Figure 1.9

1. **A1–NP1** = 5.5 cm (2⅛"), which is standard. Square down.
2. **A1–N1** = 7.5 cm (3"), which is standard. Square back towards the line squared down from **NP1**.
3. To draw in the front neck, hug the vertical line from **NP1** a short distance. Then curve the neckline towards **N1** going through a point 2.5 cm (1") diagonally from the corner. The neckline must meet the **CF** with a 90° angle for at least 0.5 cm (³⁄₁₆").
4. **XF** is 5 cm (2") above **C–C1**. Square back approximately half way across the draft.
5. **XF–F** = Front Chest pattern measurement plus 2.2 cm (¾") = 19.2 cm (7⅝"). Square up and down to the **C–C1** line.
6. Mark **X1** on the **C–C1** line.
7. **N1–SP1** = **XF–F** plus 4.3 cm = 23.5 cm (10") for dart allowance and shoulder shaping.
8. Join **SP1–NP1** to form the shoulder line. Mark the shoulder midpoint. This is the centre of the shoulder dart.
9. Mark half the Shoulder measurement on the shoulder line from **NP1**. Mark half the Shoulder measurement on the Shoulder line from **SP1**. The distance between these two points is the depth of the shoulder dart. Do not draw the dart yet.
10. Apply the **Bust Point–Bust Point** pattern measurement to the left of **CF** on line **C–C1** and drop it 3 cm (1⅛") towards the waist. This is the **Apex**. Draw a dotted line from the **Apex**, through the waist, to the **H–H1**. This is the centre of the front waist dart. For a standard size 12, mark 2.25 cm (⅞") on either side of the dotted line on **W–W1**, and connect up to the **Apex**, and down to the point where the dotted line meets **H–H1**. Calculations for depth of darts for other sizes immediately follow this draft.
11. If you do not have a **Bust Point–Bust Point** measurement, find the midpoint of **X1–C1** and drop it 3 cm (1⅛") towards the waist.
12. Draw the front shoulder dart by connecting the shoulder midpoint to the **Apex** with a dotted line, and connect the depth of dart marks to the **Apex**.

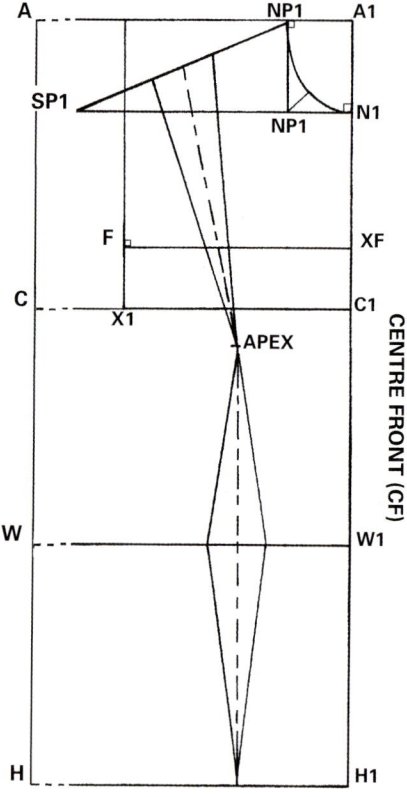

Figure 1.9 Front body.

Side Seam and Armhole

Figure 1.10

1. **U** is the midpoint of **X–X1** on the **C–C1** line. Square down a dotted line through the waist to the hip line. This is the provisional Side Seam (**SS**).
2. Mark 2.5 cm (1") on either side of the provisional **SS** on **W–W1** and connect to **U**. Call the mark on the left **SS**. Call the mark on the right **SS1**.
3. For the back armhole, draw a concave line from **SP** to **B**. Continue the line from **B** to **U** touching a point 2.5 cm (1") from **X**.
4. For the front armhole, draw a concave line from **SP1** to **F** and through to **U**, touching a point 2.3 cm (⅞") from **X1**.

For a bodice that ends at the waist, this is the end of the draft. Use the following steps for a bodice that extends below the waist.

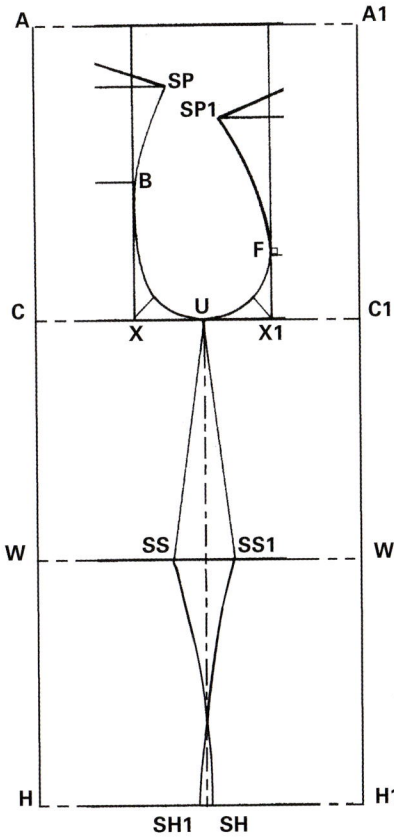

Figure 1.10 Side body.

Shaping Side Seam below Waist

1. As previously mentioned, 5 cm (2") ease has been added to the body's hip measurement. This measurement may be greater than **H–H1**.[3]
2. Compare the Hip pattern measurement from **H–H1** and record the difference.
3. On this standard size 12 pattern, the hip is 0.5 cm ($\frac{3}{16}$") larger than **H–H1**, so the difference you see is minimal.
4. Place half the difference to the left of the side seam on **H–H1**. Call this **SH1**. Place half to the right of the side seam on **H–H1** and call this **SH**. Connect from the waist side seams to the new point with a curve to reflect a hip shape. **Note:** The hips will overlap on the paper pattern.

Finessing the Pattern

1. Measure the pattern neck. If your actual neck is larger or smaller, redraw the neck curve. A small change in the curve can make a large difference in the measurement.
2. Optional – Redraw the waistline from nothing at **W** on the **CB** to a point 1.3 cm (½") below **W1** on the **CF**. As you gain experience, you will find that lowering the centre front waist in this method greatly improves the block's aesthetic appearance (see Figure 1.5).
3. Mark the straights-of-grain parallel to the **CF** and the **CB**.

Waist Reduction and Shaping with Darts for Other Sizes

1. Measure **W–W1**. It may be larger than the desired Waist pattern measurement.
2. Subtract the Waist pattern measurement from **W–W1** and record the difference.
3. Divide the difference between the side seam lines and the darts to reflect the body shape. The Front dart is usually larger than the Back dart.

Cutting out Pattern

1. Cut along the Front side seam. Flip the pattern over. Line up with the Back side seam. Trace the Front side seam onto the Back and cut along this line. This ensures that the front and back seams have the same curve and length.
2. To true up the shoulder, there are two methods; the drafting method and the folding method.

Drafting Method

Figure 1.11

1. Measure line **1** of the shoulder dart.
2. Apply this measurement to line **3**.
3. Extend line **2** a short distance above the provisional shoulder line.
4. Connect a line from **SP1** through **3**, to **2**.
5. Continue from **2** to **1**.
6. Continue to **NP1**.

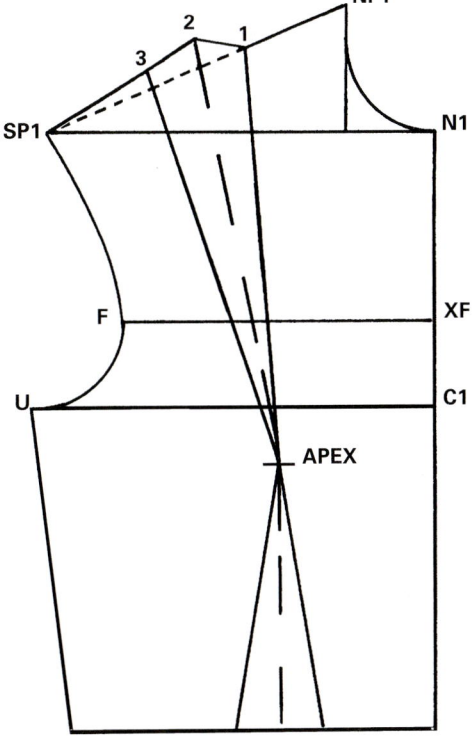

Figure 1.11 Shoulder dart.

Folding Method

1. Crease the paper along each dart line.
2. Join lines **1** and **3**.
3. Press line **2** towards the **CF**.
4. Holding firmly, draw a straight line from **NP1** to **SP1**.
5. Cut along this line.

FITTING

The previous pattern will produce a well-fitted bodice. However, because it is standardized, it may need adjustments for an individual fit. It is a good idea to make and fit a mock-up. This is especially important if the measurements were not taken by yourself. A fitting gives you an opportunity to double-check the measurements, and a chance to observe the important body stance.

Fittings are, by their nature, intensely intimate. It is important to be respectful of the client's physical and emotional comfort at all times. Not only are they presenting their unguarded body to you, but they are standing still for substantial periods of time. Establish a routine so that you remember to check each area efficiently and succinctly. I tend to start the fitting with a review of the overall fit. Then, I look at details on the back. Starting at the back establishes a certain separation between myself and the client. I then move to the more intimate front and complete a detailed check much like the back check. Next is the shoulder, neck and front underarm area. With this procedure, the level of intimacy increases as the fitter and client become comfortable with each other.

You may find that the shoulders and front armholes are the most likely areas to need adjustments. This is because the Basic Bodice Block uses a standard shoulder slope and a calculated shoulder dart. There is no way to introduce an individual's actual measurements or stance. It is only with a fitting that you are able to see the critical shoulder and armhole relationship.

SLEEVE INTRODUCTION

As the armhole of the bodice is linked to the sleeve draft, it deserves a closer investigation. With your hand, create a right angle with your thumb and fingers. Place your fingers at the armpit and your thumb pointing up towards their shoulder. Now ask the client to swing their arm forward and back. The arm should be unencumbered by your hand. This is the way the front armhole of the bodice needs to fit; neither digging into the armpit, nor too far away from the natural line of articulation. If the mock-up fabric hinders any arm movement, it is too tight. With short snips, clip into the fabric until it no longer pushes against the arm. You may find that as you clip, the top of the shoulder has excess fabric (see Figure 1.12). In that case, the client's armhole is lower than the one drafted. If the client's shoulder is very square, you will that find the opposite alteration is needed. In that case you will raise the underarm and shoulder, thereby changing the shoulder's angle.

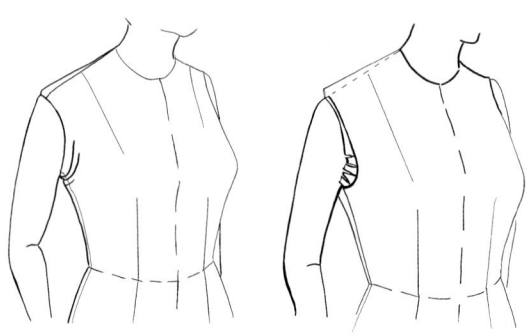

Figure 1.12 Bodice with an armhole that is too high and its correction.

Sometimes, a large triangle of extra fabric originates at the armhole and points to the bust. This means that the shoulder dart needs to be deeper at the shoulder (see Figure 1.13). (See Dart transfer in Terminology.) There is no need to remove all ease at the armhole. In fact, a small amount of ease is preferable for a comfortable sleeve. Draw a new armhole on the client from the perfected underarm to the top of the shoulder and continue along the back. Transfer any and all alterations from the mock-up fitting to the paper pattern (Figure 1.13).

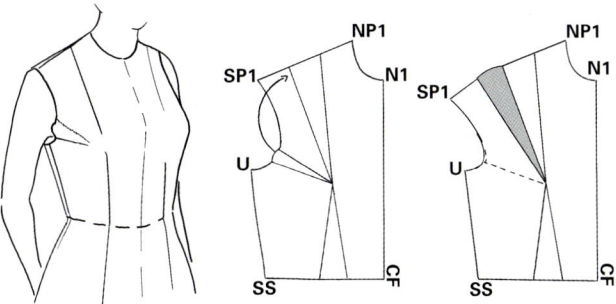

Figure 1.13 Shows the alteration needed to transfer a dart from the mock-up armhole to the paper pattern.

Modern One-piece Sleeve Block

The measurements required to draft the Modern One-piece Sleeve Block are:

1. Bodice Armhole measurement
2. Sleeve Length
3. Bicep Circumference
4. Wrist Circumference
5. Elbow Circumference – not required but useful

Because the whole, three-dimensional sleeve is mapped out in a two-dimensional pattern, the horizontal measurements are not halved.

Table 1.3 Modern One-piece Sleeve Block Measurement Chart

	MEASUREMENT + EASE	PATTERN MEASUREMENT
1 Bodice Armhole measurement This is carefully measured from the Basic Bodice Block.	43 cm (17")	**43 cm (17")**
2 Sleeve Cap ⅓ the Bodice Armhole measurement.	14.3 cm (5⅝")	**14.3 cm (5⅝")**
3 Sleeve Length Measured from shoulder to wrist.	58 cm (23")	**58 cm (23")**
4 Bicep measurement The bicep plus 5 cm (2") ease.	33 cm (13")	**33 cm (13")**
5 Wrist measurement The wrist plus 6.5 cm (2½") ease.	22.5 cm (8⅞")	**22.5 cm (8⅞")**

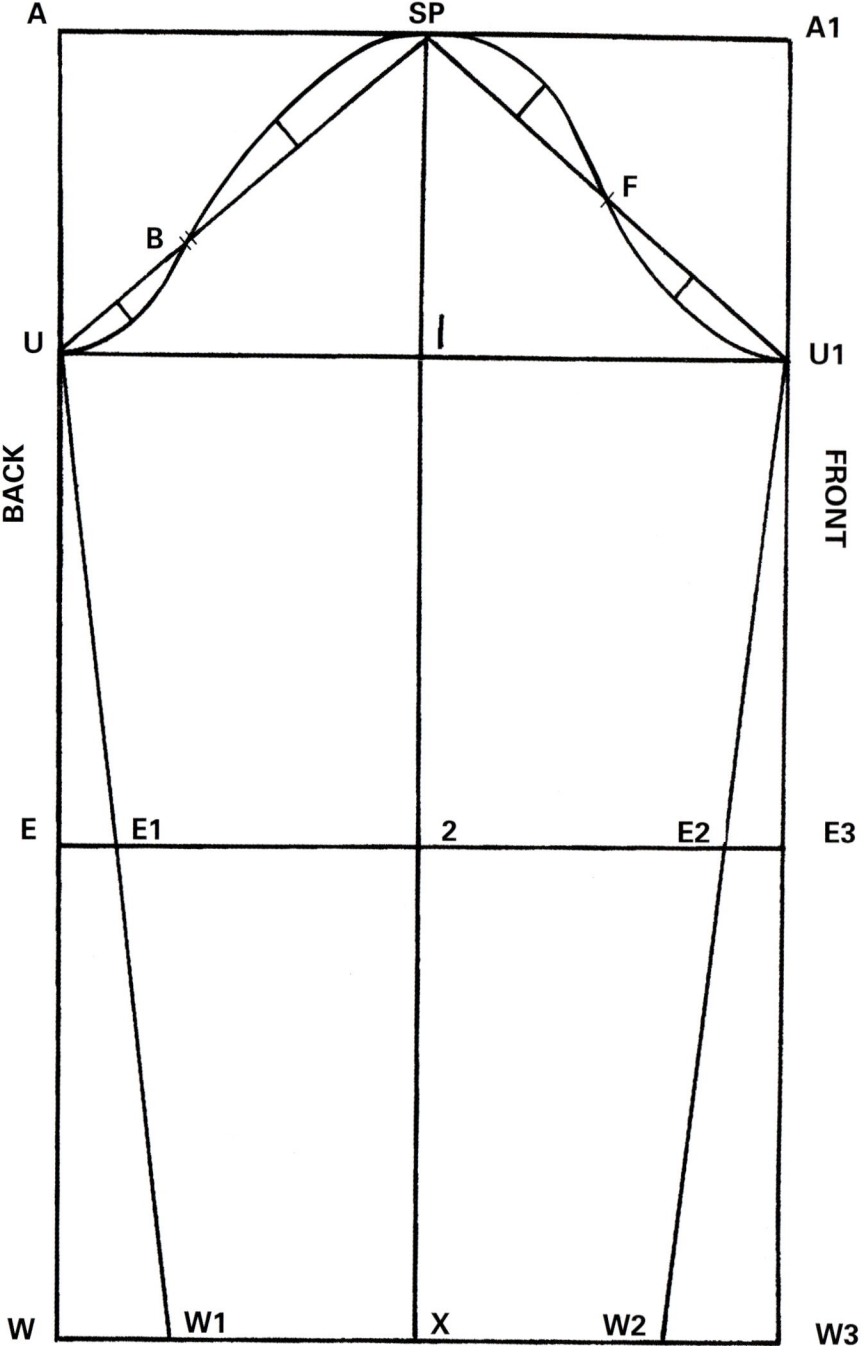

Figure 1.14 Modern One-piece Sleeve Block.

Modern One-piece Sleeve Block Instructions

Sleeve Frame

Figure 1.15
1. Take a piece of paper approximately 45 cm × 65 cm (17¾" × 25½").
2. Draw a line the length of the paper about 5 cm (2") from the left lengthwise edge.
3. Mark a point **A** on this line 5 cm (2") from the top of the paper.
4. Square a line across the paper. This is the top of the draft.
5. **A–A1** = Bicep pattern measurement = 33 cm (13").
6. Square down from **A1**.
7. **A–W** = Sleeve Length = 58 cm (23"). Square out a line across the paper. This is the bottom of the draft.
8. Mark **W3** where this line meets the line squared down from **A1**.

This completes the parameters of the sleeve draft.

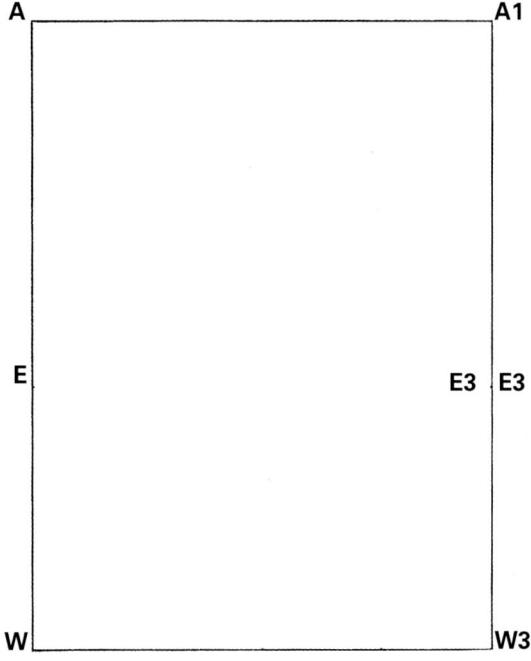

Figure 1.15 Modern One-piece Sleeve Block frame.

Sleeve Divisions and Arm Shaping

Figure 1.16

1. Find the midpoint of **A–A1**. This is the Shoulder Point (**SP**). Square down from **SP** to the bottom of the draft at **X**. This is the centre of the draft and is often used as the placement of the straight-of-grain.
2. **A–U** = ⅓ Bodice Block Armhole measurement, that is, 43 cm ÷ 3 = 14.3 cm (17" ÷ 3 = 5⅝").
3. Square a line across the draft from **U** to the line squared down from **A1**. Call this **U1**. This line indicates the underarm line. The rectangular area between **A/A1** and **U/U1** is often called the 'sleeve cap'.
4. **1** appears on the line **U–U1** along the centre line.
5. **E** is the midpoint of **U–W** and is the elbow. Square out a line across the paper to the line squared down from **A1**.
6. Call this **E3**.
7. **2** appears on the line **E–E3** along the centre line.
8. **X–W1** = half the Wrist pattern measurement = 11.25 cm (4½").
9. **X–W2** = half the Wrist pattern measurement = 11.25 cm (4½").
10. Connect **U** to **W1**. **E1** appears on this line.
11. Connect **U1** to **W2**. **E2** appears on this line.

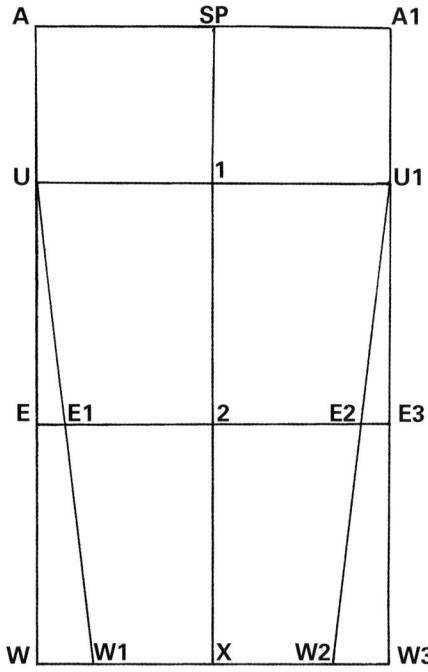

Figure 1.16 Modern One-piece Sleeve divisions and arm shaping.

Sleeve Head Shaping

Figure 1.17

The sleeve head shaping will follow the guidelines in a curvy line. This makes a sleeve that fits well into the armhole and looks smooth when the arm is resting at the side. The front differs from the back, in that it is slightly higher at the shoulder and curves more deeply under the arm.

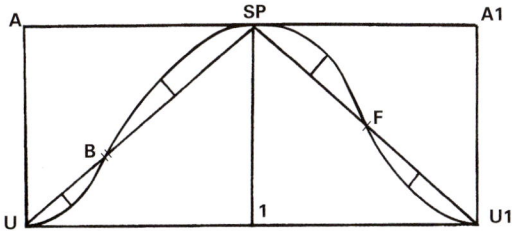

Figure 1.17 Modern One-piece Sleeve head.

1. Draw a guideline from **U** to **SP**.
2. Draw a guideline from **SP** to **U1**.
3. **B** is ⅓ of **U** to **SP**.
4. Find the midpoint of **U** to **B** and square a line 1 cm (⅜") down towards **U–U1**.
5. Find the midpoint of **B** to **SP** and square a line 1.5 cm (⅝") up towards the top of the draft.
6. **F** is the midpoint of **SP** to **U1**.
7. Find the midpoint of **SP** to **F** and square a line 2 cm (¾") up towards the top of the draft.
8. Find the midpoint of **F** to **U1** and square a line 1.5 cm (⅝") down towards **U–U1**.
9. Hitting all the previous points, draw the sleeve head.

Completion

1. Measure the sleeve head from **U** through **B** to **SP** through **F** to **U1**. **Note:** The measurement of the sleeve head must be at least equal to that of the bodice armhole. Ideally, the sleeve head is 2 cm–4 cm (¾"–1⅝") larger than the bodice armhole.
2. Sleeves usually match a Basic Bodice Block or garment at the underarm, **U**. Pattern makers add notches on the sleeves and bodice armholes to facilitate the easier setting of sleeves.
3. To determine the placement of the back notches, measure the sleeve head from **U** to **B** and record this measurement on the Basic Bodice Block back on the curve from **U** towards **B**. Mark this placement with two notches. **Note:** This may not be in the same position as **B** on the Basic Bodice Block. Refer to the Basic Bodice Block in Figure 1.5.
4. To determine the placement of the front notch, measure the sleeve head from **U1** to **F** and record this measurement on the Basic Bodice Block front from **U** to **F**. Mark the placement with one notch. **Note:** This may not be in the same position as **F** on the Basic Bodice Block.
5. Notches on sleeves are often called 'balance points'.

Modern Two-piece Sleeve Block

The measurements required to draft the Two-piece Sleeve Block are:

1. Bodice Armhole measurement
2. Sleeve Length
3. Bicep measurement
4. Wrist measurement
5. Elbow Circumference – not required but useful.

In this pattern, the sleeve is divided into two patterns that overlap. The top arm is the area we usually see. The undersleeve is the part closest to the body. There is a seam along the front of the arm and a seam along the back of the arm. It is the basis of many nineteenth-century sleeves.

Because the two patterns are drafted simultaneously, the horizontal bicep and wrist measurements are divided in half. Vertical measurements are not halved.

Table 1.4 Modern Two-piece Sleeve Block Measurement Chart

MEASUREMENT + EASE		PATTERN MEASUREMENT
1. Bodice Armhole measurement This is carefully measured from the Basic Bodice Block.	43 cm (17")	**43 cm (17")**
2. Sleeve Cap ⅓ the Bodice Armhole Measurement.	14.3 cm (5⅝")	**14.3 cm (5⅝")**
3. Sleeve Length Measured from shoulder to wrist.	58 cm (23")	**58 cm (23")**
4. Bicep Measurement The bicep plus 5 cm (2") ease.	33 cm (13")	**16.5 cm (6½")**
5. Wrist Measurement The wrist plus 6.5 cm (2⅕") ease.	22.5 cm (8⅞")	**11.25 cm (4½")**

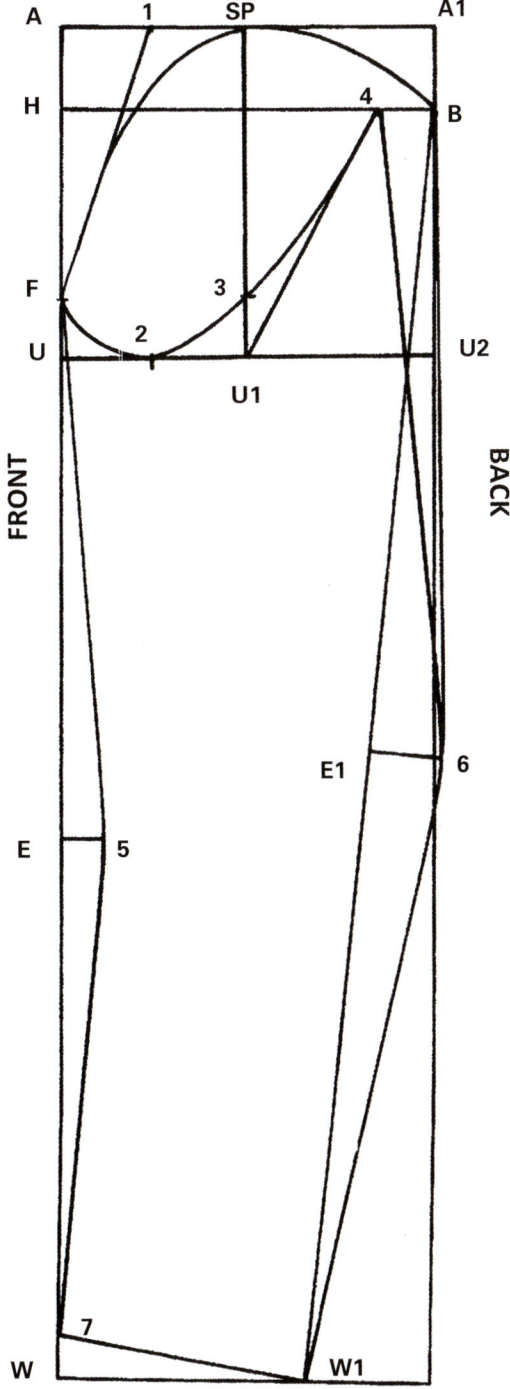

Figure 1.18 Modern Two-piece Sleeve Block.

Modern Two-piece Sleeve Block Instructions

Also called a Half and Half Sleeve

Sleeve Frame

Figure 1.19

1. Take a piece of paper approximately 25 cm × 65 cm (10" × 25½").
2. Draw a line the length of the paper about 5 cm (2") from the left lengthwise edge.
3. Mark a point **A** on this line 5 cm (2") from the top of the paper.
4. Square a line across the paper. This is the top of the draft.
5. **A–A1** = Bicep pattern measurement = 16.5 cm (6½"). Refer to Table 1.4 for this measurement.
6. Square down from **A1** the length of the page.
7. **A–W** = Sleeve Length = 58 cm (23"). Square out a line across the paper. This is the bottom of the draft. Do not attach a letter to this point where the bottom of the draft meets the line squared down from **A1**.

This completes the parameters of the sleeve draft.

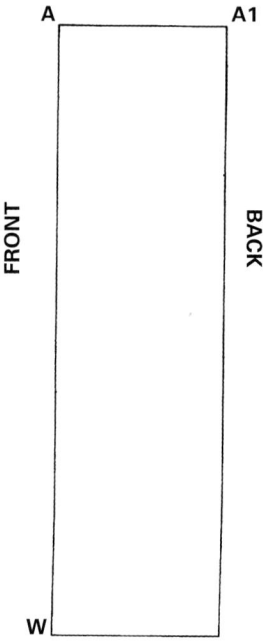

Figure 1.19 Modern Two-piece Sleeve frame.

Sleeve Divisions

Figure 1.20

1. **A–U** = ⅓ Bodice Block Armhole, that is, 43 cm ÷ 3 = 14.3 cm (17" ÷ 3 = 5⅝"). The area between **A** and **U** is often called the 'sleeve cap'.
2. Square a line out from **U**. This line indicates the underarm line. **U2** appears on the line squared down from **A1**.
3. **A–H** = ¼ **A–U**, that is, 14.3 cm ÷ 4 = 3.6 cm (5⅝" ÷ 4 = 1½").
4. Square a line out from **H**. **B** appears on the line squared down from **A1**.
5. **F** is 2.5 cm (1") above **U** on the line **A–W**.
6. **E** is the midpoint of **F–W** and is the elbow.
7. The midpoint of **A–A1** is **SP**.

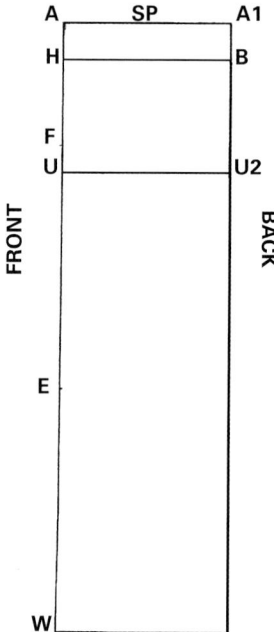

Figure 1.20 Modern Two-piece Sleeve divisions.

Sleeve Head Shaping

Figure 1.21

1. From **SP**, square down to the line drawn out from **U**. Call this **U1**.
2. **1** is the midpoint of **A–SP**.
3. Draw a guideline from **F** to **1**.
4. **2** is the midpoint of **U–U1**.
5. **3** is 2.5 cm (1") above **U1** on the line drawn down from **SP**.
6. **4** is 2.5 cm (1") to the left of **B** on the line **H–B**.
7. Draw a guideline from **U1** to **4**.
8. Following the lower part of the guideline **F** to **1**, draw the top sleeve head from **F** to **SP** to **B**. Refer to Figure 1.21 for shaping guidance.
9. Follow the lower part of the guideline **U1** to **4**, draw the undersleeve head from **F** to **2** to **3** to **4**. Refer to Figure 1.21 for shaping guidance.

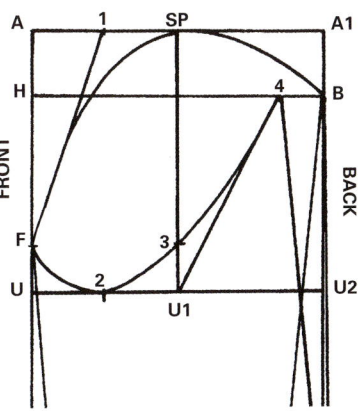

Figure 1.21 Modern Two-piece Sleeve cap.

Wrist and Arm Shaping

Figure 1.22

1. **W–W1** = Wrist pattern measurement. Refer to Table 1.4 for this measurement.
2. **7** is 1.5 cm (⅝") above **W** on the line **A–W**.
3. Connect **7** to **W1**. This is the hem line.
4. From **E**, square a line 2 cm (¾") to the right. Call this point **5**.
5. Connect **F** to **5** to **7** for the front seam of both topsleeve and undersleeve.
6. Draw a guideline from **W1–B**.
7. **E1** is the midpoint of **W1–B**.
8. From **E1**, square a line 3 cm (1⅛") to the right. Call this point **6**.
9. Connect **B** to **6** for the topsleeve back seam.
10. Connect **4** to **6** for the undersleeve back seam.
11. Connect **6** to **W1** for the back seam of both the topsleeve and the undersleeve.

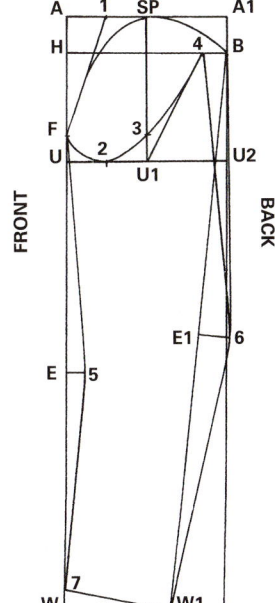

Figure 1.22 Modern Two-piece Sleeve wrist and shaping.

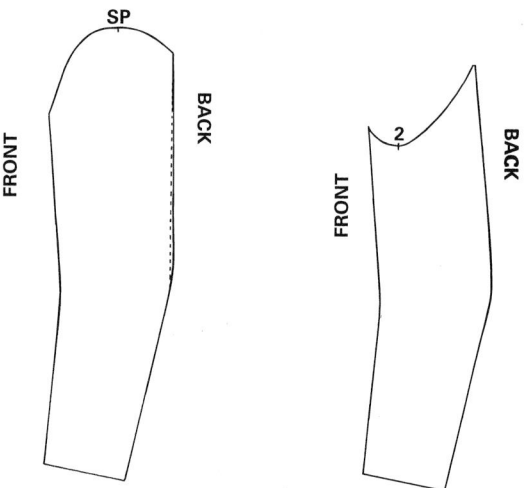

Figure 1.23 Modern Two-piece Sleeves separated.

Completion

1. Measure the total sleeve head from **F** through **SP** to **B** and from **F** through **2** and **3** to **4**. **Note:** The measurement of the sleeve head must be at least equal to that of the bodice armhole. Ideally, the sleeve head is 2 cm–4 cm (¾"–1⅝") larger than the bodice armhole.
2. To determine the placement of back notches, measure the sleeve head from **2** to **4** and record this measurement on the Basic Bodice Block back on the curve from **U** towards **B**. Mark the placement with two notches. **Note:** This may not be the same position as **B** on the bodice.
3. To determine the placement of the front notch, measure the sleeve head from **2** to **F** and record this measurement on the Basic Bodice Block front on the curve from **U** towards **F**. Mark the placement with one notch. **Note:** This may not be the same position as **F** on the bodice.
4. Many tailors use **SP** as the matching point instead of marking out single and double notches.

Introduction to Historical Sleeves

Figure 1.24

In the previous sleeve drafts, the sleeve cap depth is ⅓ the armhole measurement. In historical sleeves, the sleeve cap to armhole ratio is much smaller. As the cap is reduced in height, it becomes wider. Imagine that the sleeve head is an inflated balloon. If the balloon is squeezed from the top and the bottom, it bulges at the sides. This is essentially what happens with the sleeve head in a historical pattern. The volume is the same, but the sleeve cap is shallower and wider than in a modern sleeve. This sleeve hangs away from the body, as shown in Figure 1.24. This is a defining characteristic of a nineteenth century garment sleeve.

Note: The measurement you take for the sleeve length is from the shoulder to the wrist. Historical sleeves often start below the shoulder. Take this into account and reduce the length by the distance off the shoulder. Because the amount of shoulder drop is individual, the sleeve drafts in this book use the full length for the modern and historical sleeves. For consistency, the sleeve length is the same in this draft.

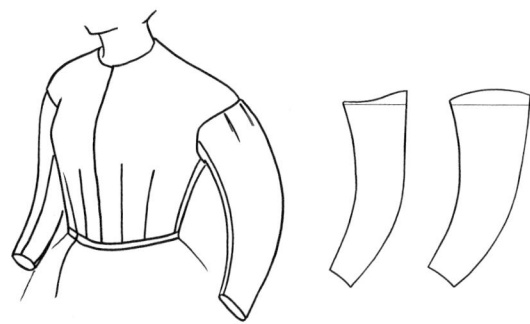

Figure 1.24 Depiction of a Historical Two-piece Sleeve.

Historical One-piece Sleeve Block

The measurements required to draft the Historical One-piece Sleeve Block are:

1. Bodice Armhole measurement
2. Sleeve Length
3. Bicep
4. Wrist
5. Elbow Circumference – not required

This sleeve is similar to a Modern One-piece Sleeve draft, but the sleeve cap is wider and shallower. Instead of adding 5 cm (2") to the bicep measurement to find the correct width, for the historical sleeve we add 10 cm (4") to the bicep measurement. Also, instead using ⅓ of the Bodice Armhole measurement for the Sleeve cap, we reduce this measurement by 5 cm (2").

Because the whole three-dimensional sleeve is mapped out in a two-dimensional pattern, the horizontal measurements are not halved.

Table 1.5 Historical One-piece Sleeve Block Measurement Chart

	MEASUREMENT + EASE	PATTERN MEASUREMENT
1. Bodice Armhole measurement This is carefully measured from the Basic Bodice Block.	43 cm (17")	**43 cm (17")**
2. Historical Sleeve Cap ⅓ the Bodice Armhole measurement minus 5 cm (2").	9.3 cm (3⅝")	**9.3 cm (3⅝")**
3. Sleeve Length Measured from shoulder to wrist.	58 cm (23")	**58 cm (23")**
4. Bicep measurement The bicep plus 10 cm (4") ease.	38 cm (15")	**38 cm (15")**
5. Wrist measurement The wrist plus 6.5 cm (2½") ease.	22.5 cm (8⅞")	**22.5 cm (8⅞")**

Historical One-piece Sleeve Block Instructions

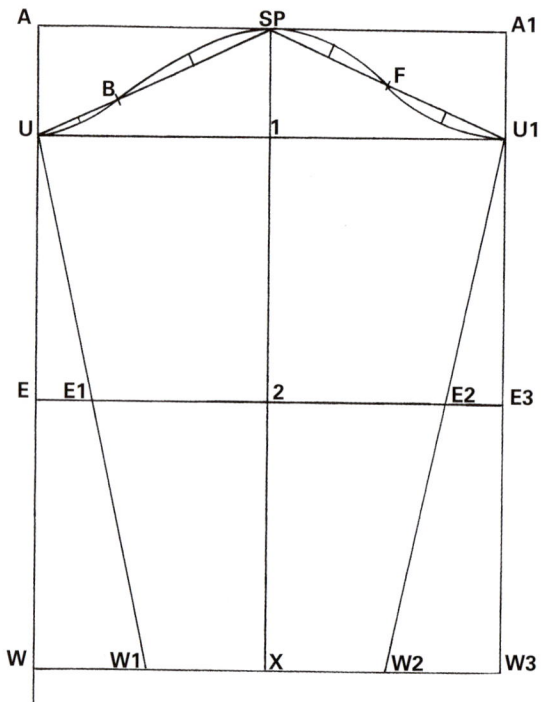

Figure 1.25 Historical One-piece Sleeve draft.

19th-Century Patterns for the Modern Body

Frame

Figure 1.26

1. Take a piece of paper approximately 60 cm × 70 cm (23½" × 27½").
2. Draw a line the length of the paper about 5 cm (2") from the left lengthwise edge.
3. Mark a point **A** on this line about 5 cm (2") from the top of the paper.
4. Square a line across the paper. This is the top of the draft.
5. **A–A1** = Bicep pattern measurement = 43 cm (17").
6. Square down from **A1** the length of the paper.
7. **A–W** = Sleeve Length = 58 cm (23"). From **W**, square out a line across the paper. This is the bottom of the draft.
8. Mark **W3** where this line meets the line squared down from **A1**.

This completes the parameters of the sleeve draft.

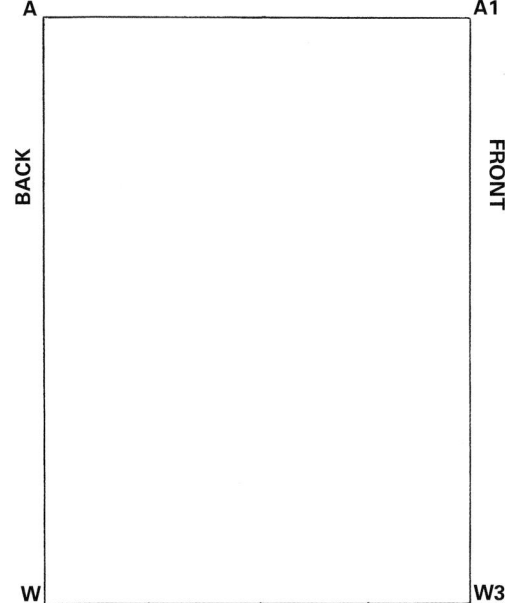

Figure 1.26 Historical One-piece Sleeve frame.

Sleeve Divisions and Arm Shaping

Figure 1.27

1. Find the midpoint of **A–A1**. This is the Shoulder Point (**SP**). Square down from **SP** to the bottom of the draft at **X**. This is the centre of the draft and is often used as the placement of the straight-of-grain.
2. **A–U** is the Historical Sleeve Cap. Refer to Table 1.5 for this measurement.
3. Repeat instructions 3–11 of the Modern One-piece Sleeve Block, Sleeve Divisions and Arm Shaping.

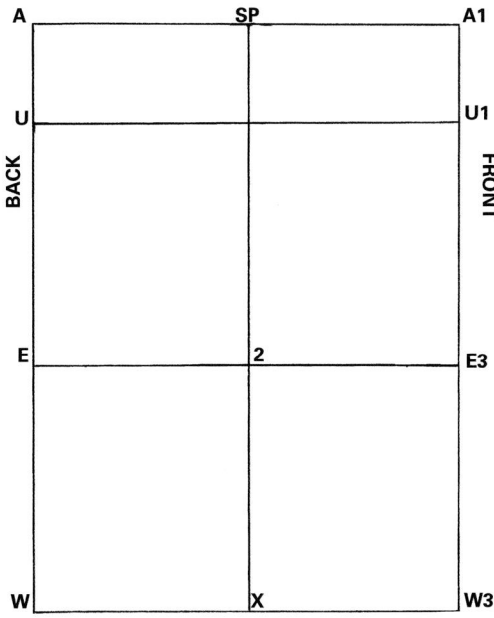

Figure 1.27 Historical One-piece Sleeve divisions.

Chapter 1 Foundation

Sleeve Head Shaping

Figure 1.28

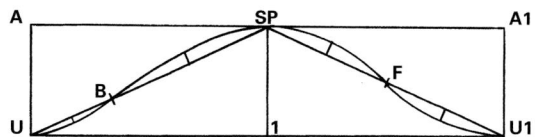

1. Draw a guideline from **U** to **SP**.
2. Draw a guideline from **SP** to **U1**.
3. **B** is a third of **U** to **SP**.
4. **F** is the midpoint of **U1** to **SP**.
5. Find the midpoint of **U** to **B** and square a line 0.5 cm (³⁄₁₆") down towards **U–U1**.
6. Find the midpoint of **B** to **SP** and square a line 1.25 cm (½") up towards the top of the draft.
7. **F** is the midpoint of **SP** to **U1**.
8. Find the midpoint of **SP** to **F** and square a line 1.25 cm (½") up towards the top of the draft.
9. Find the midpoint of **F** to **U1** and square a line 1 cm (³⁄₈") down towards **U–U1**.
10. Touching all the previous points, draw the sleeve head.

Figure 1.28 Historical One-piece Sleeve cap draft.

Completion

1. Measure the sleeve head from **U** through **B** to **SP** through **F** to **U1**. **Note:** The measurement of the sleeve head must be at least equal to that of the bodice armhole. Ideally, the sleeve head is 2 cm–4 cm (¾"–1⅜") larger than the bodice armhole. If too small, change the curve of the sleeve head until the measurement is long enough.
2. To determine the placement of the back notches, measure the sleeve head from **U** to **B** and record this measurement on the Basic Bodice Block back on the curve from **U** towards **B**. Mark the placement with two notches. **Note:** This may not be in the same position as **B** on the Basic Bodice Block.
3. To determine the placement of the front notch, measure the sleeve head from **U1** to **F** and record this measurement on the Basic Bodice Block front from **U** to **F**. Mark the placement with one notch. **Note:** This may not be in the same position as **F** on the Basic Bodice Block.
4. Many tailors use **SP** as the matching point instead of marking out single and double notches.

Historical Two-piece Sleeve Block Instructions

The two-piece sleeves in this book are developed from the tailored British half and half sleeve. Following the tailoring tradition, the front of the sleeve is always placed to the left of the page and the sleeve back is placed on the right side of the page. This is in contrast to many women's sleeve drafts, which place the sleeve in the opposite position on the page.

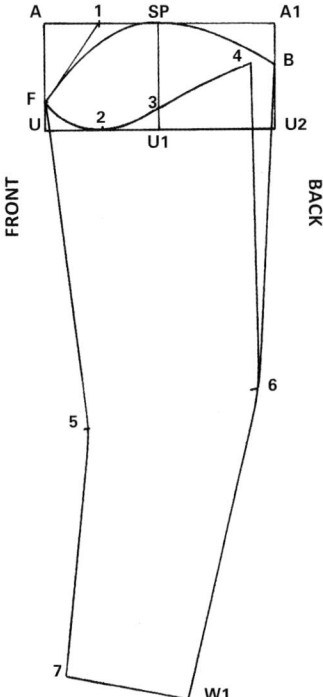

Figure 1.29 Historical Two-piece Sleeve Block.

Modifing Sleeve Cap

Figure 1.30, Figure 1.31 and Figure 1.32

1. Begin by repeating the Modern Two-piece Sleeve Block frame instructions, steps 1–7.
2. Extend the line **A–A1** to the left of **A**, 2.5 cm (1").
3. Extend the line **A–A1** to the right of **A1**, 2.5 cm (1").
4. Shift the letters **A** and **A1** to the new positions.
5. Draw a line 5 cm (2") above **U–U2**. This is the new underarm line.
6. Square down lines from **A** and **A1** to meet the new underarm line.
7. Shift the letters **U**, **U1** and **U2** to the new positions.
8. The line **H–B** remains on the same level.
9. Shift the letters **H** and **B** to the new positions.
10. **SP** remains in its former position.

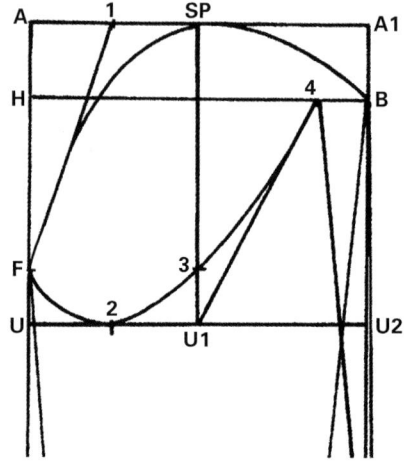

Figure 1.30 Modern Two-piece Sleeve cap.

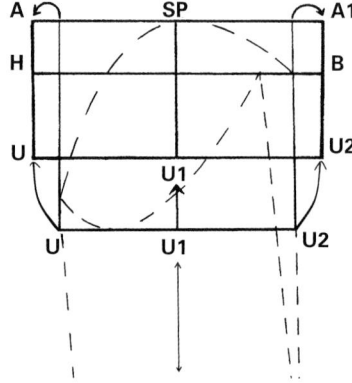

Figure 1.31 Transition of the Modern Two-piece Sleeve cap to a Historical Two-piece Sleeve cap.

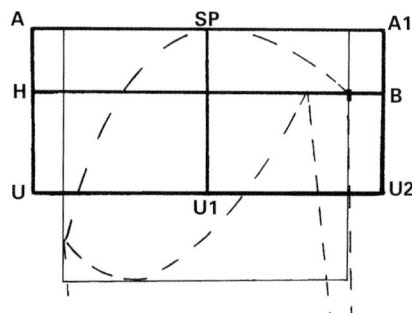

Figure 1.32 Frame of Historical Two-piece Sleeve cap.

Sleeve Head Shaping

Figure 1.33

1. **1** is the midpoint **A** to **SP**.
2. **F** is 2.5 cm (1") above **U**.
3. Draw a guideline from **1** to **F**.
4. **2** is the midpoint of **U** to **U1**.

5. **3** is 2.5 cm (1") above **U1** on the line drawn down from **SP**.
6. **4** is 2.5 cm (1") to the left of **B** on the **H–B** line.
7. Draw a guideline from **3** to **4**.
8. Using the guideline **1** to **F**, draw the topsleeve head from **F** to **SP** to **B**. Refer to Figure 1.33 for shaping guidance.
9. Draw the undersleeve head from **F** to **2** to **3** to **4**. Refer to Figure 1.33 for shaping.

Completion

Figure 1.33
1. Measure the total sleeve head from **F** through **SP** to **B** and from **F** through **2** and **3** to **4**. **Note:** The measurement of the sleeve head must be at least equal to that of the bodice armhole. Ideally, the sleeve head is 2 cm–4 cm (¾"–1⅝") larger than the bodice armhole.
2. To determine the placement of back notches, measure the sleeve head from **2** to **4** and record this measurement on the Basic Bodice Block back on the curve from **U** towards **B**. Mark the placement with two notches. **Note:** This may not be the same position as **B** on the bodice.
3. To determine the placement of the front notch, measure the sleeve head from **2** to **F** and record this measurement on the Basic Bodice Block front on the curve from **U** towards **F**. Mark the placement with one notch. **Note:** This may not be the same position as **F** on the bodice.
4. Many tailors use **SP** as the matching point instead of marking out single and double notches.

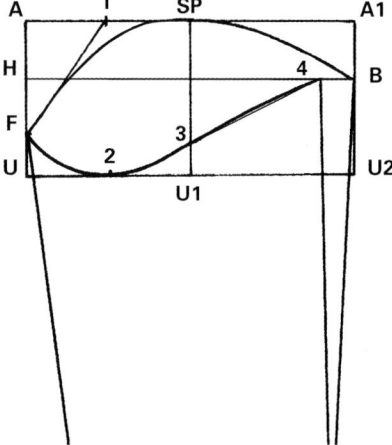

Figure 1.33 Historical Two-piece Sleeve cap shaping.

Skirt

After completing the complexities of the bodice and sleeve drafting patterns, the skirt pattern will seem quite straightforward. It is essentially a cylinder that sits comfortably around the hip area, which is reduced, with darts, to fit snugly around the waist. I have chosen to divide the waist into thirds, but it is not uncommon to place waist darts in other positions. In fact, they can be placed wherever they harmonize with the design and the client's body. In many of the historical drafts in the following chapters, I have subdivided the hip line to achieve equal skirt panels. For those patterns, the waist darts are shifted from their original positions to align with the divisions.

Despite their apparent simplicity, it would be an error to disregard skirt drafts as rudimentary or unimportant. While our attention often focuses on the area closest to the face, skirts from every period actually made the greatest impact. They were made from the largest quantity of fabric, and were therefore the most costly part of a garment. While their assemblage of straight stitching and hemming did not require the most skilful hand, they did involve long periods of arduous hand stitching. In the hands of the talented dressmaker, however, skirts provided huge scope for imagination. The method a dressmaker chose to drape an expanse of fabric, and reduce it into a small waist, is often the most telling signature of a period's silhouette.

Straight Skirt Block

The measurements required to draft the Straight Skirt Block are:

1. Waist
2. Hip
3. Waist to Hip
4. Waist to Knee

A skirt made to a person's exact measurements would be extremely uncomfortable unless the fabric has stretch. Pattern makers add extra to the body measurements to make the garment more comfortable. This extra is called 'ease'. The Straight Skirt Block includes a moderate amount of ease, for a fitted yet comfortable skirt. The hip has 5 cm (2") of ease added, and the waist has 2.5 cm (1") of ease included. Because the hip is usually the largest horizontal measurement, it determines the width of the pattern frame.

Because people are almost symmetrical, the patterns map only half of the body. Therefore, all the horizontal measurements are divided in half. Vertical measurements are not halved.

Table 1.6 Straight Skirt Block Measurement Chart

	MEASUREMENT + EASE	PATTERN MEASUREMENT
1. Waist to Depth of Dart Standard for most sizes.	15 cm (6")	15 cm (6")
2. Waist to Hip Standard for most sizes.	20 cm (8")	20 cm (8")
3. Waist to Knee Measured from shoulder to wrist.	60 cm (23½")	60 cm (23½")
4. Hip The hip circumference plus 5 cm (2") ease.	99 cm (39")	49.5 cm (19½")
5. Waist The waist circumference plus 2.5 cm (1") ease.	69 cm (27¼")	34.5 cm (13⅝")

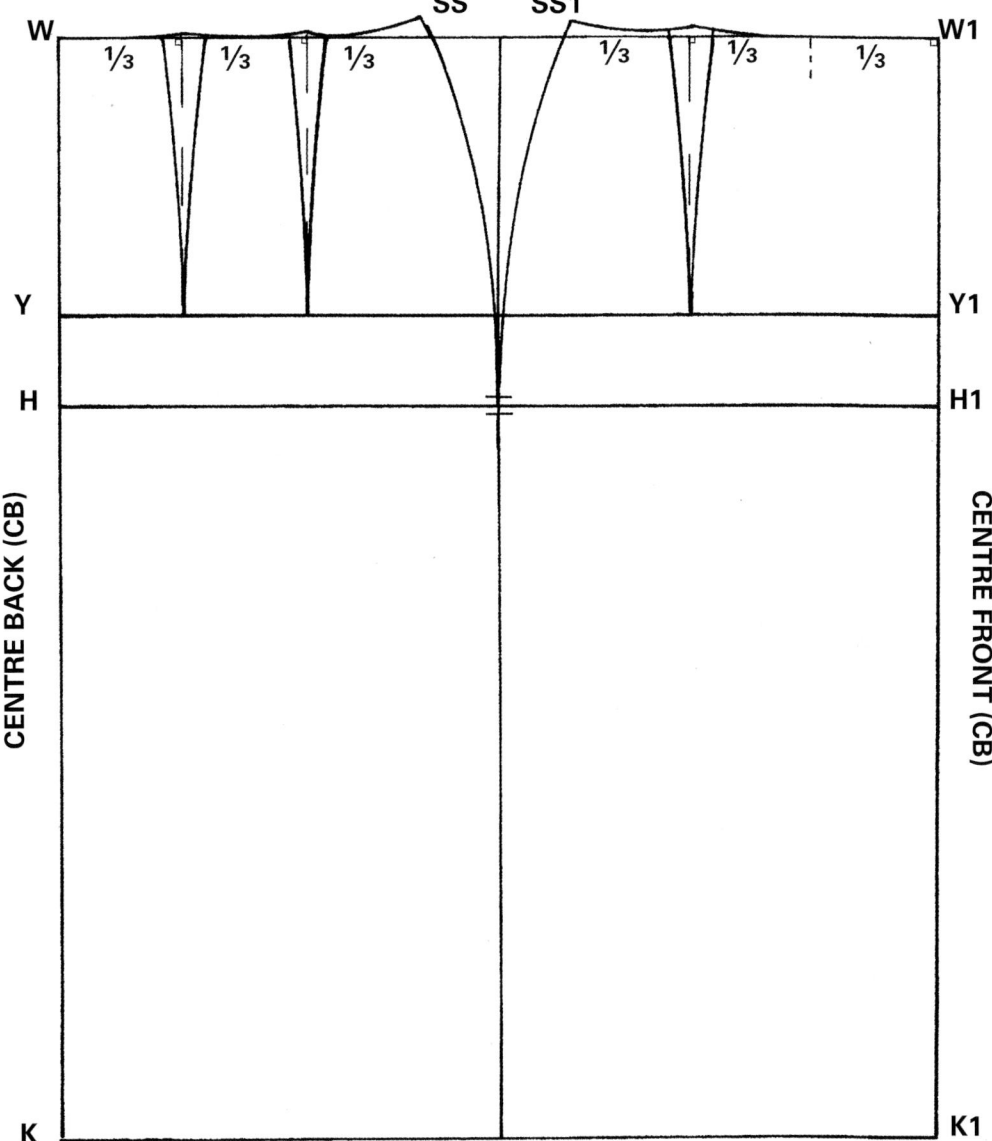

Figure 1.34 Straight and Standard Skirt Blocks.

Straight Skirt Draft Instructions

Frame

Figure 1.35
1. Take a piece of paper approximately 70 cm × 80 cm (27½" × 31½").
2. Draw a line the length of the paper about 5 cm (2") from the left lengthwise edge. Call this line the **CB**.
3. Mark a point **W** about 5 cm (2") from the top of the paper on this line.
4. Square a line across from **W** across the entire width of the paper. This is the top of the draft and is the provisional waistline.
5. **W–W1** = Hip pattern measurement, 49.5 cm (19½").
6. Square a line down from **W1**. This is the **CF** line.
7. **W–K** is the full length of the draft. In this case, it is the Waist to Knee = 60 cm (23½"), which is standard.
8. Square out a line across the paper. This is the bottom of the draft. This line connects the **CF** at **K1**.

This completes the outside parameters of the draft.

Interior Draft Lines

Figure 1.35
1. **W–H** = Waist to Hip = 20 cm (8"). This is standard.
2. **W–Y** = the dart depth = 15 cm (6"). This is standard.
3. From **H**, square out a line across the paper to meet the **CF**. Call this **H1**.
4. From **Y**, square out a line across the paper to meet the **CF**. Call this **Y1**. All the waist darts will end at this point. This line is sometimes referred to as a 'yoke line', hence the designation of **Y**.
5. Find the midpoint of **W–W1**, and square down to the bottom of the draft. This is the provisional **SS**.

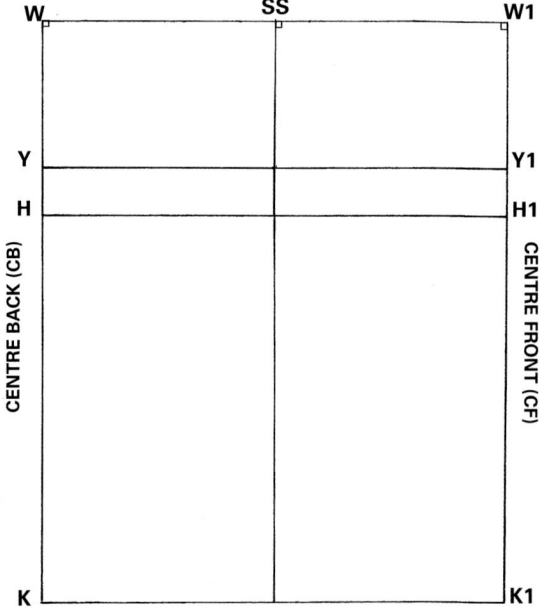

Figure 1.35 Straight and Standard Skirt frame.

Waist Reduction and Shaping with Darts

Figure 1.36

The provisional waistline, **W–W1**, is usually a larger measurement than the Waist pattern measurement. Therefore, we need to reduce **W–W1** to equal the Waist pattern measurement:

49.5 cm – 34.5 cm = 15 cm (19½" – 13⅝" = 6")

Account for half the waist reduction, 7.5 cm (3"), at the **SS**. The remaining amount of waist reduction, 7.5 cm (3"), is divided by 3 for three darts; two back darts and one front dart:

7.5 cm ÷ 3 = 2.5 cm (3" ÷ 3 = 1") per dart.

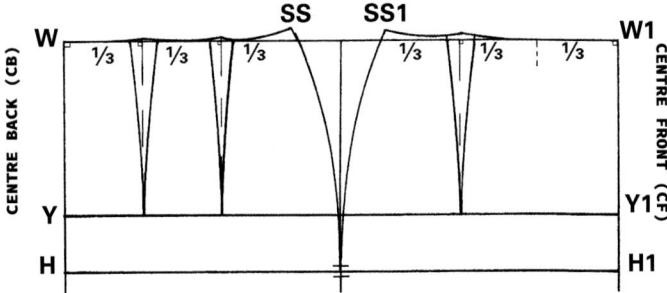

Figure 1.36 Waist reduction.

Side Seam

1. The **SS** waist reduction is 7.5 cm (3").
2. Mark a point 3.75 cm (1½") on either side of the provisional side seam and label these points **SS** and **SS1**.
3. Draw a curved line from the hip line to **SS** and **SS1**.

Back Darts

1. There are two back darts. Each dart is 2.5 cm (1") in depth on the line **W–W1**.
2. Divide **W–SS** into thirds, and square down to the line **Y–Y1**. These are the centres of the two darts.
3. Begin each dart 1.25 cm (½") on each side of the dart centres on the line **W–W1**. The darts end on the line **Y–Y1**.

Front Dart

1. There is one front dart. It is 2.5 cm (1") in depth on the line **W–W1**.
2. Divide **W1–SS1** into thirds. Square down a line from a point ⅔ from **W1**. This is the centre of the front dart.
3. Begin the dart 1.25 cm (½") on either side of the centre. The dart ends on the line **Y–Y1**.

Cutting the Pattern

Figure 1.37
Before cutting the pattern, make sure the side seams are clearly marked with two notches on the **SS** on either side of the hip line. The notches are important for matching the front and back patterns correctly.

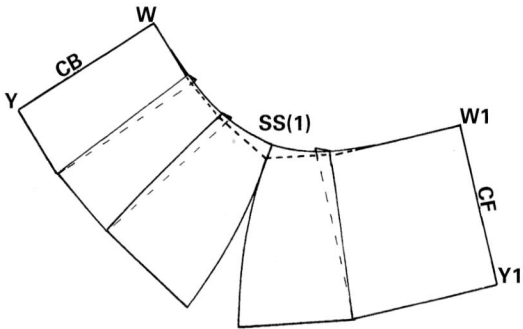

Figure 1.37 Truing and shaping waist.

1. Starting on the front, cut from the hem to **SS(1)** and beyond to the top of the paper a short distance. You will now have two pattern pieces, a front and a back.
2. Flip the front pattern over the back, matching the hem, the notches and the **SS**. Trace the front curve from the hip line to the **SS** and beyond onto the back, and cut this line.
3. Do not cut along the waist line yet.
4. Crease the front and back patterns along the line **Y–Y1**. This will make folding out the darts easier.
5. Fold the darts closed and press the bulk of the dart towards the **SS(1)**. Pin or tape the darts closed. The pattern will no longer lie flat. The paper pattern starts to take on the shape of a skirt.
6. Match the front and back patterns at the **SS(1)**. The waist will appear as an awkward, angled line.
7. Redraw the waist with a smooth and continuous curve. The curve should hit a point about 1.5 cm–2 cm (⅝"–¾") above **SS** and **SS(1)**.
8. Cut along the new waist.
9. To avoid inaccuracies, remeasure the final waist, compare this to the desired waist measurement and make any adjustments needed.

Standard Skirt Block

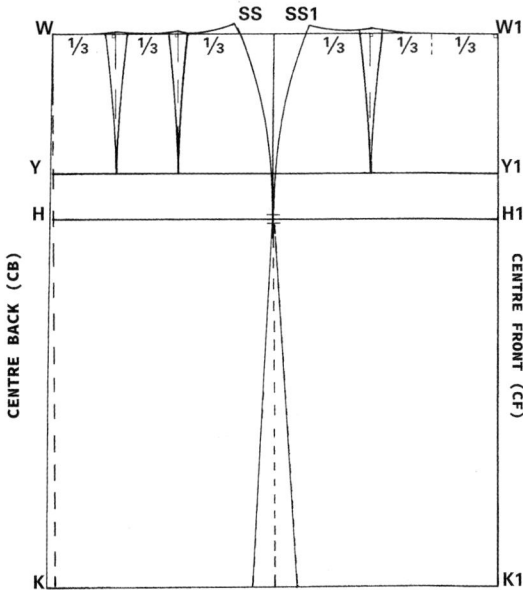

Figure 1.38 Standard Skirt Block.

The Straight Skirt Block produces a very straight skirt that may appear narrower at the knee than at the hip. A Standard Skirt Block will give more movement at the hem and is used for many skirt variations.

1. Trace the front and back pattern on a new sheet of paper.
2. Add a flare along the front **SS** and the back **SS** from 2.5 cm (1") at the hem to nothing at **H–H1**.
3. Also add flare at the **CB** with a line 1 cm (⅜") at the hem to nothing at the waist.

NOTES

1. For visual attractiveness, the stitched darts end at least 1.5 cm (⅝") away from the apex.
2. While this book is written in Canada, there are no standard women's body measurements listed with the Canadian General Standards Board. See Ann Haggar (1990) *Pattern Cutting for Lingerie, Beachwear and Leisurewear* (London: BSP Professional Books), 6, 8.
3. Note that the **SH** and **SH1** designation is not used in the subsequent drafts and is used here to describe how the hips overlap.

2
First Steps

The historical pattern maker needs to gather as much information about a garment as possible. Often, the only information is found in two-dimensional images such as fashion illustrations, photographs, or artistic renderings. These visual representations of a garment come with their own set of complications. Costume designers working in theatre, film or television usually incorporate a character's personality into their renderings, which can blur historical accuracy. Fashion illustrations show the ideal shape of the period rather than the realistic shape of an individual. Portrait artists may paint the best side of their client's visage, and exaggerate their wealth by adding greater depth to the fabric in their clothing. Photographs give a literal vision of a garment, but show it from one angle, and in two dimensions rather than three. While looking for proportion, position of seams and placement of closures, the pattern maker must also read through any creative fabrication, with an artist's eye.

This chapter discusses ways to identify specific elements found in images of historical dress and ways in which the following patterns accommodate them. The first technique a student may use to understand, or *read* a garment, is to ask and answer a series of questions about design details that are crucial to drafting a pattern.

Figure 2.1 All the focus is on the back waist of this beautiful chestnut silk jacket the pattern of which is developed in Chapter 8.

Reading an Image

BODICE

What is the silhouette or overall shape?

In addition to the knowledge accumulated by a thorough study of a period in dress history, much more can be learned through a deep examination of the image itself. Trace the outline to solidify the garment's shape in your mind. Trace any darts and visible seam lines to outline the garment's cut. Trace any gathers, pleats or tucks. This is a simple exercise, and it creates a technical drawing as a guide. See Chapter 10 for an example of tracing.

Does the bodice fit the corseted shape with or without ease?

Women in the nineteenth century almost always wore a corset. A corset provides a firm shell that moves in unison with the body. A garment of this type does not need additional ease for comfort or flexibility. Think of how snugly a tutu's bodice fits on a dancer's body, and yet the dancer has complete control. A corset works in the same manner. Historically, bodices were made to fit the corset beneath them. The Modern Basic Bodice Block has 5 cm (2") of ease included, which is too much for a historical bodice. To avoid looking oversized, some of this ease is removed from the patterns in the following chapters. For a more relaxed look, you may want to keep as much the ease as is incorporated in the Modern Basic Block.

At what level does the bust sit? Is there a bust division, or does it have one broad profile?

While body measurements taken over a corset do not differ significantly from those taken without one, body shape is dramatically altered. In particular, wearing a corset raises the fullest part of the bust. Therefore, the apex in most of the following patterns is raised to reflect the altered body shape.

Is the waist at the natural position, or is it higher or lower than the natural waist?

Some details, such as the waist position, are relatively easily observed in an image. If, however, it is in question, use the drafts in this book. Each pattern accurately reflects the waist placement of the period.

Is there a visible side seam?

A side seam equally dividing the body was not as common in the nineteenth century as it is today. An image may show a side seam that is closer to the front or the back. Find examples in this book.

Where is the shoulder seam? Where and at what angle is it placed?

Modern shoulder seams tend to sit at the highest position on the shoulder and are not noticeable when looking directly at the person. In the nineteenth century, they were often placed to the back of the shoulder as part of the bodice styling. This was not a rule, however, and some of the shoulder seams in this book have an almost modern placement.

Does the sleeve hit the natural shoulder line?

Sleeve placement is one of the clearest indications for dating historical garments. Very narrow shoulders are often indicative of an early 1800s. Extraordinarily full and wide shoulders signify an 1830s date. In mid-century, shoulders were slim and continued well beyond the point of articulation. From 1870 onwards, shoulder placement became more closely aligned with the natural shoulder.

Can you see where the sleeve seam meets the bodice? Is there one seam or two?

Sleeve seam placement is often an indication of the sleeve style. If the seam joins the armhole towards the front of the underarm, it may be a two-piece sleeve, or a one-piece sleeve that was derived from a two-piece.

What is the straight-of-grain in all garment sections?

Clothing that conforms to the body without darting or clever seaming is often due to the textile rather than the cut. It could be a weave that defies a common warp and weft arrangement like crepe or the design may be utilizing the textile's bias. Bias usage is usually connected with twentieth-century dress and the designs of Madeleine Vionnet, but it was also used to great effect in the nineteenth century. Tight sleeves were often cut on the bias to give more freedom of motion. Some bodices were cut on the bias (see Chapter 4). This allowed the bodice to be pulled over the corset tightly.

Bias was also used to actively shift fabric. If a bias edge is stitched to a straight-of-grain edge, the bias actually pushes away the straight-of-grain. Late nineteenth-century skirts were often made with a number of panels with one bias edge, each one successively pushing the next panel towards the back in a lovely sweeping motion.

SKIRTS

It can be difficult to read the volume and design of a skirt in a two-dimensional picture. If the image includes the hem, look at the hills and valleys of fabric around the hem. Variations in the colour give clues about the fabric's volume and the methods used to control it. A shallow fold will read as a slightly darker shade of the fashion fabric. This means that the skirt is relatively narrow, and there may be soft gathering or shallow pleating at the waist. A much darker shade indicates more fabric and deeper pleating at the waist. Photographic images and views show more depth of fabric.

Look also to see how often the folds occur. If they are evenly spaced, the skirt may have regular knife pleats or gathers at the waist. If the folds occur farther apart, the waist has fewer, but deeper pleats. In the 1860s, skirts had double, or even triple, inverted box pleats at the waist. They controlled a large volume of fabric and are conveyed with deep colour and lines from the waist. If fabric radiates like a starburst from a single point, it indicates a number of deep pleats with underlapping folds, which stem from the same position on the waist. This is often seen at the centre back of skirts from the second half of the nineteenth century. If there is a great deal of fabric that looks like a wave, undulating from no specific source, there is a good chance that there are cartridge pleats at the waist. Cartridge pleats are very distinctive at the waist with tiny, even cords, but are less distinctive at the hem (see Terminology for cartridge pleats).

Without a lot of experience, it is difficult to estimate the width, or diameter, of a skirt hem merely by looking at a two-dimensional image. How can one tell if the hem measures 228 cm (90") or 508 cm (200")? One technique for determining volume is referred to in Chapter 4. Using two or more measuring tapes, place them end to end in a circle on the floor and stand within the circle. It is hard to believe but this actually gives a sense of the volume as a measurement. Another method is to sew a mock-up skirt with three widths of cotton that is about 115 cm (45") wide. Gather the top to equal your waist measurement. Think of this as your base skirt, which has a hem measurement of about 340 cm (130"). Do you want less, or more, width at the hem to mimic the image? You will soon understand how a skirt of 228 cm (90") compares to a skirt of 508 cm (200").

3

Development of Period Patterns, 1800–15

Period Dress in Historical Context

This lovely ecru silk dress looks simple in cut, but between the seams it holds a rich and complex history. It is a story of revolution, escape and resettlement. It is a story of family, economy and sustainability. It is a story of the rapidly changing whims of the fashionable elite and the development of textile technology.

Following the American War of Independence in 1783, thousands who had served with the British Crown found themselves facing expulsion from their homes in the new United States. Many travelled north to settle on Crown-allotted land in the provinces of Nova Scotia, New Brunswick, Lower Canada (Quebec) and Upper Canada (Ontario). Among those who settled in the Kingston area of Upper Canada[1] were the ancestors of Agnes Etherington, the namesake of the Agnes Etherington Art Centre from which most of the garments in this collection of patterns are selected.

A few settlers, now known as United Empire Loyalists, enjoyed the privileges of rank. They could carry a few years supply of clothing and travelled with servants. However, the majority fled with little money and few possessions to 'a country yet to be formed'.[2] The conditions they experienced in their new homes were a far cry from those they had

Figure 3.1 Gown front. This crisp silk with embroidered and painted floral clusters dates from a period earlier than the cut of the gown.

Figure 3.2 The insert shows the gown back with knife pleated waist, embroidered buttons and draw-string neck tie.

known in the American states. The town built around the garrison in Kingston had but 'fifty wooden Houses and Merchant Store Houses'[3] in 1791. There were no clothiers or dressmakers in the early years before the community became more established and prosperous. All essential goods, including cloth, came to Kingston with spring and fall shipments that floated up the St Lawrence River from Britain or the United States. Some women appealed to friends and relations overseas to help them acquire suitable clothing. Elizabeth Russel was a relatively wealthy woman living in York, later Toronto, a town of similar size to Kingston, 260 km to the west. She wrote to an English friend requesting

> *a muslin gown as they are worn* and as you are very much my Size I will thank you to have it made as for yourself. … also a Calico Morning dress. The pattern of that and the muslin I leave to your choice only don't let the muslin exceed *six shillings a yard* … and be so good as to send me *a yard and a half of each to repair with.*[4]

There is no way of knowing the route that this gown from the Collection of Canadian Dress at the Agnes Etherington Art Centre followed on its way to Kingston. It could have been purchased as fabric in the United States prior to the family's travels. Alternatively, it is possible it was imported from Britain or the United States for a family wedding in 1795.[5] Regardless, the dress we see was undoubtedly remodelled from an earlier gown.

The Grecian, columnar silhouette and 'round gown' construction[6] clearly places this dress between 1795 and 1820. The long, finger-length sleeves narrow the timeframe to between 1810 and 1815. The silk is plain, with dainty tambour embroidery of green and teal foliage with celery French knots. This fabric was probably woven and embroidered in India about 1790. This crisp, silk fabric is incongruous with the aesthetic of 1810. High fashion had moved away from the heavy silks that had been popular in the eighteenth century in favour of lighter diaphanous cottons. This had become relatively inexpensive thanks to the development of the cotton gin invented by Eli Whitney in 1793. Styles in the later part of the eighteenth century were heavily pleated with yards of uncut silk. When the garments looked dated, the gowns were carefully unpicked, and often recycled into new fashions. This dress may have originally been a *robe à l'Anglaise* before it was reconstructed in this neoclassical style.

This dress is part of the time-honoured system of restructuring clothing to suit a modern aesthetic, or fit a different body shape. Noted dress historian Linda Baumgarten has written about appreciating altered clothing within a museum's collection. She suggests that 'altered clothing has value and speaks eloquently about the nature of human history as a continuum rather than isolated grand event at one particular date in the past'.[7] Development of the following pattern and the subsequent refabricating of this dress is yet another part of its continuum.

DESCRIPTION

The unlined front of the bodice has minimal shaping, with small gathers that fit tidily into a very high waistline (Figure 3.1). The back is supported by a stiff linen lining (Figure 3.2). Shoulder seams sit far to the rear, and two side back seams curve from the armholes towards the centre back waist, creating a very small, neat-looking back. Five nonfunctional embroidered buttons atop metal hooks adorn the back closure; two rows of handworked bars provide some sizing flexibility. The modest neckline is edged with a drawstring to adjust any potential gaping. Straight sleeves, long enough to cover the hands to the fingertips, are pleated into a high shoulder with a moderate fullness. The front skirt hangs straight from the high waist with only a hint of gathering. The back skirt is more generous, with seven knife pleats on each side facing into the centre back.[8]

Primary Step-by-Step Drafting Instructions

The key to developing a period pattern from a Modern Basic Block is to isolate specific differences, and determine how to accommodate them into the final draft. Raising the waist and bust line are the most obvious adjustments that must be made to the modern draft. Equally important is the division of a single back panel into two shaped pattern pieces to create the neat, diamond-shaped back that is essential for the period look. Before beginning a new draft, it is a good idea to remeasure the client. In addition to the basic measurements listed in Chapter 1, take a horizontal measurement directly under the bust. This is not necessary for the following draft, but may be used to double-check the draft before construction. The original pattern is indicated with short dotted lines. The longer dotted lines indicate the centre of darts.

To start this draft, you will need a completed front and back Basic Bodice Block pattern without the optional back shoulder dart.

New Waist

Figure 3.3

1. To find the new waist on both patterns, draw a horizontal line 7.5 cm (3") below **C–C1**. This is standard for a bust measurements of 88 cm–95 cm (34½"–37½"). Increase this depth by 0.5 cm (³⁄₁₆") for every 5 cm (2") larger bust measurement. For example, for a bust of 100 cm (39½"), draw the line 8 cm (3⅛") below **C–C1**.
2. Remove the pattern portions below this line and set aside (Figure 3.3).

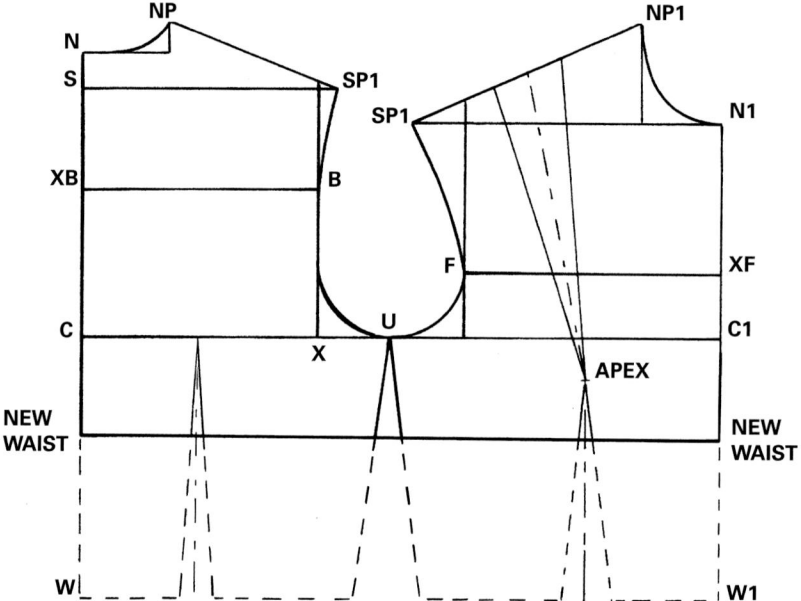

Figure 3.3 Basic Bodice with shortened waist.

BODICE BACK

Bodice backs from this period are composed of two pattern pieces. The primary gown has a back closure and the Centre Back (**CB**) is placed on the straight-of-grain. The seam dividing the back is called the Side Back (**SB**) seam. Historically, its curve is a matter of choice, from straight to quite rounded. The following instructions produce a moderate curve for the primary bodice. The alternative bodice will have a straighter line.

Back Guideline

Figure 3.4 and Figure 3.5

1. Draw a line from **B** to the top of the dart and continue to the desired position on the new waist, approximately 3 cm (1⅛") from the **CB**. This is the guideline for the new **SB** seam.
2. Using the guideline, draw a curved line. The crest of the curve is about 2 cm (¾") from the midpoint of the guideline.
3. Cut along the **SB** seam line.

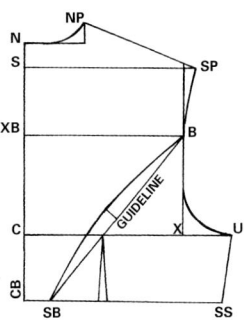

Figure 3.4 Side Back guideline.

Side Back Panel

Figure 3.6

1. Extend the dart to the cut along the **SB** seam.
2. Close the back dart. Fold one side of the dart and place it along the other side of the dart so the two branches meet. Secure this in position with pins or tape.
3. Closing the dart produces an awkward line on the **SB** seam and the new waist.
4. Smooth **SB** seam and waist by blending a new line and discarding the angle (see Blending in Terminology).
5. Measure both branches of the **SB** seam. They must be equal. If one side is longer than the other, trim off the excess at the armhole. This is called truing up, or truing (see True up in Terminology).

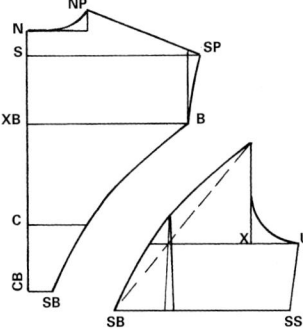

Figure 3.5 Side Back seam.

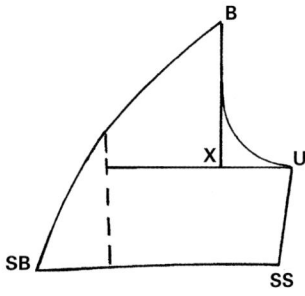

Figure 3.6 Side Back panel.

Front Bodice

Figure 3.7, Figure 3.8 and Figure 3.9

1. Raise the **Apex** to the line **U–C1** (see Figure 3.7).
2. Redraw the shoulder and waist darts to reflect the new **Apex** position.
3. Cut along one branch of the waist dart from the waist to, but not through, the **Apex**.
4. Fold one side of the shoulder dart. Place the fold along the other side of the dart. This is called 'closing the dart'. Secure the shoulder dart closed with pins or tape. With the shoulder dart closed, the waist dart will automatically open (see Figure 3.8). This is a process known as 'dart transfer', as all the shaping capacity of one dart is transferred into another area (see Dart transfer in Terminology).
5. True up the shoulder seam.
6. Record the new waist dart's depth at the waist.
7. Redraw the waist as a smoothly curved line blending the area of the former dart.
8. Mark the position of two small tucks under the bust area. These two tucks will equal the depth of the original waist dart.
9. When making up the garment, the total waist should equal one half of the under bust measurement plus about 1 cm (⅜") for ease.

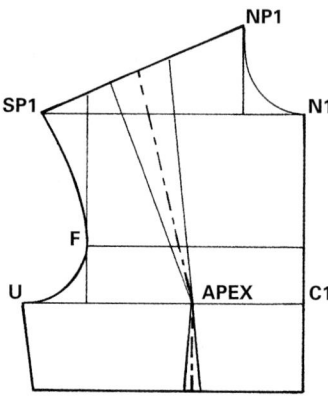

Figure 3.7 Raising Apex.

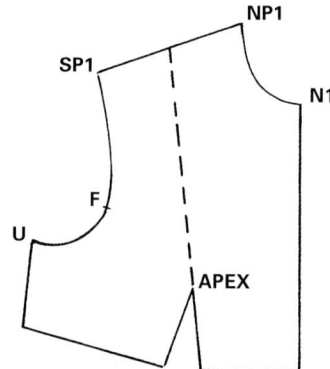

Figure 3.8 Transfer shoulder dart.

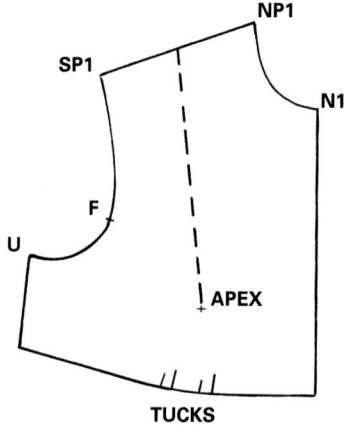

Figure 3.9 Front tucks.

Shoulder and Neckline

Figure 3.10

1. With the neck dart still closed, match the back and front pattern pieces from **NP** to **SP**.
2. Mark a point 2 cm (¾") from **NP** towards **N**.
3. Mark a point 4 cm (1⅝") from **SP** towards **B**.
4. Draw a line between the two points. This is the new shoulder.
5. Indent the back armhole 2.5 cm (1") from **B**, as indicated in Figure 3.10.

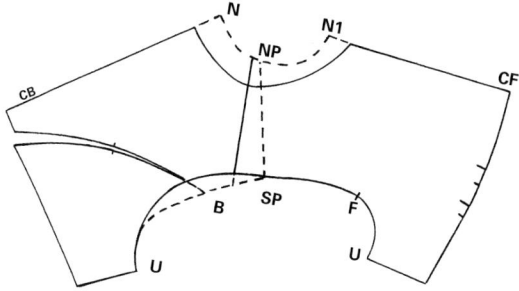

Figure 3.10 Shoulder and neckline.

Sleeve

Figure 3.11

1. Use the One-piece Historical Sleeve Draft.
2. Extend the back sleeve head 2 cm–3 cm (¾"–1⅛") to fit into the deeper back armhole.
3. Draw a horizontal line approximately 7 cm (2¾") below the line drawn out from **W**.
4. Square down a line from **W1** and **W2**.
5. Add flare of 1 cm–2 cm (⅜"–¾"). The new hem is a little wider than the original so as to sit comfortably over the hand.
6. Smooth any sharp angles.
7. The straight-of-grain is the centre length of the sleeve.

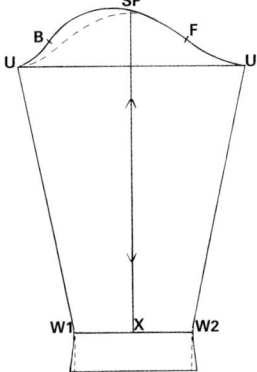

Figure 3.11 Primary sleeve.

Skirt

Figure 3.12

Skirts of this period are essentially large rectangles. This skirt will need two panels of 115 cm (45"). This will give a width of approximately 230 cm (90"). The length is the measurement from the raised waist to the floor.

The front is flat, the sides are gently gathered at the waist, and the back has seven knife pleats per side facing towards the **CB**.

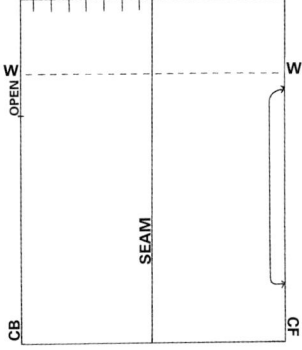

Figure 3.12 Skirt diagram.

Figure 3.13 Soft fabric sways with the wind in this sweet fashion plate. The fabric is gathered around the raised waist and the skirt hangs straight without angled shaping.

Figure 3.14 The diminutive back and raised waist of this dress project a youthful look that was appreciated during the first decade of the nineteenth century.

Alternative Regency Gown Drafting Instructions

The draft for the alternative bodice is similar to the primary pattern, but has more fullness in the bodice and skirt. The neckline is much lower both front and back. The shortened sleeves are also much fuller. The back bodice has a sharper diamond-shape back, which is one of the most common characteristics of the Regency/Federalist period. It can be easily visualized in the outline of sharply angled shoulders and **SB** seams. The soft front gathering, a popular aspect of the period's aesthetic, is produced by modifying the primary draft with a technique called 'cutting and spreading' (see Cutting and spreading in Terminology).

Alternative Back and Side Back

Figure 3.15 and Figure 3.16

1. On a clean sheet of paper, draw a vertical and horizontal grid. Place the **CB** along the vertical gridline and the waist along the horizontal gridline.
2. Draw a new neckline.
3. From the neckline to the waist, draw a number of lines, as shown in Figure 3.15.
4. Record the neck and waist measurements from **CB** to the last line drawn.
5. Cut the pattern along the drawn lines.
6. Being careful to line up the new waist along the horizontal gridline, spread out the sections as desired. The total width should measure at least one and a half times the original width.
7. Redraw the neckline blending into a smooth and continuous line.
8. In making up, gather the top and bottom to equal the original measurement, or encase a drawstring. Concentrate the gathers in the areas of the spreading.
9. The **SB** guideline is used as the **SB** seam.

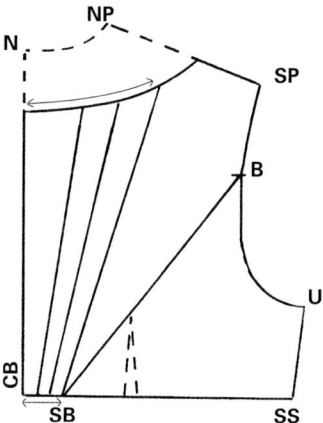

Figure 3.15 Lines for cutting.

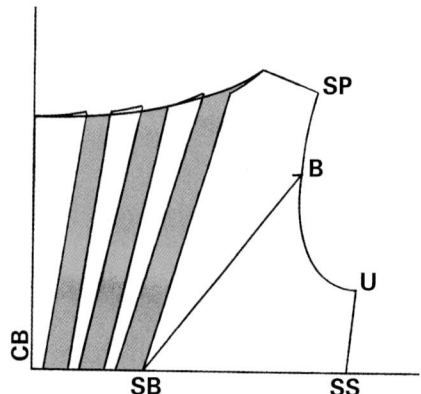

Figure 3.16 Cutting and spreading.

Alternative Front

Figure 3.17, Figure 3.18 and Figure 3.19

1. On a clean sheet of paper, draw a vertical and horizontal grid. Place the **CF** along the vertical gridline and the new waist along the horizontal gridline.
2. Draw a new neckline.
3. From the neckline to the waist, draw a number of vertical lines, as shown in Figure 3.17.
4. Record the neck and waist measurements from the first vertical line to the **CF**.
5. Cut the pattern along the lines.
6. Being careful to line up the waist along the horizontal gridline, spread out the sections as desired. The total width should measure about 1½ times the original width (see Cutting and spreading in Terminology).
7. Redraw the neckline blending into a smooth and continuous line.
8. Optional, add a seam to divide the shoulder strap from the bodice.
9. In making up, gather the top and bottom to equal the original measurement, or encase a drawstring.

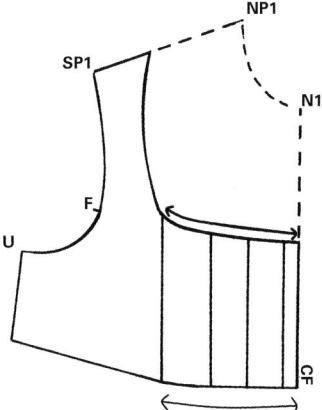

Figure 3.17 Lines for cutting.

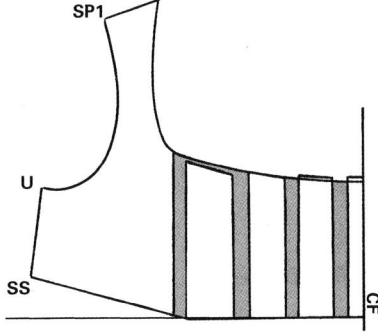

Figure 3.18 Cutting and spreading.

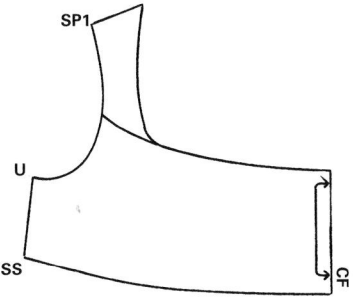

Figure 3.19 Completed Front showing the optional shoulder strap.

Shoulder and Neckline

Figure 3.20

1. Match the front and back patterns at the shoulders from **NP** to **SP** and secure this with tape (see Figure 3.20). The dotted lines indicate the original pattern before cutting and spreading.
2. Mark a point 2 cm (¾") from **NP** on the back neck. Mark a point approximately 6 cm (2½") below **SP** on the back armhole.
3. Connect these two points for the new shoulder seam.
4. For an even smaller back, indent the back armhole up to 4 cm (1⅝").
5. Separate the Front and the Back along the new shoulder seam.
6. To finesse the pattern, raise the waist at the **CB** 2 cm (¾") and curve to nothing at the Side Seam **(SS)**.
7. To further finesse the pattern, you may shift the **SS** towards the back, or even eliminate it altogether. The placement of the **SS** was not standardized at the time.

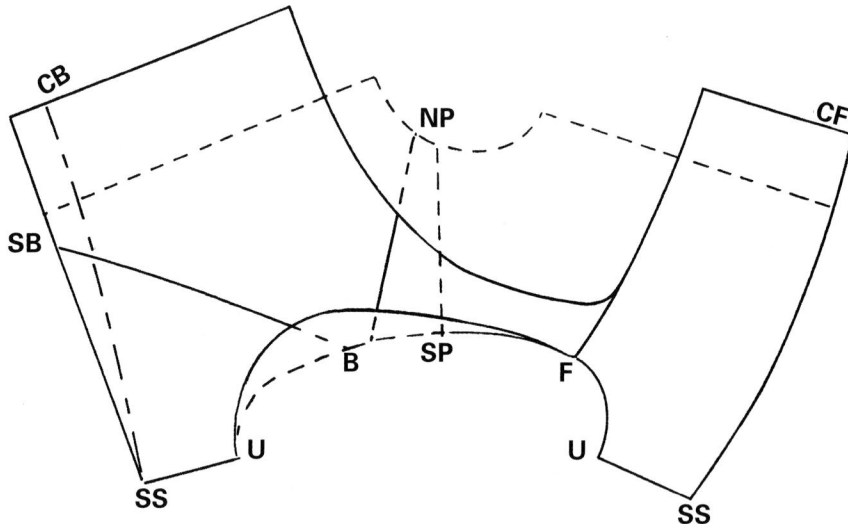

Figure 3.20 Shoulder and necklines.

Alternative Sleeve

Figure 3.21 and Figure 3.22
Both alternative sleeves are very full. The fullness does not rise above the shoulder.

1. Complete this chapter's primary sleeve cap instructions.
2. On a clean sheet of paper at least twice as wide as the sleeve pattern, make a grid to correspond to **U–U1** and the centre line from **SP**.
3. Draw a line 5 cm (2") parallel to and below **U–U1**. This is the new bottom of the sleeve.
4. Divide the sleeve into equal quarters. It is helpful to number the sections, as seen in Figure 3.21.
5. Cut along the dividing lines. The sleeve is now in four pieces.
6. Keeping the **U–U1** line on the grid-line, spread the sleeve pieces to achieve a sleeve at least two times the original width. Depending on the weight of the fabric, you may find that three times the original width gives a better look.
7. Trace the tops and bottoms of the spread pieces.
8. Redraw the sleeve head, remembering to blend the jagged tops. Add 1 cm–2 cm (⅜"–¾") to the height. Add extra on the back sleeve head to accommodate for the narrowing of the Across Back.

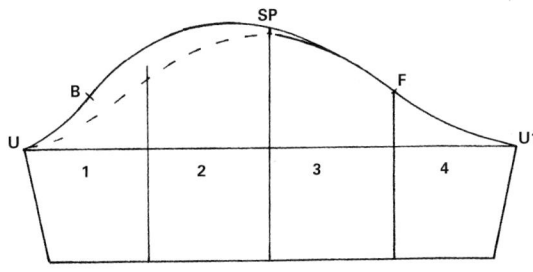

Figure 3.21 Alternative short sleeve.

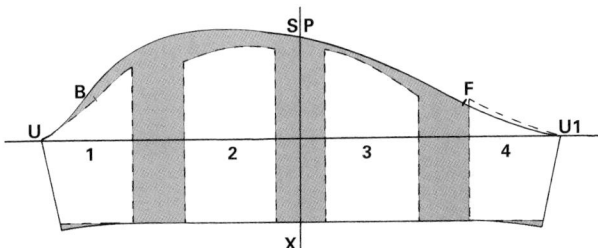

Figure 3.22 Alternative sleeve cut and spread.

Alternative Skirt

Figure 3.23

Like the primary pattern, the alternative skirt is essentially a large rectangle made up of three panels of 115 cm (45") fabric. This will give a width of approximately 340 cm (133"). The length is measured from the high waist to the floor. Adding gores, or triangles of fabric, will add volume to the skirt hem. You have the option to cartridge pleat the back of the skirt instead of knife pleating it. Instructions for cartridge pleats are found in Chapter 5.

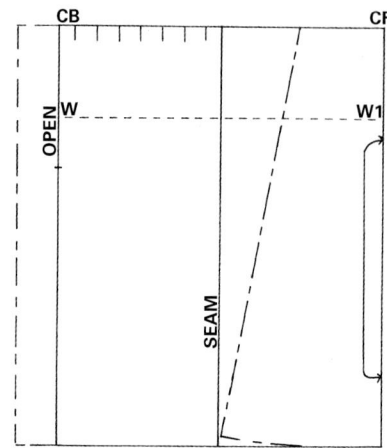

Figure 3.23 Alternative skirt diagrams.

NOTES

1. The Crawford Purchase is one of the earliest land agreements between the British Crown and the Indigenous people of what is now Canada. It was for a large track of land along the northern shore of the St Lawrence River and the end of Lake Ontario, and extended inland from the lake 'as far as a man can travel in a day'. It was exchanged for clothing and firearms.
2. Elizabeth Errington (1995) *Wives and Mothers, Schoolmistresses and Scullery Maids: Working Women in Upper Canada, 1790–1840* (Montreal & Kingston: McGill-Queen's University Press), 5.
3. Errington, *Wives and Mothers*, 12.
4. Mary Holford (1983) 'Dress and Society in Upper Canada, 1791–1841', *Costume*, 17(1): 84.
5. Unknown Maker, Day Dress, 1815, Agnes Etherington Art Centre, 3 March 2023. Available at https://agnes.queensu.ca/explore/collections/object/day-dress-7.
6. The term 'round gown' refers to a dress in which the bodice and skirt are joined together and wrap around the body. This is common now, but the term was used to distinguish this construction from gowns that opened at the front exposing an ornate petticoat.
7. Linda Baumgarten (1998) 'Altered Historical Clothing', *Dress*, 25(1): 42.
8. M. Elaine MacKay (2007) *Beyond the Silhouette: Fashion and the Women of Historic Kingston* (Kingston: Queen's University), 14.

4

Development of Period Patterns, 1820–35

Period Dress in Historical Context

Fashion trends overlap before one is considered obsolete and another de rigueur. By 1815, the statuesque figure that had been the standard silhouette for twenty years showed signs of softening, with gored skirts and decorated hems. By the late 1820s, all the trappings of neoclassicism had vanished. A new curvilinear line replaced the elongated shape. It resembled an hourglass, and would become the dominant silhouette for the rest of the century. Wide shoulders, exuberant puffed sleeves, an inserted waistband and a full skirt with padded hem all contribute to the appearance of a small waist and an hourglass silhouette. This beautiful dress embraces the new, romantic age, and exudes youthful buoyancy with an airy, sylph-like quality.

This dress was owned by Helen Mowat, the wife of John B. Mowat, a prominent merchant and aspiring politian in Kingston, Canada. Helen would have had access to 'an assortment of Woollens and Cottons, [and] Silks',[1] through her husband's store, and the financial means to procure it. She could have had it made in Montreal; however, the needlework trades had secured a foothold locally. Dressmakers, who often called themselves 'mantua makers', 'milliners', 'embroiderers' and even 'stay makers', all advertised in the Kingston newspapers.[2]

Figure 4.1 Dress front. This lovely cotton dress expresses the romanticism of the period.

Figure 4.2 Back sleeve detail.

These advertisements can be confusing. Sometimes, businesses claimed to carry 'ready-made' dresses. These were not completed dresses, but rather dress lengths of fabric with partially constructed skirts, which would need to be made up in the client's choice of style. Other dressmakers used the term 'to measure', which might suggest that a client could send her body measurements to the dressmaker, and in short time would receive a completed dress. While in some cases a dressmaker would have had the client's measurements on file, this was not an option for most women in Kingston. Another, more descriptive term for creating a dress or pattern was 'pin-to-the-form'.[3] With this technique, dressmakers draped a pattern directly on the client who stood before her wearing only a chemise and corset. It was accurate, but time-consuming and only practical for the more affluent members of society. Therefore, many women used the traditional and practical method of pattern making by unstitching an existing garment and using the individual pieces as the pattern for a new garment. 'When you have once procured a pattern … which fits a Lady's figure, and this you ought to make of soft paper or cloth, you will not require to measure a fresh one for every new dress.'[4]

I believe that Helen Mowat's dress was pinned-to-the-form. The striped, bias-cut front panel would have followed the shape of the corset beneath. Bias can be extremely unstable and unpredictable. The only way to ensure a perfect fit would be by draping the fabric directly on the body. The dressmaker would have encouraged fabric into the darts a little at a time until the bias was fully stretched. The bodice bears out this theory, with darts that are much deeper than we would expect. Only a professional with years of experience would have the skill to accomplish that manipulation.

Paper patterns were not widely available, but professional dressmakers found plenty of inspiration from hand-coloured fashion plates. *Ackermann's Repository of the Arts*, *La Belle Assemblé* and *Costume Parisien* are three illustrated fashion magazines that are often referenced in dress histories. I am unaware of any surviving paper patterns from this era, but Figures 4.4 and 4.5 show details of published sleeve patterns. There is a lovely contrast between the fine drawings of sleeve drafts in *The Tailor's Masterpiece* (1838) by George Walker,[5] and those from *The Workwoman's Guide* by A Lady, also published in 1838.[6]

Figure 4.3 From the *Book of Trades*, this is a rare picture showing a dressmaker using the pinned-to-the-form method of pattern making.

George Walker was addressing other tailors; highly skilled professionals who served an elite clientele, and who had had a long history of pattern secrecy. His draft shows the process of developing different sleeves with precise mathematical calculations. Each point of reference comes directly from a previously charted point. It is clean, measured, balanced and beautifully drawn. This is a scientific method of drafting and the results would be predictable and repeatable (see Figure 4.4).

By comparison, the *Workwoman's Guide* gives patterns for simple items needed in an average home (see Figure 4.5). The Lady's readership were 'Clergymen's Wives, Young Married Women, School-mistresses, and Ladies Maids'.[7] The bulk of patterns, like pinafores, bonnets and simply cut men's shirts, could be cut directly from rectangular lengths of fabric. There are no complete patterns for adult women's gowns, but the book includes a variety of fashionable sleeves, collars and cape designs. The sketches are naive, the instructions are minimal and the measurements are rudimentary, but they show skill in developing patterns. Indicating that a sleeve is cut on the bias by drawing it on a square folded from corner to corner is straightforward and very clever. No training or apprenticeship was needed to understand that crucial bit of information. The Lady had the experience to formulate calculations and translate that information into simple drawings.

Laid out side by side, they illustrate the premise of this book and my philosophy of pattern drafting. A solid grasp of drafting techniques is key. But to go beyond the draft, you must internalize its geometry, embrace your artistic ability and draw. Both skills are necessary to draft current fashion trends, reinterpret designs of the past or develop styles for the future.

DESCRIPTION

This dress (Figures 4.1 and 4.2) is constructed out of delicately woven cotton, with alternating stripes of fine lawn and closely woven warp, and decorated with sprays of printed pink roses. The bodice is unlined. All the hand-stitched seams are piped with a very fine cord, providing some structure. A heavily corded corset and a number of petticoats would have determined its overall shaping. The centre front of the bodice is cut on a bias fold. Two large angled darts would have removed any ripple of excess fabric.

The main decorative theme found at the base of the topsleeve and at the join of the skirt flounce is a series of triangular points. These were a popular trim that was coined 'vandyking', after Sir Anthony van Dyke's famous portraits. A secondary decorative technique is the use of bias. This not only produces a wonderful play of stripes, giving the dress visual movement, it also produces a skirt with a flouted and weighted edge that would stand away from the body.[10]

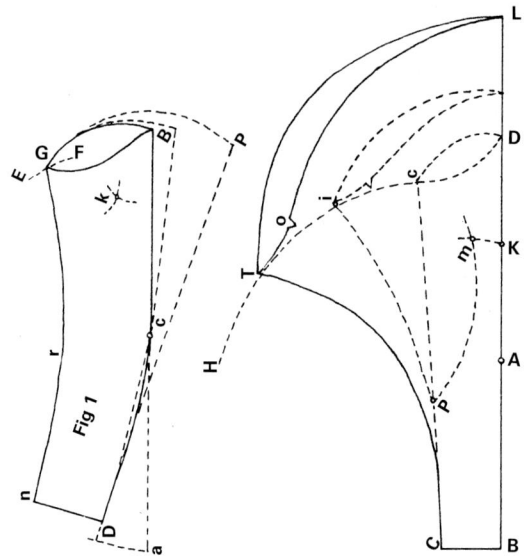

Figure 4.4 Beautifully drawn sleeve drafts by George Walker in 1838.[8]

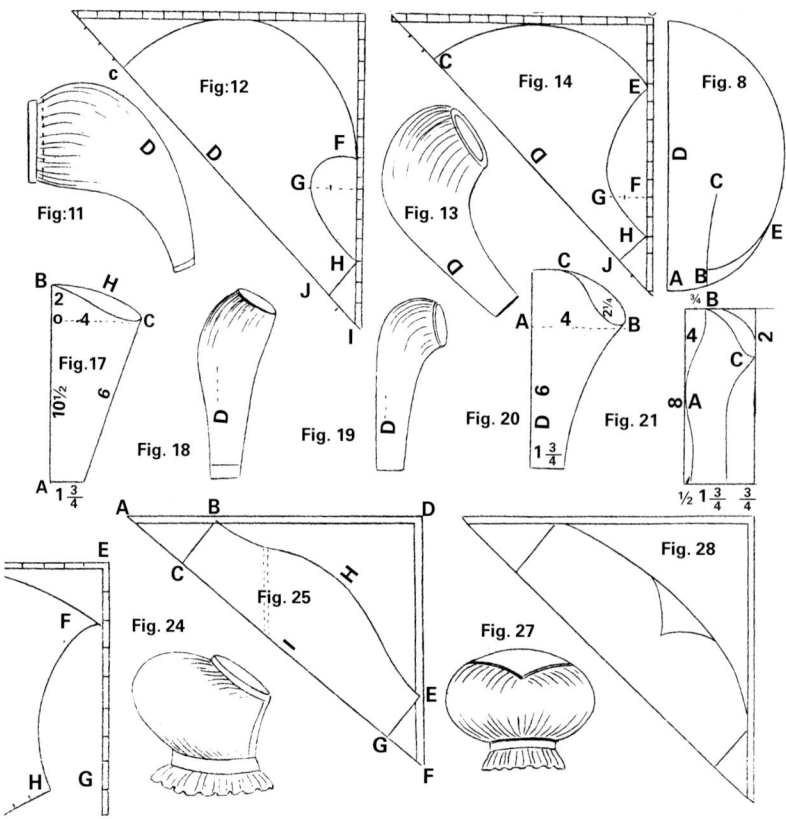

Figure 4.5 Detail of a full page of sleeve options from *The Workwoman's Guide* by A Lady.[9]

Primary Step-by-Step Drafting Instructions

To start this draft, you will need completed front and back Basic Bodice Block patterns without the optional back shoulder dart. The primary gown's waist appears to be at the natural level. It can stay at the natural waist, or you can raise the pattern waist for a more recognizably period shape. An inserted waistband further shortens the appearance of the waist. Bodices of the period have little structure of their own and take on the fit and shape of the corset. This bodice front is cut on the bias, which indicates that it was worn tightly with no ease. Therefore, some of the ease included in the Modern Basic Block must be eliminated for the period block (see Figure 4.6).

The original pattern is indicated with short dotted lines. The longer dotted lines indicate the centre of darts.

Remove Excess Ease

Figure 4.6

1. Draw a line 5 cm (2") above W–W1. This is the top of the waistband. The inserted waistband will be removed from the pattern in due course, but it is helpful to keep it connected to the bodice pattern until manipulations are completed.
2. Remove excess ease:
    a. Draw a new Centre Front 0.5 cm (³⁄₁₆") from the Centre Front.
    b. Draw a new Centre Back 0.5 cm (³⁄₁₆") from the Centre Back.
    c. At the Side Seam, remove 1 cm (⅜") from each side at **U**, to nothing at the new waist.

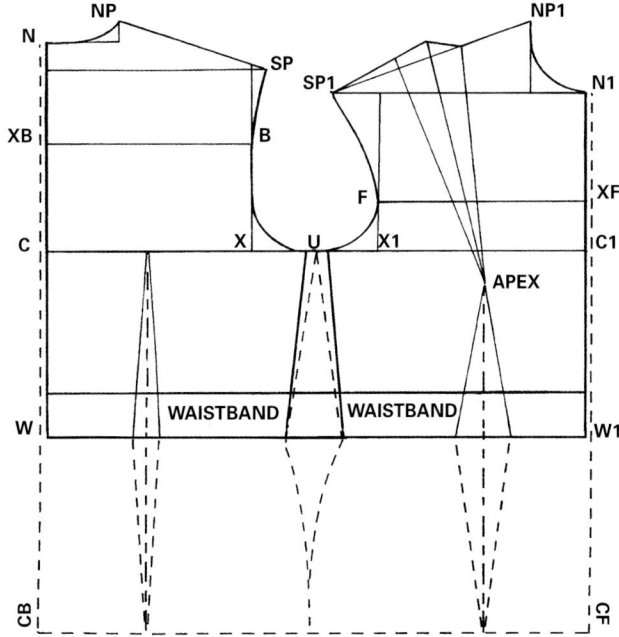

Figure 4.6 Modern Bodice Block with reduced ease.

BODICE BACK

The bodice closure is at the Centre Back, which is placed on the straight-of-grain. Backs from this period are often cut with two pattern pieces. The seam dividing the back is called the Side Back (**SB**) seam.

Side Back Guideline

Figure 4.7
Draw a line from **B** to the top of the dart and continue to the top of the waistband approximately 2.5 cm–3 cm (1"–1⅛") from the **CB**. This is the guideline for the new Side Back (**SB**) seam. Continue in a straight line to the new waist (see Figure 4.7).

1. Using the guideline, draw a curved line touching all points (see Figure 4.8).
2. Remove the inserted waistband portion and set aside.
3. Cut along the **SB** seam line to separate the pattern pieces (see Figure 4.9).

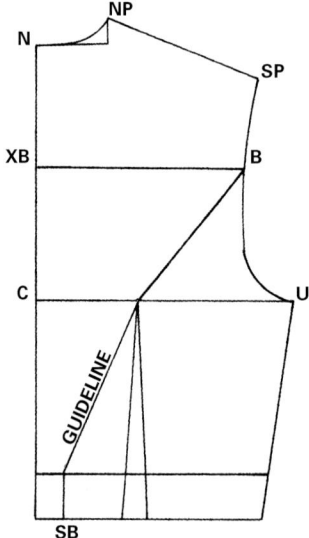

Figure 4.7 Side Back seam guideline.

Side Back

Figure 4.8 and Figure 4.9

1. Close the back dart: to do this, fold one side of the dart and place it along the other side of the dart so the two branches meet. Secure this in position with pins or tape. Closing the dart produces an awkward line on the **SB** seam and the waist.
2. Smooth the **SB** seam and waist (see Blending in Terminology).
3. Measure both branches of the **SB** seam. They must be equal. If one side is longer than the other, extend the shorter branch at the armhole. Any excess will be removed when the armhole is redrawn. This is called truing up, or truing (see True up in Terminology).

This completes the Back and Side Back pattern pieces.

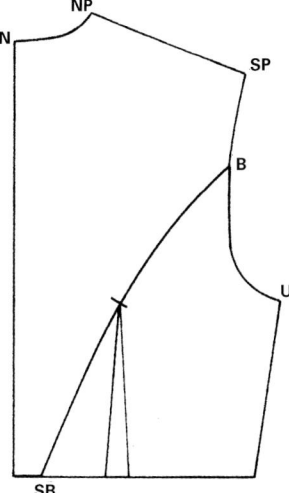

Figure 4.8 Side Back seam.

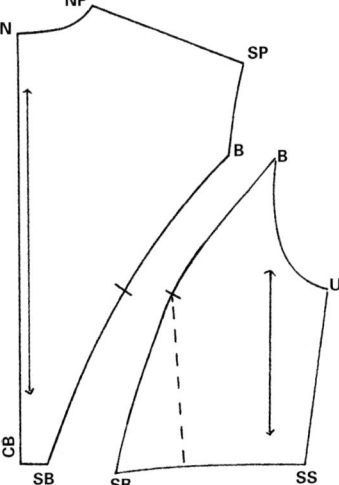

Figure 4.9 Separated Back and Side Back patterns.

Chapter 4 Development of Period Patterns, 1820–35

Bodice Front

Figure 4.10 and Figure 4.11

The placement of the front waist darts is key to the development of the desirable hourglass shape. In terms of fit, their direction determines the position of the fullest part of the bust. In this period draft, darts point slightly towards the armhole, which produces a broader look.

Darts also visually reinforce the hourglass shape. Starting close to the Centre Front and angling outward, they form a 'V' shape.

1. Raise the **Apex** to the line **U–C1**.
2. Redraw the shoulder and waist darts to reflect the new **Apex** position.
3. Cut along one branch of the shoulder dart to, but not through, the **Apex**.
4. Close the waist dart. To do this, fold one side of the waist dart. Place the fold along the other side of the dart. Secure the dart closed with pins or tape. With the waist dart closed, the shoulder dart will automatically open (see Dart transfer in Terminology). This is an important step, as it provides a clean surface on which we can draw a new dart.
5. Remove the inserted waistband and set aside.
6. Mark a point 2 cm–3 cm (¾"–1⅛") to the left of the **Apex** on **U–C1**. This is the point of the new dart.
7. Mark the new base of the dart 4 cm–5 cm (1⅝"–2") from **CF**.
8. Connect the two points. This is the new dart placement.
9. Draw a line from the new dart point to the **Apex** (see Figure 4.10).
10. Cut along the new dart to the point and continue to the **Apex** (see Figure 4.11).
11. Close the shoulder dart and secure it closed with pins or tape. With the shoulder dart closed, the waist dart will automatically open along the newly drawn line (see Figure 4.11). (See Dart transfer in Terminology.)
12. True up the shoulder.

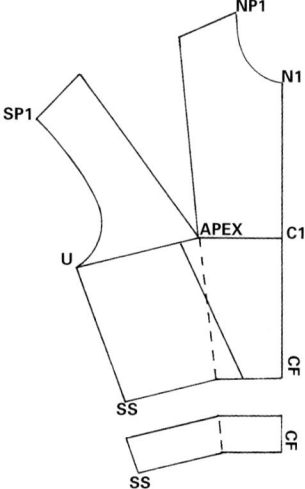

Figure 4.10 Front modification.

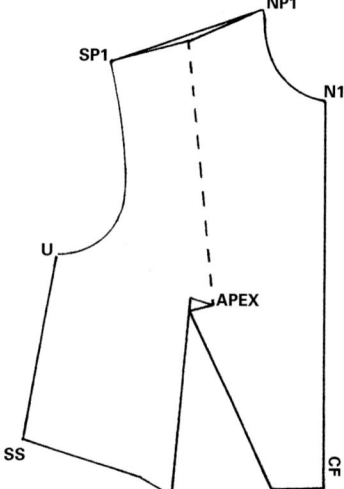

Figure 4.11 Closed shoulder dart.

13. Shape the dart, gently sculpting the curve under the bust.
14. Measure both branches of the dart. They must be equal. If they are not, true up at the waist.
15. Indicate the grain line, and that the **CF** is on a bias fold.

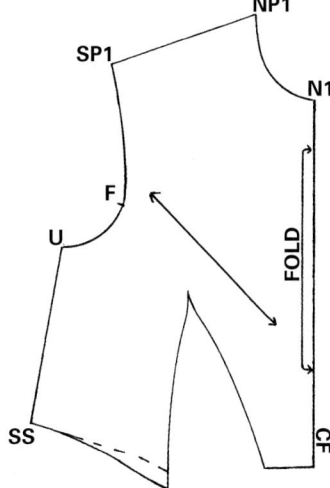

Figure 4.12 Shaped dart.

Shoulder and Neckline

Figure 4.13
As jaunty sleeves amplified the visual upper globe of the hourglass, bodice shoulders started to spread beyond the body's natural line. This shoulder seam extends into the armhole and sits further to the back than a modern shoulder.

1. With the shoulder dart still closed, match Front and Back patterns from **NP** to **SP** and secure this with tape.
2. Draw a new armhole from **B** to **F** going through a point approximately 1.5 cm (⅝") away from **SP**.
3. Mark a point approximately 4 cm (1⅝") below **SP** on the new back armhole. Connect to **NP**. This is the new shoulder seam.
4. With the shoulder seam still connected, redraw the neck line.

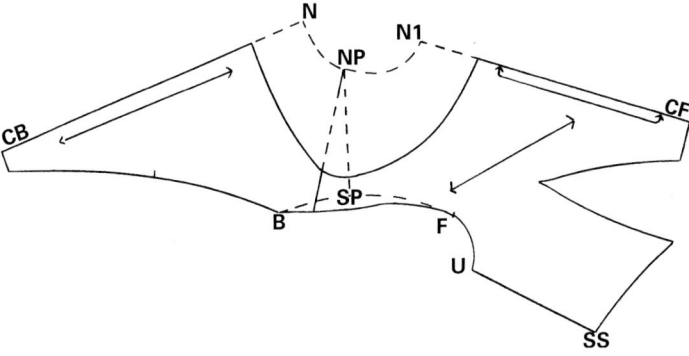

Figure 4.13 Shoulder and neckline.

Waistband

Figure 4.14

Join all sections of the inserted waistband together, matching the top and bottom.

1. On a clean piece of paper, trace the pieces, and blend the angles.
2. Place a fold indication at **CF**.

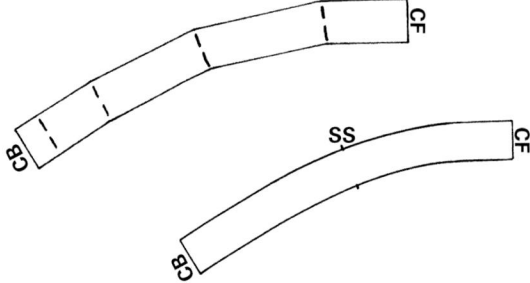

Figure 4.14 Inserted waistband.

SLEEVES

Long Sleeve

Figure 4.15

The primary long sleeve fits closely to the arm with little ease. Placing the straight-of-grain on an angle creates some flexibility for more comfortable movement. Piping along the front and back seams give shape and stability to the cotton.

1. Use the Historical Two-piece Sleeve draft.
2. Scoop the front and back seams 1 cm–1.5 cm (⅜"–⅝"), as indicated in Figure 4.15.

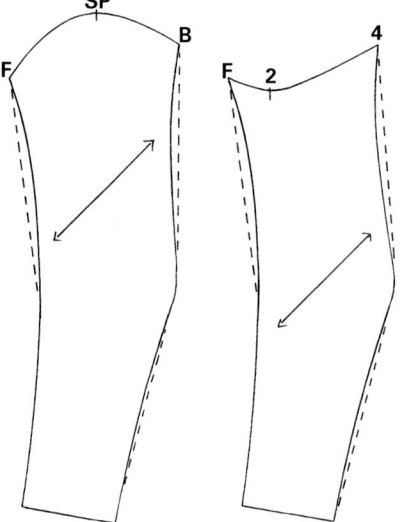

Figure 4.15 Long sleeve.

Short, Puff Sleeve

Figure 4.16, Figure 4.17, Figure 4.18 and Figure 4.19

With such a large puffed sleeve, it can be difficult to know how much volume to add to the pattern. This is where art, skill, practice and a good toile overtake mathematical calculations. Try holding a measuring tape in the desired shape to estimate the size you want. For a sleeve of this size, you will need to spread the sleeve to equal about 66 cm (26") in width. The total height, from shoulder to the gathered band, equals about 41 cm (16").

1. Use the Historical One-piece Sleeve draft in Chapter 1.
2. On a clean sheet of paper, draw a horizontal and vertical gridline corresponding to **U–U1** and **SP–X**.
3. Draw a parallel line 10 cm (4") below **U–U1**. This is the bottom of the topsleeve. Draw three lines dividing the sleeve into quarters. It is useful to number the sections (see Figure 4.17).
4. Cut through the lines.
5. Spread the centre sections approximately 3.5 cm (1½") at the **U–U1** line.
6. Repeat with the two outer sections.
7. Redraw the sleeve head with extra height. In this case, the raised **SP** is 33 cm (13") above **U–U1**. Keep the curve relatively shallow at **SP**.
8. Redraw the hem in a curve.
9. This sleeve may be cut on the bias or straight-of-grain.

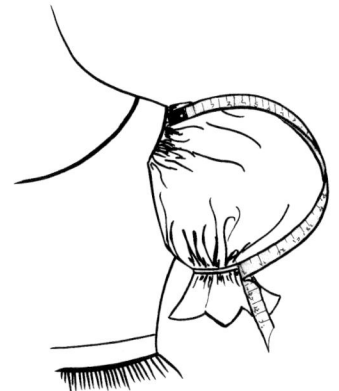

Figure 4.16 Using a tape measure to estimate volume.

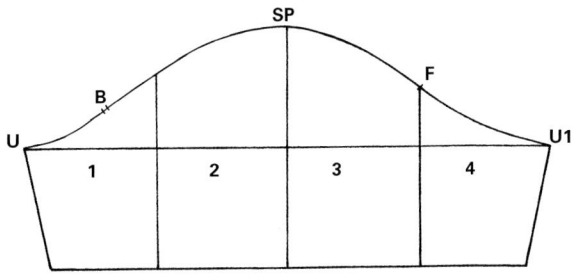

Figure 4.17 Sleeve divisions.

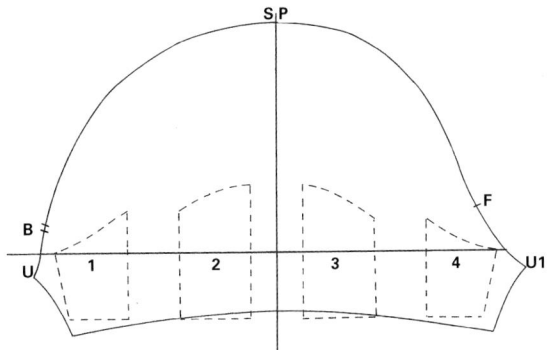

Figure 4.18 Puffed sleeve spread out.

Figure 4.19 Decorative sleeve cuff.

RUFFLE

The puff sleeve is finished with a 2.5 cm (1") band and ruffle. The ruffle consists of six cleverly pieced sections, each shaped with a vandyked edge.

SKIRT

Skirts of this period are essentially large rectangles. The full length is from the waist to the ankle; approximately 10 cm (4") above the floor. The closure is at the back. The upper half of this skirt is cut on the straight-of-grain. Its top edge is finely and evenly gathered into a reinforced waistband and its bottom is finished with a very fine piped pinked or vandyked edge. To reproduce this portion, you will need three panels of 115 cm (45"). This will make a skirt width of approximately 330 cm (130"). The lower half of the skirt is cut on the bias. It is a little more than 1½ times wider than the top. It is gathered and secured along the piped points. A self-covered cord of 1 cm (⅜") slightly stretches the hemline.

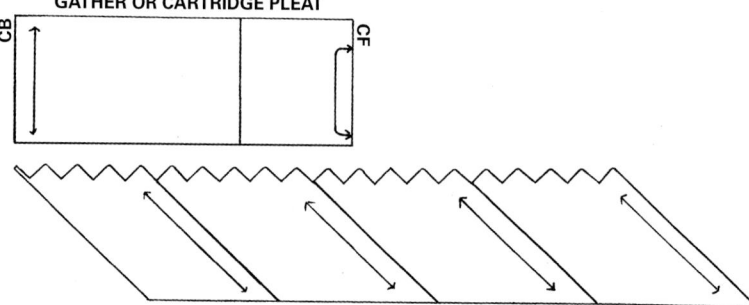

Figure 4.20 Skirt diagram with bias flounce.

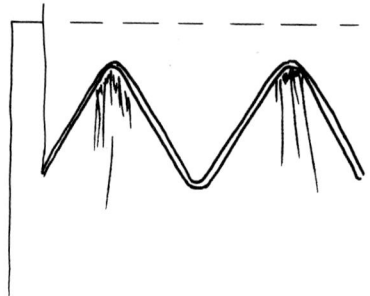

Figure 4.21 Detail of vandyking on skirt.

Figure 4.22 This is another period dress that uses ornamental edging with triangular points known as 'vandyking'.

Alternative Day Dress Draft Adaptations

This alternative day dress provides a broad range of pattern options. Its compound sleeve has two new drafts, which can be used together or individually. It is gathered at the neckline and waist. The amount of gathering will depend on what is pleasing to the eye. As a general rule, gathers need to be at least one and a half times the ungathered measurement in order to read as gathers. However, much depends on the weight of the fabric used. A light cotton lawn will need more gathering than a heavy velvet fabric. Always make a sample to determine how much gathering is required for a project.

Alternative Back

Figure 4.23 and Figure 4.24
This Bodice Back is cut with one pattern rather than two. Gathers replace the back waist dart. Complete the Remove Excess Ease instructions and follow the Shoulder and Neckline instructions to prepare the Alternative Back for alterations.

1. On a clean sheet of paper, draw a vertical and horizontal grid.
2. Place the **CB** along the vertical gridline, and the waist along the horizontal gridline.
3. From the neckline to the waist, draw two or more lines, as shown in Figure 4.23.
4. Record the neck and waist measurement from **CB** to the last line drawn.
5. Cut the pattern along the drawn lines.
6. Being careful to line up the waist along the horizontal gridline, spread out the sections to achieve the desired concentration of gathers. This is called 'cutting and spreading'.
7. Redraw the neckline, blending it into a smooth and continuous line.
8. In making up, gather the neckline to equal the original measurements.
9. Gathers at the waist spread across the back including the dart area. Concentrate most of the gathers closer to the **CB**.

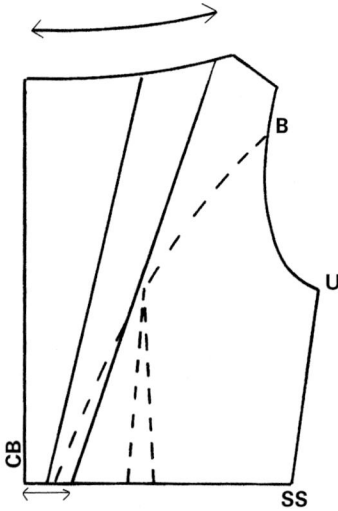

Figure 4.23 Alternative Back with cutting lines.

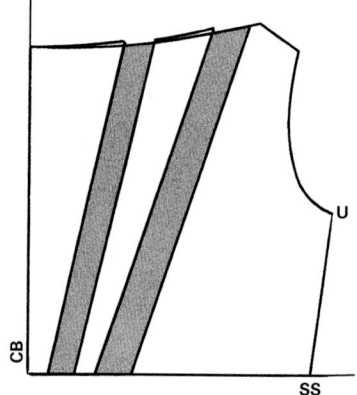

Figure 4.24 Alternative Back spread out.

Alternative Front

Figure 4.25 and Figure 4.26

1. Complete the primary Front instructions and Neck and Shoulder instructions.
2. Separate front and back on the new shoulder seam.
3. On a clean sheet of paper, draw a vertical and horizontal grid.
4. Place the **CF** along the vertical gridline and the waist along the horizontal gridline.
5. From the neckline to the waist, draw a number of straight lines, as shown in Figure 4.25.
6. Record the neck and waist measurement from the drawn lines to the **CF**.
7. Cut the pattern along the lines.
8. Being careful to line up the waist along the horizontal gridline, spread out sections as desired.
9. Redraw the neckline blending into a smooth and continuous line.
10. In making up, gather the neck to equal the original measurements.
11. Gathers at the waist spread across the front, including the area of the dart. Concentrate most of the gathers closer to the **CF**.

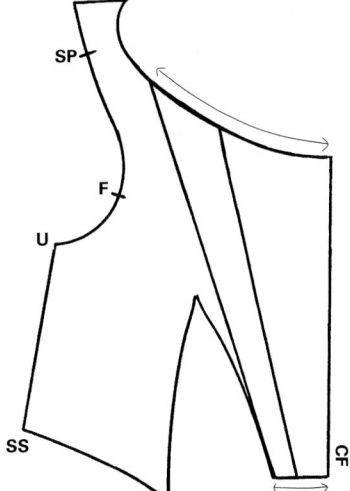

Figure 4.25 Alternative Front with cutting lines.

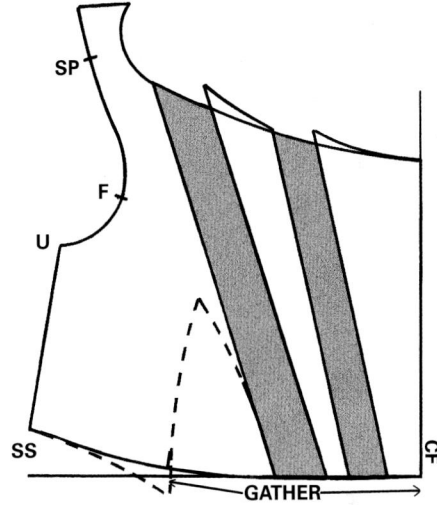

Figure 4.26 Alternative Front spread out.

BELT

Use the primary waistband for the separate belt. Shape the lower edge into a point at the front, as shown in Figure 4.27. The shape is developed from the Basic Bodice Block. In practice, it may be too curved for the body and may be straightened in a fitting.

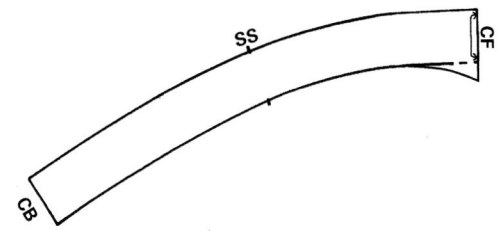

Figure 4.27 Belt.

ALTERNATIVE DESIGN: COMPOUND SLEEVE

Beret Sleeve

Figure 4.28 and Figure 4.29

You could use the primary pattern for the small puff sleeve, but a beret sleeve also would work well, and is a wonderful shape. The beret sleeve is very full at the armhole, but without gathers at the bicep. It is essentially a large circle of fabric with a smaller circle cut out for the armhole. Use the measuring technique seen in Figure 4.16 to determine the distance from the top of the sleeve to its hem. This will give you an idea of the circle's size.

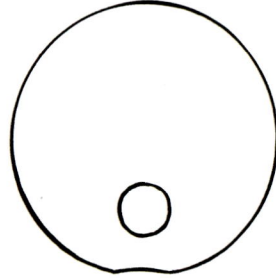

Figure 4.28 Beret Sleeve draft.

1. In this draft, the circle has a diameter of about 51 cm (20").
2. Flatten the circle in one area for about 10 cm (4"). This is the underarm.
3. Draw another circle starting about 5 cm (2") from the flattened area. The circumference of this circle should equal the bicep.
4. This is your sleeve pattern.
5. The outer circumference is gathered to fit the armhole. The circle within will fit the bicep.
6. You may cut the inner circle to be larger than the bicep if desired. In that case, the inner circle will be gathered as well, and some of the height will be lost.

Figure 4.29 Beret Sleeve with gathered outer edge to fit armhole.

Oversleeve

Figure 4.30 and Figure 4.31

Ideally, this is made from silk organza for optimal lightness and transparency.

1. Use the Historical One-piece Sleeve draft.
2. On a clean sheet of paper, draw a horizontal and vertical gridline corresponding to **U–U1** and **SP–X** (see Figure 4.30).
3. Trace the sleeve.
4. Cut from **SP** to **2**.
5. From **2**, cut to just before **E1** and **E2**. Leave a small hinge.

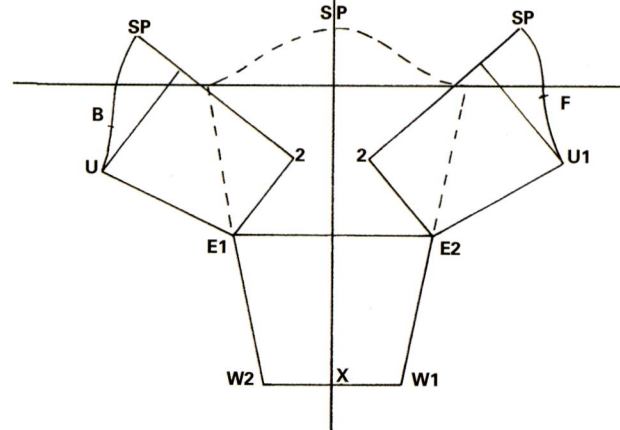

Figure 4.30 Opened topsleeve.

6. Align the lower sleeve with the horizontal and vertical grid.
7. Spread the topsleeve.
8. Redraw the sleeve head starting at **U**, adding height to the original, and returning to **U1**. In this drawing, the new **SP** placement is placed 40 cm (16") above the original line **U–U1**.
9. Redraw the underarm seam **U** to **W1** and **U1** to **W2** curving into the original sleeve.

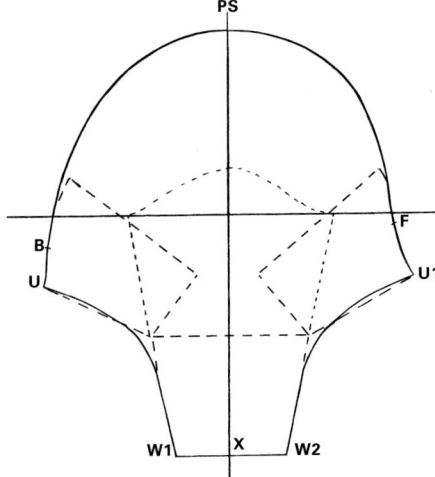

Figure 4.31 Redrawn Sleeve head and underarm seam.

Sleeve Cuff

Figure 4.32

1. Copy the lower 7 cm (2¾") of the sleeve.
2. Divide the section equally into four sections.
3. Cut the divisions from the top to the bottom, leaving a small hinge.
4. Open the cuts 1 cm (⅜").
5. Draw new top, curving both the top and bottom.
6. Redraw the top as a vandyked edge.

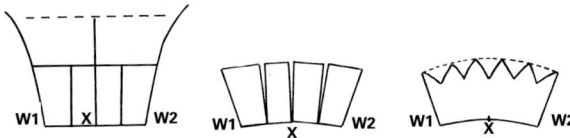

Figure 4.32 Process of drafting cuff.

ALTERNATIVE SKIRT

Skirts of this period were very simply cut in a rectangle. Like the primary dress, you will need three panels of 115 cm (45") fabric. The length is from the waist to the ankle, approximately 10 cm (4") above the floor. The fabric is pleated or gathered into the waist, with the closure at the back. There are two rows of vandyked trim placed on the bottom of the skirt, starting just shy of the half way point. This is an awkward proportion to our eye, but was very common at the time.

NOTES

1. *Kingston Chronicle & Gazette* (1834) 'The Subscriber Has For Sale', 3 February, p. 3, col. 3.
2. Elizabeth Errington (1995) *Wives and Mothers, Schoolmistresses and Scullery Maids: Working Women in Upper Canada, 1790–1840* (Montreal: McGill-Queen's University Press), 199–203.
3. Claudia Kidwell (1979) *Cutting a Fashionable Fit: Dressmakers' Drafting Systems in the United States* (Washington: Smithsonian Institution Press), 13.
4. Quote from Anon (1825) *The Duties of a Lady's Maid: With Directions for Conduct and Numerous Receipts for the Toilette*, 318, cited in Hilary Davidson (2019) *Dress in the Age of Jane Austen: Regency Fashion* (New Haven: Yale University Press), 130.
5. Janet Arnold (1982) *Patterns of Fashion 1: Englishwomen's Dresses & Their Construction c. 1660–1860* (London: Macmillan/Drama Books), 12.
6. A Lady (1986) *The Workwoman's Guide by A Lady: A Guide to 19th Century Decorative Arts, Fashion and Practical Crafts* (Boston: Opus Publications), 85.
7. Ibid., 4.
8. G. Walker (1835) *The Art of Cutting Ladies' Riding Habits, Pelisses, Gowns, Frocks, &c. Fifth Edition* (https://books.google.com), detail of Plate 18.
9. *Workwoman's Guide*, 85.
10. M. Elaine MacKay (2007) *Beyond the Silhouette: Fashion and the Women of Historic Kingston* (Kingston: Queen's University), 25–7.

5

Development of Period Patterns, 1840–49

Period Dress in Historical Context

If the dress in Chapter 4 exemplifies the inventiveness of the late 1820s and 1830s, this dress, worn by Zelicia Batt for her marriage to Hugh Cope Rothwell in 1848, epitomizes the controlled and restrained aesthetic of 1840s fashion. Its clean, quiet lines seem at odds with the steady pace of transformation within the fashion industry. Publications catering to the amateur and professional dressmaker alike had became widespread and informative. The tailoring industry was keenly developing new and improved methods of charting the body's contours onto flat paper patterns. Everyone involved in the fashion industry was eagerly awaiting word of the newly patented sewing machine, which promised to take the drudgery out of plain stitching long seams. Each stream proceeded along parallel paths during the 1840s. It would be another decade or so before the paths converged, and the home sewer had the resources to challenge the professional.

Daydreaming about fashion probably became an enjoyable pastime for the home sewer while leafing through periodical magazines. In the 1830s, inexpensive publications had became easily obtainable for the general public. Among them was a group that became known as 'women's magazines'. They offered women the prospect of hours of leisure with stories, poetry, editorial essays and sheet music. For artistic inspiration, these magazines included needlework patterns and embroidery designs. One of their most popular regular features was a fashion page. These pages included beautifully hand-painted illustrations of

Figure 5.1 Front of dress. This beautiful silk is woven with variegated plum and copper threads to create colourful stripes.

Figure 5.2 Sleeve detail.

seasonal fashions. As they were published in regular intervals, the journals developed a loyal following who looked forward to the newest dress design and the next story instalment. In Britain, *The World of Fashion and Continental Feuilletons*, *The Lady's Magazine* and *The Ladies' Pocket Magazine* satisfied a clientele interested in the newest styles. In the United States, *Godey's Lady's Book*, published in Philadelphia from 1830 to 1878, and *Peterson's Magazine*, first published as *The Lady's World of Fashion* in 1842, did the same.

By the 1840s, journals for the professional dressmaker sold full-sized paper patterns with all the components needed for a bodice with sleeves. The various pattern pieces often overlapped and needed to be individually traced onto another sheet of paper before use. There was no attempt to personalize the paper pattern with a client's measurements. Fitting the pattern to the client was the responsibility of the dressmaker. The bodice patterns were beautifully drawn, and much can be deduced from analysing their lines. However, since they were always used as only a starting point, they cannot be used as literal, finished drafts. Patterns for skirts were never included. As Mrs Cory, author of *The Art of Dressmaking, containing Plain Directions in Simple Language from the Fitting of the Pattern to the Finish of the Dress* (1849), stated: 'Skirts are so simple, that I conclude anyone who would attempt a body would know how to make them.'[1]

Trade journals still taught the pin-to-the-form method of pattern making. Known today as 'draping', paper or light fabric was pinned directly onto the client:

> You commence by folding down the corner the length of the front, and pinning it to the middle of the stay bone. Then let the paper be spread as smoothly as possible along the bosom to the shoulder, and fold it in a plait (dart) so as to fit the shape exactly, and bring the paper under the arm, making it retain its position by a pin.[2]

This method was perfectly adequate for the short, soft bodices of the 1810s, or even the the waist-length bodices of the 1830s, but when the trend for extremely tight bodices that extended below the waist became fashionable in the 1840s, pin-to-the-form must have been more difficult. Wrangling larger pieces of paper to cover more surface would require greater dexterity on the part of the professional and more patience on the part of the client. Having a full-sized paper pattern to assist with draping must have made a huge difference in the dressmaker's ability to produce well-cut garments.

Even though tailors did not make women's dresses, they had traditionally made women's riding habits and stays, so any development within the tailoring industry had an effect on women's wear. Throughout the nineteenth century, tailors devised and published drafting system after drafting sytem, all

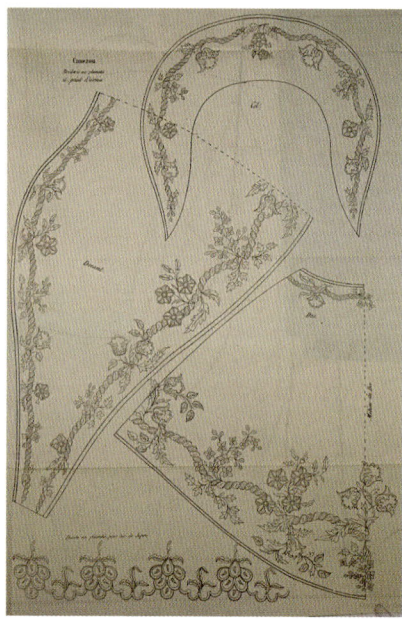

Figure 5.3 A pattern for a cape-like garment with embroidery in satin stitch and gun stitch, in *Petit Courrier des Dames*, 20 April 1846.[3]

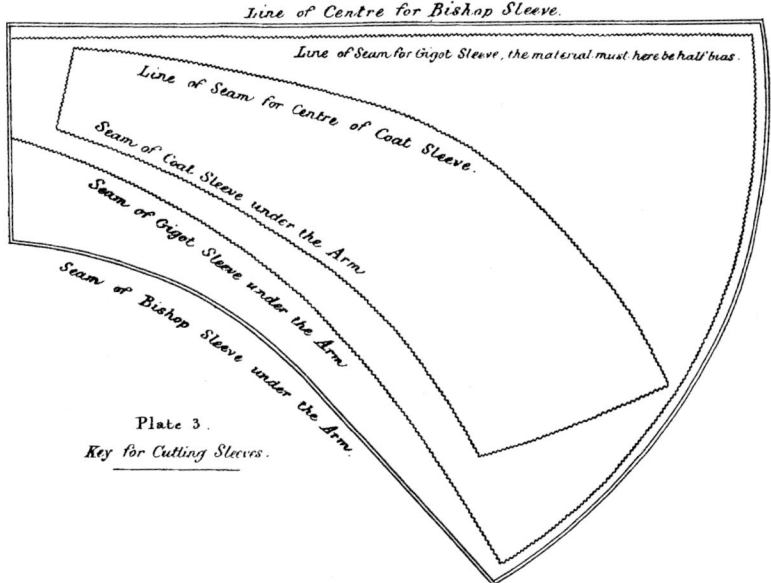

Figure 5.4 Sleeve patterns in Mrs Howell's 1845 *The Hand-book of Dress-making*.[4]

with the purpose of improving on the last. Many of these publications followed a proportional method of pattern making. This was a mathematical approach, in which all applied measurements were a ratio of one body measurement, usually the chest. For example, the front, side and back might each be calculated as one-third of half the chest measurement. It followed the premise that rather than mapping the body's shape with precision, a well-cut garment should form the perfectly shaped man. Another process used by tailors was with the application of direct measurements. With this method, every conceivable body measurement was translated onto the page. Rarely did one system work perfectly for every body, so most tailors used a combination of systems. In the early development of women's patterns, the direct measurement system was seen to be the best way to accommodate the vast and diverse combination of measurements that represent women's bodies.

DESCRIPTION

This one-piece dress is a fine example of the lean silhouette of the day (see Figure 5.1). The bodice has a rounded centre front point that sits well below the natural waist. Three darts on either side of the front taper from the deep waist to a very high bust, accentuating the torso's length. It is kept rigid with baleen on the darts and the seams. A high neck, dropped shoulders and small capped sleeves produce the long, sloping and rounded shoulder characteristic of the period. The shoulder seam sits slightly to the back of the natural shoulder line. The one-piece, moderately bell-shaped sleeves are edged with delicate lace. They are cut on the bias, providing both visual appeal and comfort. The sleeve caps and bell hems are trimmed with self-fabric trim. The skirt, cut in straight panels, is gathered at the waist into cartridge pleats. These are gathered more densely in the back. The dress's relatively simple silhouette, and the clever use of self-fabric trim, encourage the eye to focus on the extraordinary silk taffeta fabric.

Primary Step-by-Step Drafting Instructions

Before beginning the 1840s block, it is a good idea to remeasure the client, especially if the garment is going to be worn over a corset. In that case, take the measurements with the corset laced as tightly as it is expected to be worn. Note that the following measurements are suggestions and work well with the standard sizing used in this book. You may find the darts will be closer, or further apart, in your draft.

To start this draft, you will need a completed front and back Basic Bodice Block pattern without the optional back shoulder dart.

Remove Excess Ease

Figure 5.5

1. Draw a new Centre Front 0.5 cm (3/16") in from the Centre Front.
2. Draw a new Centre Back 0.5 cm (3/16") in from the Centre Back.
3. On the Side Seam, remove 1 cm (3/8") from each side seam at **U** to nothing on the line **W–W1**.

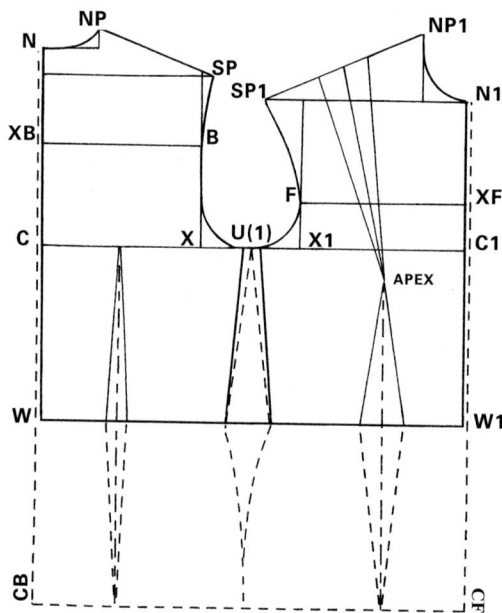

Figure 5.5 Remove ease.

Bodice Back

Figure 5.6

The primary dress back is cut in one piece, with the pattern on the fold. There is no waist dart in the garment, so the dart in the pattern must be removed.

1. Mark a point the width of the dart to the left of the **SS** on the line drawn out from **W**.
2. Draw a line from **U** to this point. This is the new **SS**.
3. To finesse the pattern and exaggerate the long bodice appearance, draw the waist 1.5 cm–2 cm (⅝"–¼") higher than the original.

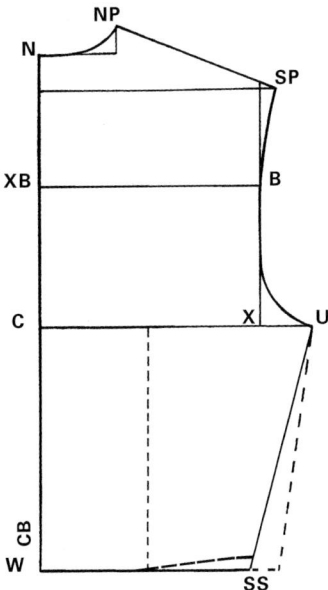

Figure 5.6 Dart transfer.

Bodice Front

Figure 5.7

A dropped waist and six long, curved darts create the elongated torso that is typical of the 1840s. The look is improved when a corset supports the bust in an unnaturally high position. Raising the bust point in the pattern goes a long way to recreating the look.

1. Raise the **Apex** to the line **U–C1**.
2. Redraw the shoulder and waist darts to reflect the new **Apex** position.
3. Cut along one branch of the shoulder dart to, but not through, the **Apex**.
4. Close the waist dart:
    a. Fold one side of the waist dart. Place the fold along the other side of the dart.
    b. Secure the dart closed.
    c. With the waist dart closed, the shoulder dart will automatically open.

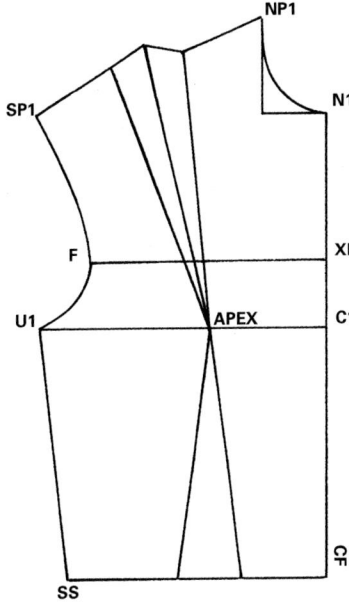

Figure 5.7 Raise Apex.

5. Mark the bottom of the first dart 2.5 cm (1") from the **CF** and the dart point 3 cm (1⅛") from **CF** on the line out from **C1**. Connect the points.
6. Mark the bottom of the next dart 3 cm (1⅛") from the first, and the dart point at the **Apex**. Connect the points.
7. Mark the base of the third dart 2.5 cm (1") from the second dart, and the point about 3 cm (1⅛") from the **Apex** on **U–C1**. Connect the points.

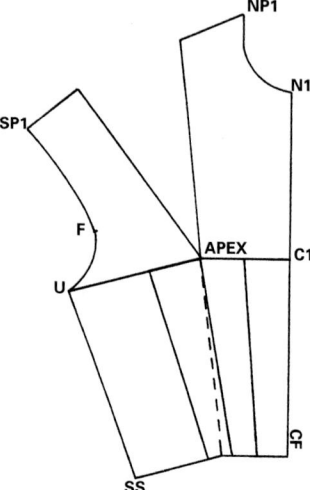

Figure 5.8 Draw three darts.

8. Add a length of about 8 cm (3") to the **CF** below the waist.
9. Draw the new, dropped front waist.
10. Draw a line from the new dart points to the **Apex**.
11. Cut along each new dart from the hem to the new dart point, and continue to the **Apex**. Leave a small hinge.

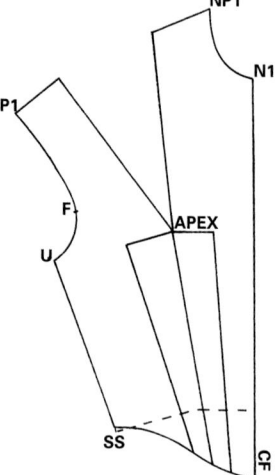

Figure 5.9 Lower Centre Front waist.

12. Close the shoulder dart. The waist darts will open automatically.
13. Arrange the three waist darts so they open equally.

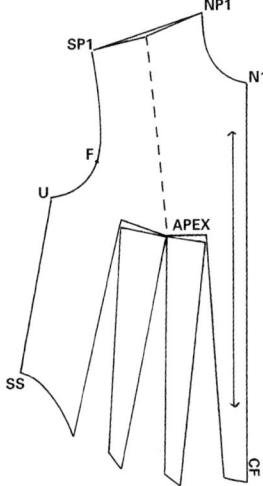 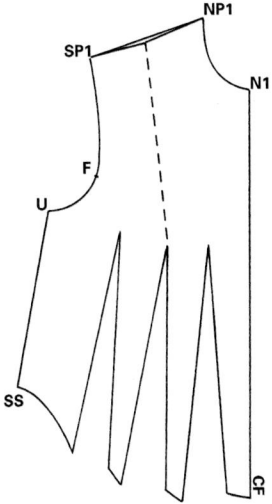 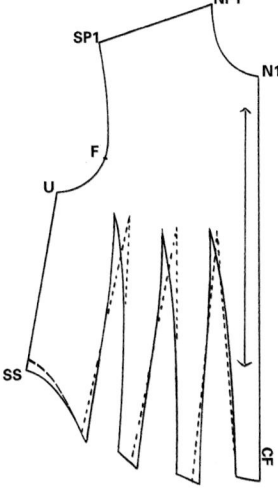

Figure 5.10 Dart transfer. **Figure 5.11** Three equal darts. **Figure 5.12** Shaped darts.

14. Redraw the darts as curves:
    a. Move the point of each dart 1–2 cm (⅜"–¾") towards the armhole.
    b. Redraw each dart curving into the new points.
    c. Below the waist, add a small amount of fulness to the abdomen by curving the left side of each dart 0.5 cm–1 cm (³⁄₁₆"–⅜").
    d. Measure both branches of each dart. They must be equal. True up as necessary.
15. To finesse the pattern and exaggerate the long bodice appearance, start drawing the waist 1.5 cm–2 cm (⅝"–¾") higher at the **SS**. Repeat this on the back bodice pattern. To further finesse the pattern, you may want to raise the front neck and the underarm as much as possible. These changes are best addressed after the first toile fitting. They will add to the illusion of a long and lean torso, but can cause some discomfort.

Shoulder and Neckline

Figure 5.13 and Figure 5.14

Bodice shoulders hugged the body well beyond the natural point of articulation. The shoulder seam of the primary design lies slightly behind, and parallel to, the natural shoulder line.

1. Match Front and Back patterns at the shoulder from **NP** to **SP** and secure this with tape.
2. Draw a new armhole from **F** to just below **B** going through a point approximately 3 cm (1⅛") away from **SP**.
3. Mark a point approximately 1.5 cm (⅝") below **NP** on the Back pattern.
4. Mark a point approximately 1.5 cm (⅝") below **SP** on the Back pattern.
5. Connect the points. This is the new shoulder seam.
6. To finesse the pattern, draw the shoulder line with a curve. This brings the shoulder closer to the neckline, and rounds the shoulder at the join of the arm (see Figure 5.14).

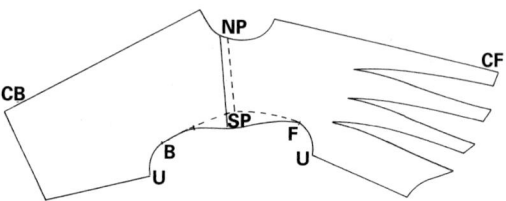

Figure 5.13 Neck and shoulder.

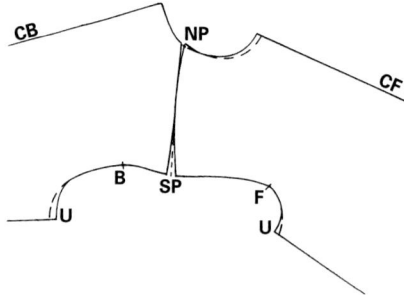

Figure 5.14 Neck and shoulder detail.

Sleeve

Figure 5.15 and Figure 5.16

1. Use the Historical One-piece Sleeve draft in Chapter 1.
2. Lower **SP** 3 cm (1⅛").
3. Redraw the sleeve head to reflect the lowered **SP** (see Figure 5.15).
4. Drop perpendicular lines from **E** and **E2** to the line drawn out from **W**.
5. Cut **X–2**, **2–E1** and **2–E2**.
6. On a clean sheet of paper, draw a horizontal and vertical gridline corresponding to **U–U1** and **SP–X**.

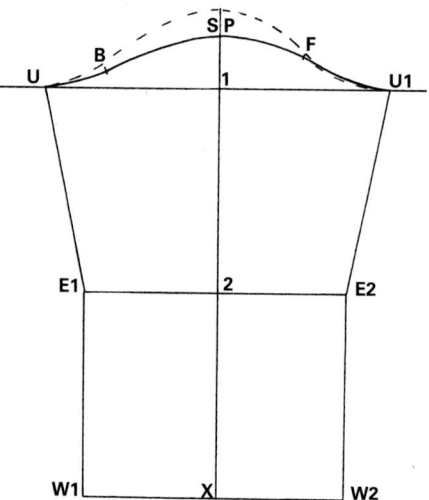

Figure 5.15 Lowered sleeve head.

7. Spread the lower arm equally on either side of the **SP–X** gridline for a total of 10 cm–12 cm (4"–4 ¾").
8. Scoop the underarm seam 1 cm–1.5 cm (⅜"–⅝"), as indicated in Figure 5.16.
9. Redraw the sleeve hem.
   1. Measure the sleeve head from **U–U1**. **Note:** The measurement of the sleeve head must be at least equal to the measurement of the bodice armhole.
   2. Measure the sleeve head from **U–B** and record this measurement on the back Bodice Block pattern on the curve from **U** towards **B**. Mark the placement with two notches. **Note:** This may not be in the same position as **B** on the Basic Bodice Block.
   3. Measure the sleeve head from **U1–F** and place this measurement on the front Bodice Block pattern from **U** to **F**. Mark the placement with one notch. **Note:** This may not be in the same position as **F** on the Basic Bodice Block.
   4. If the sleeve head measurement is not large enough, extend the sleeve beyond **U** and **U1** in 1 cm (⅜") increments until the measurements are correct. Connect the new **U** and **U1** to **E1** and **E2**.
   5. This sleeve is cut on the bias.

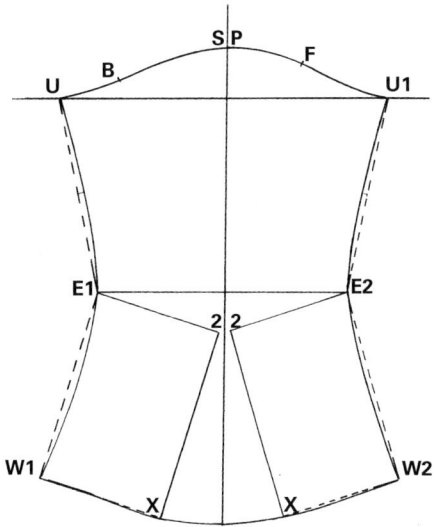

Figure 5.16 Bell sleeve.

Cap Sleeve

Figure 5.17
1. Use the sleeve drafted in Figure 5.15.
2. Drop perpendicular lines from **U** and **U1** for 10 cm (4").
3. Divide into quarters and number the sections 1–4 from left to right.
4. Cut to, but not through, each line from the hem to the sleeve head.
5. Spread each section 0.75 cm (⅛").
6. Draw a new hem (see Figure 5.17).

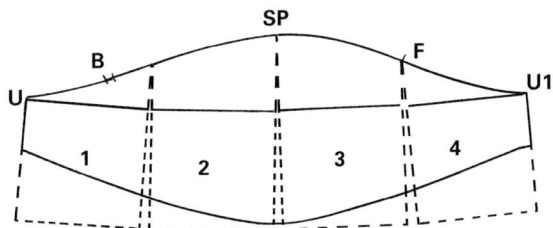

Figure 5.17 Cap sleeve divided into sections.

SKIRT

Skirts of this period are essentially large rectangles with a closure at the back and pleating at the waist. The most reasonable method of developing the skirt pattern is to use the full width of the fabric. Today, fabrics are woven in relatively predictable widths. Therefore, it is useful to think in terms of fabric with a standard 115 cm or 45" width.

An 1840s skirt can range from 300 cm to 500 cm (120"–200") at the hem. Therefore, three or four panels are needed for one skirt, depending on the fabric type and volume desired. Three panels of fabric will be approximately 330 cm (130") when made up. This measurement accounts for seams and an overlap for the closure. The length of each panel depends on the measurements of the client. You need to measure from the waist to the floor over any petticoats. Add to that at least 7 cm (3") for a hem, and 7 cm (3") for turning down the fabric at the waist. These calculations give the general size of the rectangle.

Drafting a rectangular skirt may sound simple, but notice that the horizontal stripes of the primary gown are perfectly straight and parallel to the hem, despite the fact that the bodice front waist drops to form a rounded point. Add to that the further complication that the skirt is gathered with cartridge pleats (also known as 'organ pleats'), and you will understand that its draft needs additional information.

The first step in determining the skirt waist pattern is to make a sample of cartridge pleating with the fashion fabric. This will give the information needed to estimate the skirt front (see Cartridge pleat in Terminology).

Cartridge Pleat Sample

Figure 5.18

1. Take a long narrow strip of fashion fabric about 10 cm × 50 cm (4" × 20").
2. Fold one of the long edges about 2.5 cm (1") to the wrong side.
3. Mark one row of dots 1 cm (⅜") from the folded edge and 1 cm (⅜") apart.
4. Mark a second row of dots 1 cm (⅜") below the first row, being careful to keep the rows and dots parallel and an equal distance apart.
5. Stab stitch each dot along one row using one long thread. Repeat the process for the second row of dots.
6. Pull the gathering threads until the strip pleats into 2".
7. If the pleats are very loose, there are a couple of options. You may need to add tape, or a strip of fabric under the fold to make the pleat thicker. If the fabric is still loose, you may need more fabric than used in the sample. If the gathers feel too tight, give the gathering threads some slack. This will give an approximate measurement of fabric needed to match the bodice front waist.

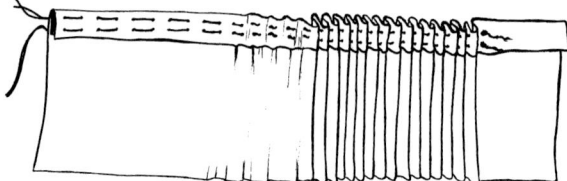

Figure 5.18 Cartridge pleats.

Draping the Skirt Method

1. Complete the mock-up skirt using fabric that is the same weight as the fashion fabric.
2. Place it, and the bodice, on a dress-form over any underpinnings.
3. Trace the hem of the bodice onto the mock-up skirt with a heavy pencil.
4. When the mock-up is laid flat, the markings will clearly delineate the contour of the skirt waist.

Cut and Spread Method

Figure 5.19

1. With the front bodice darts closed, trace the lower part of the bodice pattern.
   Note: The pattern pieces will overlap above the waist.
2. On another clean piece of paper, make a grid. The vertical line will represent the **CF**, and the horizontal line will represent the waist.
3. Cut and spread the lower bodice pattern to the width of the skirt front.
4. Draw a smooth connecting line for the skirt waist.

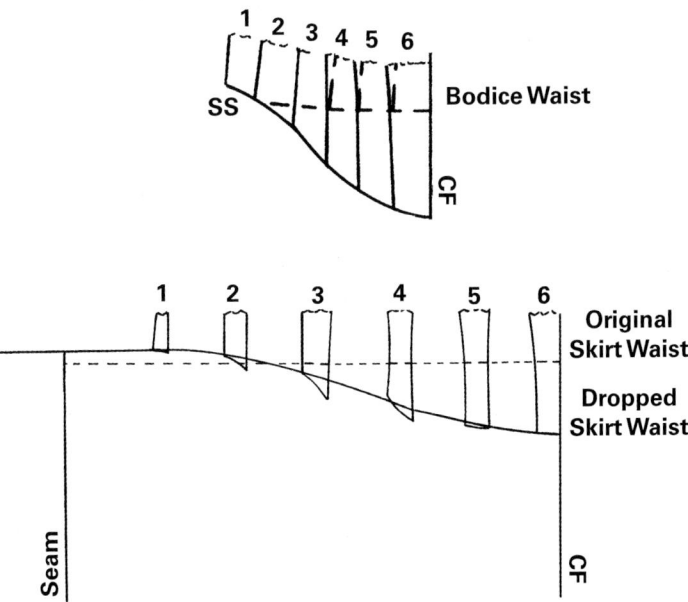

Figure 5.19 Skirt waist development.

Figure 5.20 Both of these alternative dresses show what would become known as a 'princess seam'. In the white dress, the SF seam goes into the armhole and in the turquoise dress, the SF seam goes to the shoulder seam.

Alternative Day Dress Draft Adaptations

These alternative designs use a single seam rather than multiple darts to create the long line. This seam, called the Side Front (**SF**) seam, is achieved by modifying the shoulder and waist darts.

White Dress Adaptations

Figure 5.21 and Figure 5.22

1. Trace the front with the extended shoulder.
2. Close the waist dart and open the shoulder dart.
3. Mark a point on the **CF** 3 cm–4 cm (1⅛"–1⅝") below the waist.
4. Redraw the waist to this point with a moderate curve. This is the new waist.
5. Mark a point on the new waist approximately 2.5 cm (1") from the **CF**. Mark a point approximately 4 cm (1⅝") above **F**. Draw a smooth line from the waist, through the **Apex** area, and to the armhole. This is the new **SF** seam. Measurements for this line are only approximate, because it is determined visually.
6. Mark a notch at the **Apex** for ease of truing.
7. Cut through along the **SF** seam to separate the single pattern into two pattern pieces.
8. Shape under the bust.
9. True up the **SF** seam.
10. The straight of grain is either parallel to the **CF**, or bias on the **CF**.

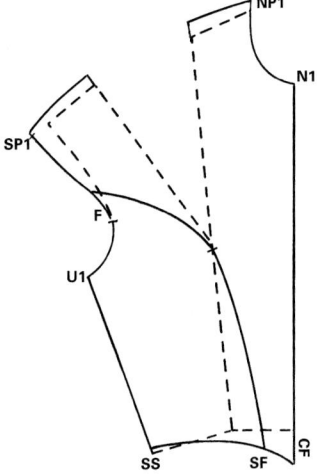

Figure 5.21 The Side Front seam placement.

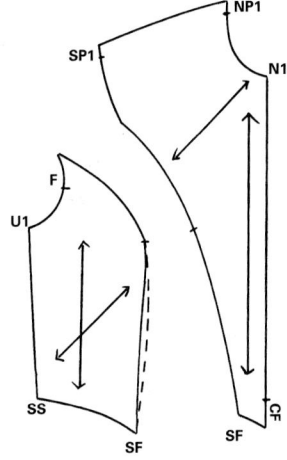

Figure 5.22 Front and Side Front panel patterns.

Turquoise Dress Adaptations

Figure 5.23
1. Trace the front with an extended shoulder.
2. Close the waist dart and open the shoulder dart.
3. Mark a point on the **CF** 3 cm–4 cm (1⅛"–1⅝") below the waist.
4. Draw a line from this point to the Apex.
5. Redraw the waist to this point with a moderate curve starting 1.5 cm–2 cm (⅝"–¼") above the waist at **SS** to the lengthened **CF**. This is the new waist.
6. Draw a new shoulder dart from a point closer to the original **SP** placement to the **Apex**.
7. Cut along this line to the **Apex**, leaving a small hinge.
8. Close the original shoulder dart. This is called pivoting the dart.
9. Using the shoulder and waist darts as a guide, draw a smooth and continuous line. This is the new **SF** seam.
10. Mark a notch at the **Apex**.
11. Draw the front band with the inner edge along the **SF**. Extend 1 cm (⅜") beyond the shoulder. The band width is about 10 cm (4") wide at the shoulder and 0.75 cm (¼") at the CF.
12. Draw the back band to fit the back bodice pattern.

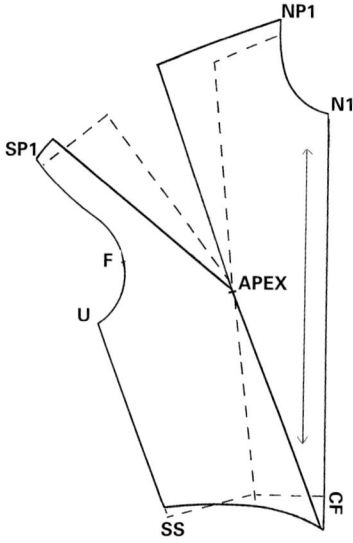

Figure 5.23 Pivot shoulder dart.

COLLAR BAND

The collar is drawn from the pattern. Add 0.75 cm (¼") to both front and back collar band at the shoulder. This is to account for the rounding of the shoulder. It must be fitted on the body to ensure a perfect fit. It is stitched by hand onto the bodice.

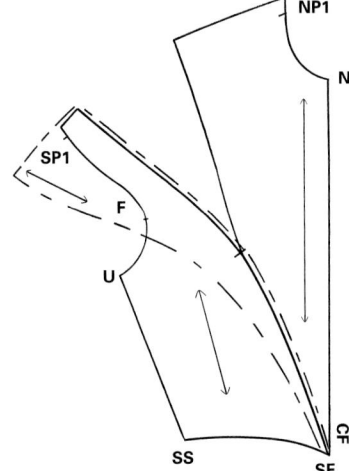

Figure 5.24 Collar band front. **Figure 5.25** Collar band back.

Alternative Sleeve

Figure 5.26

1. For both dresses, use the Historical Two-piece Sleeve draft from Chapter 1.
2. Scoop the front and back seams 1 cm–1.5 cm (⅜"–⅝"), as indicated in Figure 5.26.
3. For the turquoise dress, shorten the hem length to reflect the design.
4. Add a ruffle 5 cm (2½") × one and a half times the hem width.

Skirt Design for Alternative Dress 1 and 2

1. Use the instructions for the primary design for determining the skirt waist line.
2. Use knife pleats instead of cartridge pleats. A complete description of knife pleating is found in Chapter 6, pages 110 and 111.

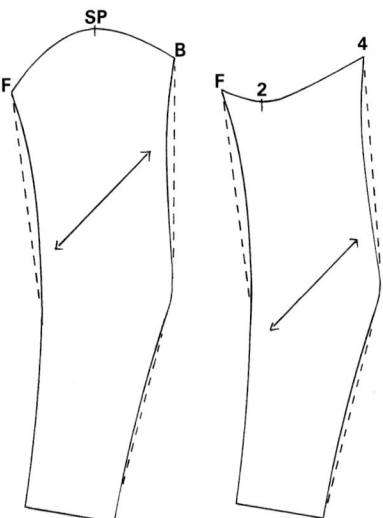

Figure 5.26 Sleeve.

NOTES

1. E. A. Cory (1849) *The Art of Dressmaking, containing Plain Directions in Simple Language from the Fitting of the Pattern to the Finish of the Dress.* Available at https://books.google.co.uk/books/about/The_Art_of_Dressmaking_Containing_Plain.html. Accessed 2 December 2024.
2. Anon (1843) *The Ladies Hand-book of Millinery, Dress-making and Tatting*, 25, 26. Available at https://books.google.com.
3. *Petit Courrier des Dames* (1846), 20 April.
4. M. J. Howell (1845) *The Hand-Book of Dress-Making*, Plate 3, https://archive.org/details/TheHandBookOfDressMaking. Also found in Arnold (1982) *Patterns of Fashion 1* (London: Macmillan/Drama Books), 14; and Arnold (2021) *Patterns of Fashion 1* (London: School of Historical Dress), 5.

6

Development of Period Patterns, 1850–59

Period Dress in Historical Context

The middle years of the nineteenth century were a fulcrum, equally balancing the clothing industry before, and after, extensive industrialization. For many key players in the fashion industry, it was a period of technological development and industrial expansion. As always, the style of dress symbolized society's collective spirit. The aesthetics of fashion mirrored the thriving industry with an ever-expanding silhouette, buoyed by the invention of the steel wire crinoline.

Without question, the introduction of the sewing machine in the middle of the century set the pace for clothing industries across the world. During the second half of the century, the well-known publication *The Tailor & Cutter* estimated that a shirt was constructed with approximately 20,000 stitches. By hand, a sewer could average 35 stitches per minute.[1] The machine worker could average between 1,000 and 2,000 stitches per minute. Throughout the 1850s, and then the 1860s, the production and distribution of the sewing machine increased at a huge rate, and was embraced by professionals and home sewers alike.

Speed was not the only consideration. One contemporary writer, John W. Urquhart noted that 'Hand work is always irregular, no matter how well performed, and is constantly

Figure 6.1 Dress front. This lovely lilac and white checked dress is the epitome of an 1850s look. If made in modern fabric, it would be substantial and heavy, but this silk is light and airy.
Figure 6.2 Dress back.

subjected to strains at particular points, while machine work, being regular, receives the strain upon larger portions of the seam and suffers less.'[2] He further compared the single thread, chain-stitch sewing machine with the less common, dual thread, lock-stitch ones. A single thread chain-stitch had the advantage of being slightly elastic, which protected it from breaking. It also simplified the process of using an old garment as the pattern for a new one 'because the seams are readily removed by releasing the finishing end and drawing out the thread in one continuous length.'[3] Lock-stitch machine seams had a greater tendency to unravel if the thread was broken, but its stitches were also slightly elastic and lay flat on both sides of the fabric. When bobbin and top threads were equally balanced for proper tension, Urquhart concluded that lock-stitching was undoubtedly better adapted for ordinary work than hand-stitching.[4]

Another quintessential innovation that defined the 1850s was the crinoline. The crinoline, whether made of crisp horsehair or hoops of steel, allowed for larger and larger bell-shaped skirts. By the time the steel cage crinoline was developed by R. C. Millet in Paris in 1856, the fashion was ubiquitous. The addition of flounces and fringes increased the square footage a woman inhabited to a greater degree than ever before. Yards of silk were light and buoyant, and created the illusion of skirts, and the women who wore them, almost floating above the ground. It was a fashion that crossed the class divide and was worn by the elite and shopgirls alike. In a effort to reinforce their wearability, this W. S. and C. H. Thomson Skirt Factory advertisement shows a workroom of women appearing to wear the product they are producing (see Figure 6.3).

For the first time, the silhouette was truly representative of the hourglass, and any woman could achieve the desired look. There are only two ways to amplify a body's natural shape into an exaggerated hourglass figure: illusory design and body manipulation. During the first half of the nineteenth century, silhouettes changed primarily by the former method. For example, even though the gigot sleeves and padded hemmed skirts of the 1830s created an hourglass shape, the core's armature was the body. The cage crinoline was the century's first manufactured item that created an unnatural body shape over which a garment was built. It would undergo successive changes over the decades; from the bell shape, to an inverted cone, to an ellipse, and finally to a bustle. When it fell out of fashion in the 1880s, another body modifier, the corset, took on the lion's share of manipulatory work, as waists became tighter and busts more rounded.

There is one more invention that may have had an influence on dress of the day. Photography had been introduced in the 1830s by Louis Daguerre and Joseph Niépce in France, and W. Henry Fox Talbot in Britain. By the 1850s, improvements to the process had made photography both popular and accessible. It became a viable and permanent means for a woman to construct her appearance. It seems more than possible that dress fabrics with strong graphic designs became popular during this period, at least in part because of their photographic merits. Skirts with multiple flounces, each with strong

Figure 6.3 W. S. & C. H. Thomson's Skirt Manufactory. Wood-engraved illustration from *Harper's Weekly*, 19 February 1859.

vertical stripes, would add interest to a composition with the design elements of line and texture. This would not be lost on photographers, who were often accomplished portrait painters as well. As photographs reflected the physicality of the sitter, they also projected the skill of the artist.

DESCRIPTION

This two-piece, lavender checked silk dress exemplifies the popular styling of the 1850s (see Figures 6.1 and 6.2). An hourglass shape is achieved with broad shoulders, a trim waist and a peplum that flares over a full skirt. A wide shoulder band that extends beyond the natural shoulder line, and angles to a point at front and back, reinforces the silhouette. This band is trimed with impressive gold and black silk fringe. The slender waist is balanced with broad two-tiered pagoda sleeves, also trimmed with fringe. Nonfunctional plum pudding buttons, crocheted with two-toned purple silk thread, define the front closure.

Three-tiered skirts were the height of fashion in the late 1850s. This skirt is cut from straight panels of fabric that are pleated into a plain cotton waistband using a combination of techniques. A box pleat marks the centre front. Knife pleats, facing the front, continue to approximately 6 cm (2½") on either side of the centre back, where tiny cartridge pleats control the greatest amount of fullness at the back.

Primary Step-by-Step Drafting Instructions

To start this draft, you will need a completed front and back Modern Basic Block pattern without the optional back shoulder dart. The Modern Basic Block has more ease than is needed for the 1850s block, so most will be removed in creating the historical block. Additional adjustments may be needed during the first fitting. The original pattern is indicated with short dotted lines. The longer dotted lines indicate the centre of darts.

Remove Excess Ease

Figure 6.4

1. Draw a new **CF** 0.5 cm (³⁄₁₆") to the left of **CF**.
2. Draw a new **CB** 0.5 cm (³⁄₁₆") to the right of **CB**.
3. Remove 1 cm–1.5 cm (⅜"–⅝") from each side seam from **U** to nothing at the line **W–W1**.

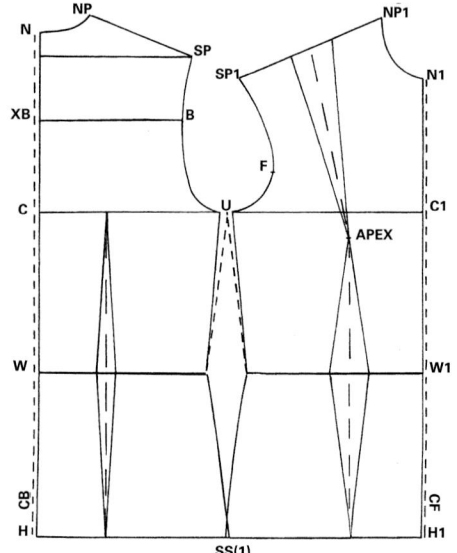

Figure 6.4 Remove excess ease.

Back Bodice

Figure 6.5

1. From **B**, mark a point 2.5 cm (1") towards **XB** along the line **XB–B**.
2. Draw a line from that point to the left side of the waist dart. This defines the back panel and will become the left **SB** seam line.
3. Cut the pattern separating the panels along the left **SB** seam line.
4. The right side of the dart ends at the line **C–U**. This defines the side back panel. Smooth any angles. This is the right side of the new **SB** seam.
5. There are now two pattern pieces; the back panel and the side back panel.

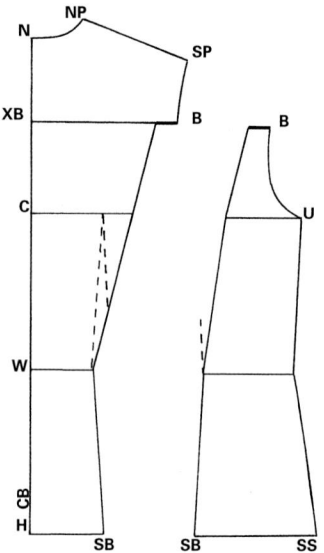

Figure 6.5 Back panel, side back panel and SB seam.

Back Panel Peplum

Figure 6.6

The basque, or peplum, is the skirt of the bodice.

1. On the back panel, draw an angled line from nothing at the waist, to 8 cm–10 cm (3¼"–4") away from the original **SB** hem. There is an option to angle this line closer or further away for more or less flare.
2. Extend the **CB** below **H** approximately 10 cm (4").
3. Draw a new provisional hem.

Side Back Peplum

Figure 6.6

1. Separate the side back panel at the waist.
2. Divide the section below the waist in half, vertically.
3. Cut along the division from the hem to the waist leaving a small hinge.
4. Spread apart 8 cm–10 cm (3¼"–4").
5. The waist will automatically form an angle. Smooth this into a curve.
6. Create a curve on the top waist. These two opposing waist curves produce a dart that will result in more waist defined shaping.
7. Draw a new provisional hem that corresponds to the back panel hem in length and shape.

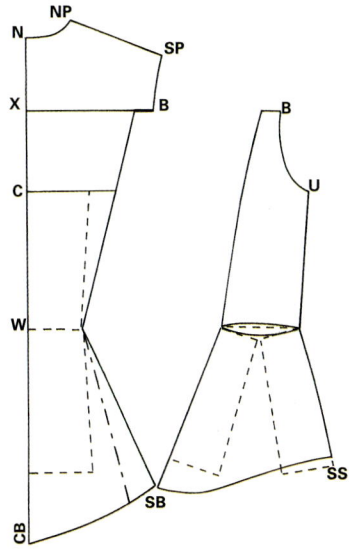

Figure 6.6 Back and side back peplum.

Front Bodice Positioning Darts

Figure 6.7 and Figure 6.8

1. Raise the **Apex** to the line **U–C1**.
2. Mark a point 1.5 cm–2 cm (⅝"–¾") from this point towards **U**. This is the point of **dart 1**, and is the new **Apex**.
3. Redraw the shoulder dart to reflect this position.
4. Using the **Apex** as the high point of the waist dart, draw its centre from the **Apex** to the original dart position on the hem.
5. Shift depth of **dart 1** to the right of this drawn line. This brings the dart closer to the **CF**.
6. Mark a second point approximately 4.5 cm–5.5 cm (1¾–2¼") to the left of the **Apex**. This is the point of **dart 2**.
7. Draw a line parallel to **dart 1** from the point of **dart 2** to the hem. This is the placement of **dart 2**.

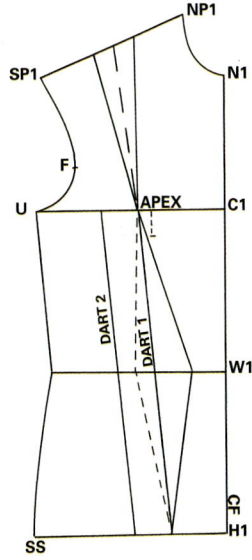

Figure 6.7 Front dart positions.

8. Cut up **dart 2** to its point and then continue along the line **U–C1** to the **Apex**, leaving a small paper hinge.
9. Close the shoulder dart. The cut will automatically open up as the volume of the shoulder dart is transferred to **dart 2**.
10. Below the waist, even up the two darts by removing some volume from **dart 1** and adding the same amount to **dart 2**.
11. Add volume to **dart 2** with an additional 1 cm–2 cm (⅜"–¾") **with a curve from the waist to the hem. This extra front volume is needed to sit over the crinoline shape.**
12. True up the darts. This is crucial because the sides are no longer equal in length.

Figure 6.8 Transferring shoulder dart.

Front Peplum

Figure 6.9 and Figure 6.10

1. Separate the peplum from the main body along the waist from the **SS** to **dart 2**.
2. Divide the section below the waist in half, vertically.
3. Cut along this division from the hem to the waist, leaving a small hinge.
4. Spread open 8 cm–10 cm (3¼"–4").
5. The waist will automatically form a curve at the waist. Smooth this curve.
6. Create a curve on the top waist. These two opposing curves produce a dart resulting in closer waist shaping.

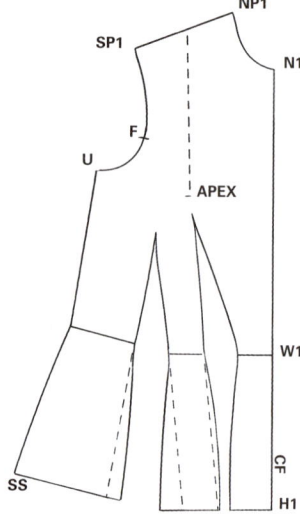

Figure 6.9 Shape waist darts.

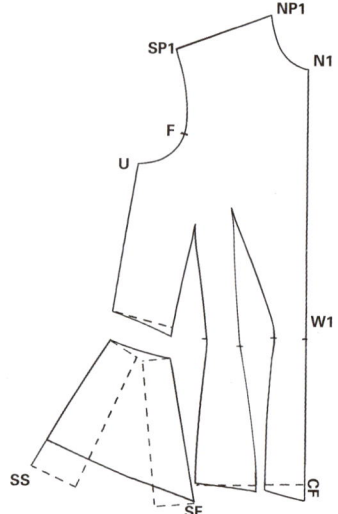

Figure 6.10 Remove the peplum.

Finishing

1. Match the panels from the waist to the hem.
2. Draw a new hem from the lowered **CB**, above the original hip line at the **SS**, and then to a lowered **CF**.

Shoulder and Neckline

Figure 6.11 and Figure 6.12
The bodice shoulders in this period extend well beyond the natural point of articulation. This shoulder seam is parallel to the modern shoulder line, and is placed towards the back.

1. Match front and back patterns at the shoulder from **NP** to **SP** and secure this with tape.
2. Mark a point approximately 1.5 cm (⅝") below **NP** on the back pattern.
3. Mark a point approximately 1.5 cm (⅝") below **SP** on the back pattern.
4. Connect the points. This is the new shoulder seam.
5. Draw a new armhole from **B** to **F** going through a point approximately 3 cm (1⅛") away from **SP**.
6. Draw the front and back shoulder line with a slight curve beyond **SP**. This rounds the shoulder at the join of the arm.
7. Extend the rounded shoulder seam lines about 10 cm (4"). This extension is the shoulder of the collar band.
8. Continue drawing the collar band. In this case, the collar band is about 20 cm (8") at the **CB** and 12 cm (4¾") at the **CF**.
9. Add 0.5 cm (³⁄₁₆") to both front and back collar band at the shoulder. This is to account for the rounding of the shoulder. This must be fitted on the body to ensure a perfect fit.

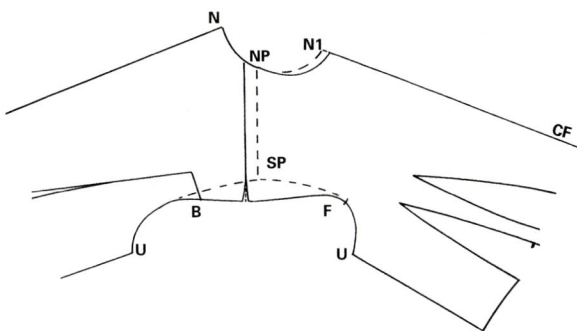

Figure 6.11 Shoulder and neckline.

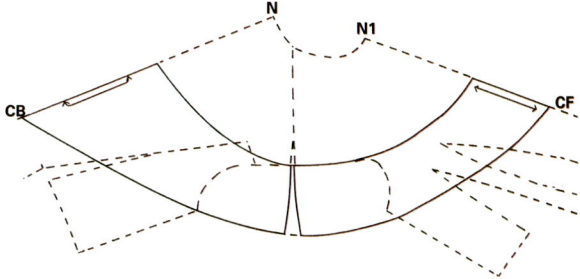

Figure 6.12 Shoulder band.

Pagoda Sleeve

Figure 6.13, Figure 6.14 and Figure 6.15

The demure bell sleeve of the 1840s gave way to the much more extreme Pagoda sleeve in the 1850s. This draft uses the cut and spread technique to draft a sleeve designed to reveal a billowing undersleeve called an 'engageante'. Start with the Historical One-piece Sleeve block with a wider wrist.

1. Divide the sleeve into four equal sections.
2. Number the sections 1–4, left to right.
3. Cut the dividing lines.
4. Place section 4 in front of section 1, matching **U1** to **U**, **E3** to **E** and **W3** to **W**.
5. Spread sections 2 and 3 about one and a half times the width of the section (see Cutting and spreading in Terminology).
6. Redraw the sleeve head with a very shallow cap.
7. Redraw the hem with added length and a small point at the back (see Figure 6.15).
8. This is the undersleeve. In practice, the top of this sleeve would probably be constructed in linen or cotton rather than silk.
9. The topsleeve flounce reaches the elbow on the line drawn out from **E**.
10. Draw the top flounce hem to mirror the under hem.
11. For more flare, angle the seam, making sure to join the original seam about 1 cm (⅜") below **F**.
12. In making up, pleat and gather both sleeves into the armhole.

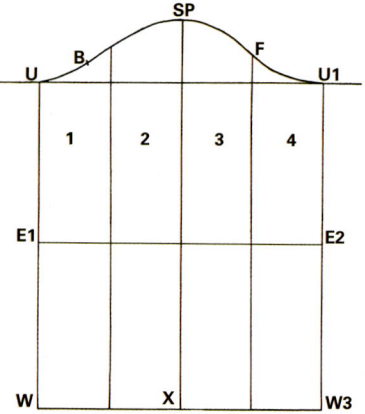

Figure 6.13 Historical One-piece Sleeve in sections.

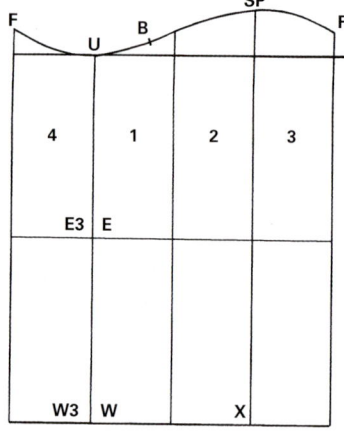

Figure 6.14 Rearrange sleeve sections.

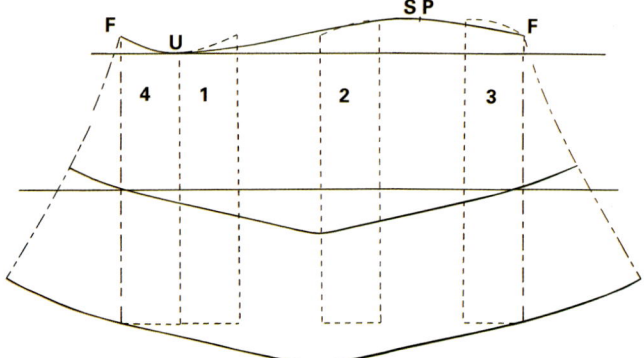

Figure 6.15 Cut and spread sleeve sections divided into two tiers.

Setting the Sleeve

U on the sleeve matches **U** on the bodice. This places the seam forward and higher on the bodice than with a regular one-piece sleeve. It corresponds to the front sleeve seam placement on a man's jacket.

SKIRT

The primary skirt, like all skirts in this period, is a rectangle made of equally long sections of fabric that are joined along the selvages. Jean Hunnisett notes that skirt hems varied from the beginning to the end of the period, from 275 cm (108") to 411 cm (162"). Historically, fabric widths varied. Today, most yardage is 115 cm (45") wide. Therefore, three lengths of fabric work well for the base of this skirt. The length of each piece is from the waist to floor measurement taken over the crinoline, plus 5 cm (2") for seam allowance and a measure of error at the top, plus 7 cm (3") for the hem. Each flounce is about 26 cm–30 cm (10"–12") in length and one and a half times the skirt hem in width. The top flounce is positioned just below the bodice hem. The hem of the bottom flounce sits 5 cm (2") above the base skirt hem. Throughout the 1850s, the knife pleats or inverted box pleats were more fashionable than cartridge pleats. However, the 6 cm–10 cm (2½"–4") on either side of the **CB** was usually cartridge pleated.

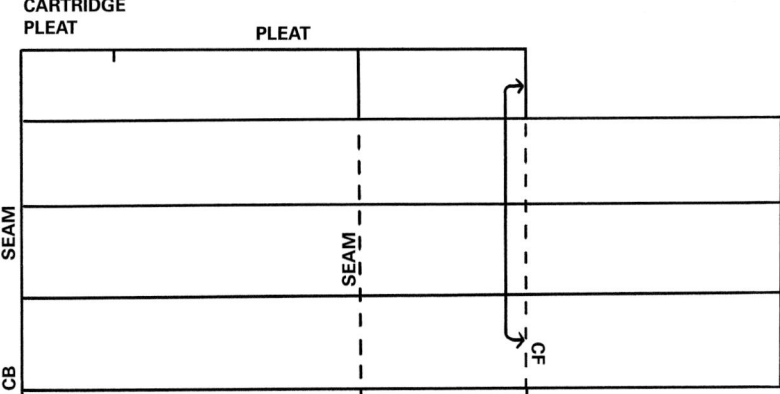

Figure 6.16 Skirt diagram.

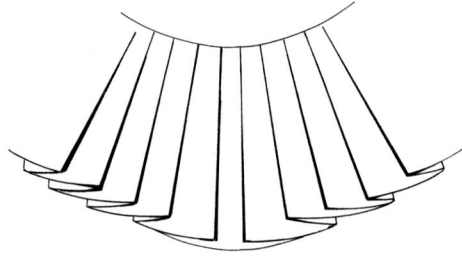

Figure 6.17 Knife pleats with an inverted box pleat at the centre.

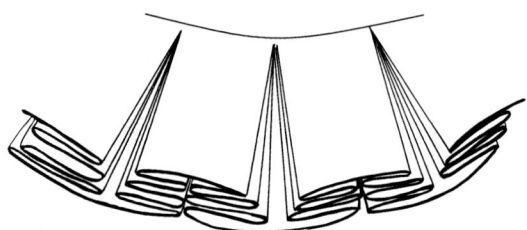

Figure 6.18 Triple inverted box pleats.

PLEATING

Pleating a large amount of fabric into a waist can be very daunting. On the visible side, pleats must be equal in width, but on the underside, they are much larger and can be varied in width. There are two methods of pleating a rectangle of fabric; using a mathematical formula, or draping. Because pleats provide a great deal of elasticity, it is unnecessary to add ease to the formula. To simplify the calculations, try rounding up the increments.

Mathematical Formula

The following instructions are for knife pleats. Cartridge pleating is addressed in Chapter 5. Three widths of fabric equalling approximately 330 cm (130") are needed for a skirt in this period. In historical designs, the visible pleats are often smaller in the back than in the front.

The standard waist measurement used in this book is 68 cm (27").

1. Determine the width of pleats in the design. In this case, choose 2.5 cm (1") pleats for the front and sides and 1 cm (⅜") pleats for the back.
2. Determine how many pleats of each width are needed for the waist. In this case, 20 pleats are needed for the front and sides and 12 are needed for the back, giving a total of 32 pleats.
3. Determine how much fabric is left over after the visible pleats are accounted for. Subtract the waist measurement from the width of fabric: 330 cm (130") − 68 cm (27") = 262 cm (103").
4. Divide the remaining fabric by the number of pleats: 262 cm ÷ 32 = 8.18 cm (103" ÷ 32 = 3.21"). Thus, rounding the numbers for easier calculations, each pleat will have an 8 cm (3¼") turnback.

DRAPING INSTRUCTIONS

If you have access to a dress-form, the pleats can be draped. Always drape the fashion fabric over the petticoat or bustle that will be used under the completed garment. Jean Hunnisett suggests using a length of elastic tied tightly around the waist with the fabric between the elastic and the dress-form. The elastic holds the weight of the fabric while it is manipulated into pleats. Each pleat must be perpendicular to the floor.

1. While manipulating the fabric, envision each pleat as a straight line from the hem.
2. Fold each pleat evenly.
3. Pin each pleat into position on the dress-form.
4. Place a tape around the pleated waist.
5. Carefully secure tape onto the pleats with pins or basting.
6. Machine stitch the tape onto the pleated waist. This can be the interfacing for the waistband, or simply a means to hold the pleats into position until the waistband is applied.

FINESSING THE DRAFT

Note the horizontal lines of this garment (Figures 6.1 and 6.2) and you will notice the regularity of the lines. The skirt is equally divided. The hem of the bodice is roughly close to the top of the first skirt flounce. The undersleeve hem is at the same level as the bodice hem. The top flounce equally divides the sleeve, and is at the height of the waist. The sleeves mimic the hem line of the bodice. The collar band reinforces the gentle angle of the sleeves and bodice hem. Another way of looking is to see a cone shape with a head at the top. The tiers from the bottom to the top get slightly smaller. Despite the magnificence of the garment, the head and face are still the most important aspect of the ensemble.

Figure 6.19 Alternative Dress 1. This chestnut and blue colour combination was popular.

Figure 6.20 Alternative Dress 2. The copper watered silk and velvet is resplendent.

Alternative Day Dress Draft Adaptations

ALTERNATIVE DRESS 1

This beautiful chestnut dress has a typical 1850s silhouette with a fitted bodice and three-tiered skirt (see Figure 6.19). The bodice has open fan pleating on the shoulder. Fan pleated bodices were very popular throughout the 1840s and 1850s. The design had wide pleating on the shoulders, which was folded into very small pleats or shirring at the centre front waist. This style provided the visual hourglass shaping, and was relatively easy for an average dressmaker to produce using the 'pin-to-the-form' method of pattern making. There is even some evidence that this styling was used for dress during pregnancy, as the pleats could be let out and repleated as necessary.[5] This particular dress looks like a subtle version of the fan pleated bodice. As this fashion plate illustration is from 1859, a fully fanned bodice may have seemed rather old-fashioned.

This style is more successfully draped than drafted. In recreating this bodice, complete a sturdy cotton backing according to the primary drafting instructions without the peplum. Use this backing as the foundation of the bodice. Place the completed backing on a dress-form and drape the fashion fabric onto it. By draping it on a form, you will mould the fashion fabric over the rounding of the shoulder. Place the folds in the most pleasing positions. Join the fashion fabric and the backing by stitching them together under the pleats.

The sleeve is similar to the primary bell-shaped sleeve in Chapter 5. It fits smoothly into the armhole without gathers. It also fits the bicep without a great deal of fullness. However, it seems to follow the curve of the elbow more closely than the 1840 pattern would have done. This leads me to believe that it is a two-piece sleeve with a curved arm.

To make this sleeve, start with the Historical Two-piece Sleeve draft in Chapter 1. Note that the front seam sits higher than in the draft.

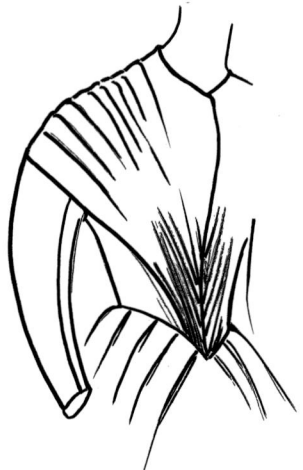

Figure 6.21 Fan-shaped bodice.

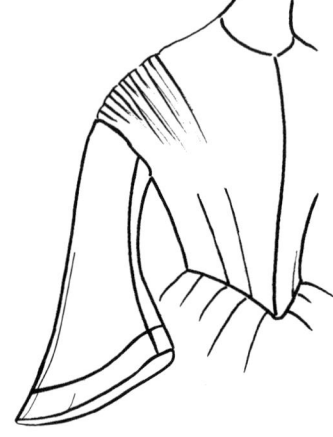

Figure 6.22 Modified fan-shaped bodice with Two-piece Bell Sleeve.

Two-piece Bell Sleeve

Figure 6.23

1. On the line **H–B**, mark a point 2 cm (¾") to the left of H. This is the new placement for **F**. Note: F will not meet F on the bodice, rather it creates a front seam that starts high on the armhole.
2. Draw a smooth curve from **F** to **SP**, and from **SP** to **B**. This is the new sleeve head for the topsleeve.
3. Draw a scooping line from **F** to **4** as indicated. This is the new sleeve head for the undersleeve.
4. Cut the elbow from **6** to **5**, leaving a small paper hinge.
5. Spread **6** open about 8 cm (3").
6. Draw the new front seam from **F** to **5** to the desired hem length. In this case, about 5 cm (2") above the wrist.
7. Shape the back seam into a bell, as illustrated in Figure 6.23.
8. Draw the hem as desired.

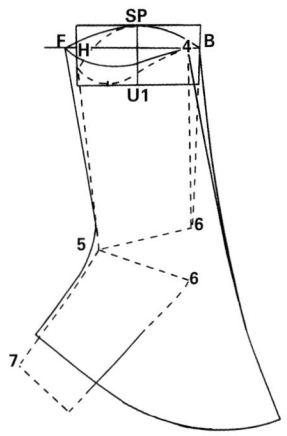

Figure 6.23 Two-piece Bell Sleeve pattern.

ALTERNATIVE DRESS 2

The alternative copper dress has a fitted bodice that can be drafted with the primary techniques without the peplum (see Figure 6.20). The skirt has two tiers rather than three. The skirt appears to have a deep inverted box pleat at the front, followed by very deep knife pleats facing towards the front. They probably change direction at the sides with pleats facing the **CB**. The sleeve is open from a point high on the armhole, and opens to show an extremely full engageante.

ALTERNATIVE DRESS 2 SLEEVE

There are three pattern pieces for this sleeve. The patterns needed are: the sleeve cap, which would be constructed out of inexpensive cotton, the sleeve body, and the mancheron, which is a decorative cap that covers the sleeve cap and the horizontal seam.

Sleeve Cap

Figure 6.24

1. Refer to the Alternative Dress 1 sleeve for the shape of the sleeve head.
2. Cut along the line of **U** and remove the sleeve pattern below this line.

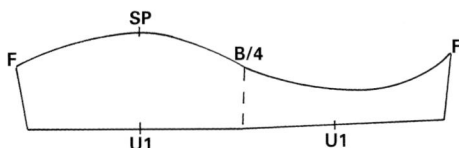

Figure 6.24 Sleeve cap.

Chapter 6 Development of Period Patterns, 1850–59

3. Trace the topsleeve head and the undersleeve head patterns.
4. On a clean sheet of paper, join **B** to **4**. This is the sleeve cap. It would be constructed out of cotton.

Sleeve Body

The pattern for the sleeve body below the sleeve cap is essentially a large triangle with a rounded point. The top width is at least twice the width of the sleeve cap's base. The length is the full length of the arm or longer. The triangle is pleated onto the sleeve cap, with the greatest concentration on the topsleeve and less on the undersleeve.

Mancheron

Figure 6.25 and Figure 6.26
1. Copy the sleeve cap pattern.
2. Add length to the hem to cover the horizontal undersleeve and body seam.
3. Add a little width to the hem below **F** to accommodate the extra width needed to cover the sleeve cap and gathered sleeve body.

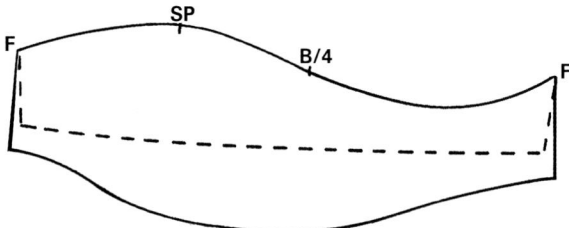

Figure 6.25 Mancheron.

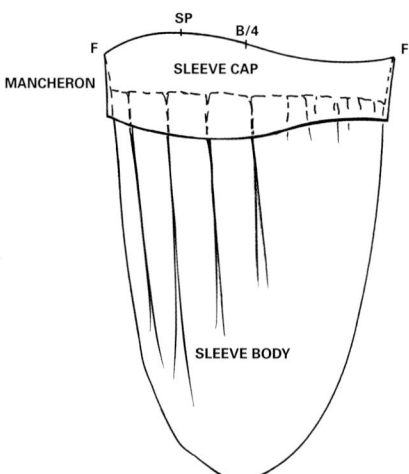

Figure 6.26 Sleeve construction in sequence.

NOTES

1. James A. Schmiechen (1984) *Sweated Industries and Sweated Labor: The London Clothing Trades, 1860–1914* (Chicago: University of Illinois Press), 9.
2. P. Sykas (2014) 'Investigative Methodologies: Understanding the Fabric of Fashion', in S. Black et al. (eds) *The Handbook of Fashion Studies* (London: Bloomsbury), 236. J. W. Urquhart (1881) *Sewing Machinery, Being a Practical Manual of the Sewing Machine …* (London: Crosby Lockwood), 17, 18.
3. Ibid.
4. Ibid.
5. In a 5½" × 4½" daguerreotype of Mrs John (Sarah) Macaulay, c. 1855, from the Queen's University Archives, V-23 P-7, Sarah Macaulay sits wrapped in a figured shawl. Her bodice is controlled with stitching just under the bust. The silk splays out just below control stitching covering what appears to be a pregnant belly. Discussed in M. E. MacKay (2012) 'Through the Lens of Fashion: An Analysis of the Clothing of Women in Early Victorian Ontario', Master's Thesis, Toronto Metropolitan University, 54.

7

Development of Period Patterns, 1860–69

Period Dress in Historical Context

This stunning two-piece dress exhibits a sleek line that is devoid of any surplus ruffling (Figures 7.1 and 7.2). It is a celebration of the clean uncluttered lines and vibrant colours that characterize 1860s fashion. In addition to symbolizing the youth and purity of its owner, the colour is a signifier of Victorian devotion to the scientific process and commitment to discovery and commerce.

This dress was made for Mrs Eliza Gordon, of Ottawa, Ontario, in the year of her marriage in 1869. Its silk taffeta fabric was known as 'changeable' silk. This term was used to describe a textile in which the warp is one colour and the weft is a different colour. In this case, the silk is a weave of blue and green producing a striking peacock colour. With any kind of movement, the chromatic scheme would undulate from turquoise to a dark blue-green with an olive cast, hence the label 'changeable'. While Mrs Gordon's dress is definitely chemical in its colouring, its exact formula cannot be assertained without a chemical analysis.

The discovery of chemically synthesized aniline dyes introduced the professional chemist to the fashion industry. William Henry Perkins is credited with the discovery and subsequent patenting of the first aniline dye in 1856. While distilling coal tar in search of pharmaceutical compounds, he became sidetracked by the reaction of aniline, one of the

Figure 7.1 Dress front.

Figure 7.2 Dress back. A remnant of this peacock silk was donated with the dress. It is possible that the extra fabric was to be made into a ball gown bodice for evening events.

byproducts of the processing, when it was combined with dichromate. Perkins extracted a rich purple compound, which proved to be colour-fast and stable when used as a dye on protein fibres such as silk and wool. Purple had long been a valued colour for textiles but was reserved for the aristocracy. Perkin's discovery, which he called 'mauvine', sparked a huge trend for aniline purples in various hues. When Queen Victoria and Empress Eugénie were seen sporting the new shades, the craze became fixed. Charles Dickens noted:

> As I look out of my window, the apotheosis of Perkin's purple seems at hand – purple hands wave from open carriages – purple hands shake each other at street doors – purple hands threaten each other from opposite sides of the street; purple-striped gowns cram barouches, jam up cabs, throng steamers, fill railway stations: all flying countryward, like so many birds of purple paradise.[1]

Recognizing the commercial implications of aniline dyes, chemists rushed to develop a variety of synthetic dyes from the same coal tar base. By heating and mixing aniline with acids, often with soluble metals such as mercury and iron compounds, they produced a whole spectrum of brilliant colours.

At the same time, pattern makers began appealing to a broader clientele. Ebenezer Butterick was a merchant tailor from Worcester, Massachusetts. He was schooled in tailoring systems that were based on using proportional calculations to develop the parametres of a pattern. With this methodology, a tailor needed only a few measurements to produce a pattern. It was a short step from drafting with one or two measurements directly from the body, to drafting with measurements only, without the presence of a body. By assessing and formularizing gradations between one size and another, drafting a full range of sizes became a relatively straightforward process. Butterick was not alone is developing sized patterns, but he was an early purveyor in selling them to the public. In the early 1860s, he began marketing patterns for men's shirts and children's clothing. By 1867, he branched out to selling women's clothing patterns as well. These patterns were cut out of light tissue

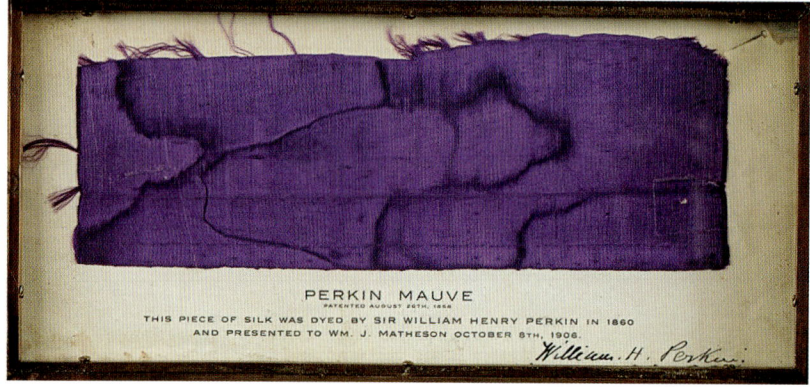

Figure 7.3 Swatch of silk dyed in mauvine.

Figure 7.4 Cox and Minton American Dress Chart, Front of Lady's Dress, 1868.

paper, which made them easier to distribute through the mail than traditional heavy brown paper had been. The patterns did not have printed instructions, but were cut to shape with notches to indicate how they were to be joined together. A keen businessman, Butterick used multiple means to expand his business. He advertised with larger clothing operations and sewing machine companies. By distributing patterns by mail order, he opened up the market to include women in rural communities as well as small town dressmakers. In 1873, he started publishing a semi-annual catalogue of his patterns called *The Delineator*. By the time he published his first *Delineator*, Butterick had sold an astonishing 6 million paper patterns, and had laid the foundation for the paper pattern industry.

DESCRIPTION

This shot silk two-piece dress has a fitted bodice with equally placed darts (see Figures 7.1 and 7.2). Every dart and seam is stabilized with baleen in cotton channels. It has a rounded neck, with a small stand collar with double folded bias trim. It has a front closure with nine half ball-shaped buttons worked in thread of a darker blue. Fringe and bias trim follow the armhole and over the shoulder to a very sharp and deep 'V' point coming to the centre back waist. The two-piece sleeve is slim and slightly curved. It tapers to the wrist and is decorated with double folded bias and fashion fabric leaf shapes.

As was the fashion in the late 1860s, this skirt was cut in an inverted cone with smooth waist and full hem. Gored panels were a way to increase the hem's width without adding bulk to the waist. As the decade proceeded, fullness was swept to the back, creating a dramatic ellipse. This skirt has nine wedge-shaped panels. The skirt fits into the waist with knife pleating at the sides, and cartridge pleating on either side of the back opening. The bustle and bow are each separate accessories to the dress. The bustle is four pieces gathered and joined together. The double lobed bow has a central rosette and is attached to a narrow waistband with a hook and eye closure. The bustle and bow are trimmed with silk fringe.

Primary Step-by-Step Drafting Instructions

The 1860s period block begins with minor revisions to the Modern Basic Block found in Chapter 1. The Modern Basic Block has more ease than is needed for the 1860s block, so some will be removed in creating the historical block. Additional adjustments may be needed during the first fitting. The original pattern is indicated with short dotted lines. The longer dotted lines indicate the centre of darts.

To start this draft, you will need a completed front and back Modern Basic Block pattern without the optional back shoulder dart. Only the portion above the waist is needed for this period draft.

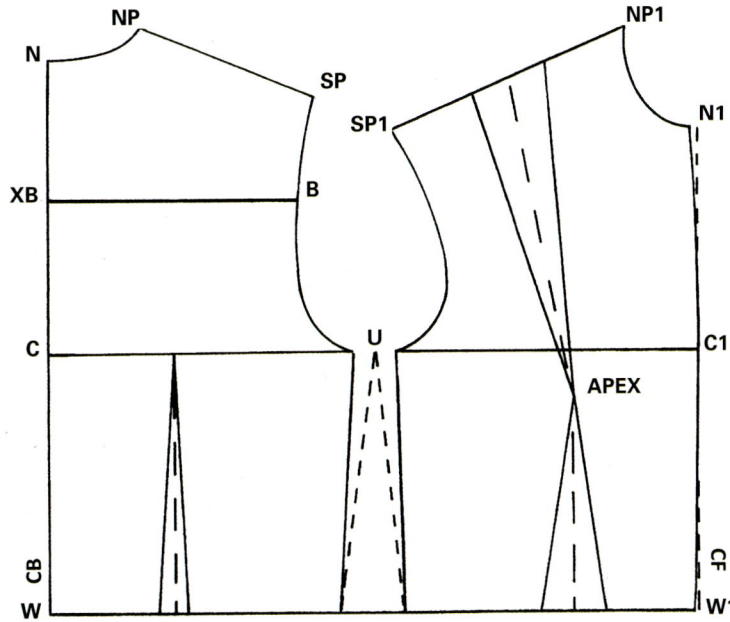

Remove Excess Ease

Figure 7.5 Removal of excess ease.

Figure 7.5
1. Draw a new Centre Front by removing 0.5 cm (3/16") at **N1** and **W1**.
2. Remove 1 cm–1.5 cm (3/8"–5/8") from each side seam from **U** to nothing on the line **W–W1**.

Bodice Back

Figure 7.6
The primary gown back is cut in one piece with the pattern on the fold. There is no waist dart in the garment, so the dart in the pattern must be removed.

1. Measure the depth of the dart at the waist.
2. Mark a point, equal to the depth of the dart, to the left of the **SS** on the line drawn out from **W**.
3. Draw a line from **U** to this point. This is the new **SS**.

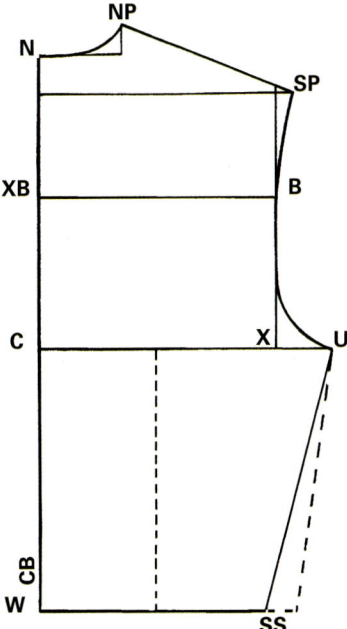

Figure 7.6 Remove back waist dart.

Bodice Front

Figure 7.7, Figure 7.8, Figure 7.9 and Figure 7.10

The 1860s aesthetic tended towards symmetry. Two darts were often equally placed on either side of the bust. This configuration seems to give the bodice a neat and clean appearance. In some cases, the dart closest to the **SS** angled towards the armhole.

1. Drop a line from **F** to the line **U–C1**.
2. Find the midpoint of this line and draw a perpendicular line to the armhole. Call this **F1**. **F1** is the front balance point for the two-piece sleeve.
3. Raise the **Apex** to the line **U–C1**.
4. Redraw the shoulder and waist darts to reflect the new **Apex** position.
5. Close the waist dart and open the shoulder dart.
6. Draw two waist darts.
   a. **Dart 1** starts about 5.5 cm (2¼") from the **CF** waist and ends about 7.5 cm (3") from the **CF**. The dart point is 1 cm (⅜") below the line **U–C1**.
   b. **Dart 2** starts about 3 cm (1⅛") from the first dart on the waist and angles slightly towards the armhole. The dart point is 1 cm (⅜") below the line **U–C1**.
7. Draw a line from the **Apex** to the point of each waist dart.
8. Cut up **darts 1** and **2** to the **Apex**, leaving a small hinge.
9. Close the shoulder dart and open **darts 1** and **2** equally.
10. True up the shoulder from **SP1–NP1**.
11. True up the darts at the waist.
12. Shape the darts to soften the straight lines and more closely conform to a body.

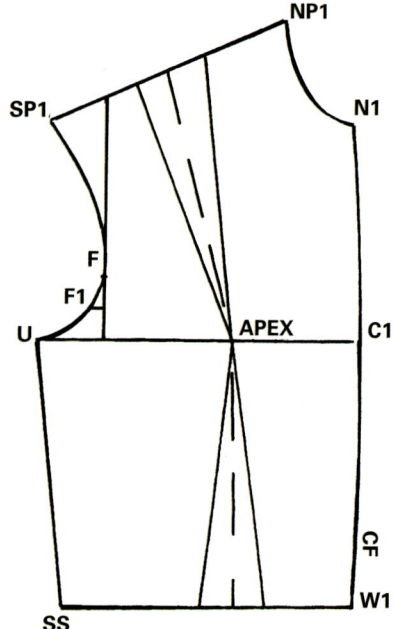

Figure 7.7 Raise Apex, find F1.

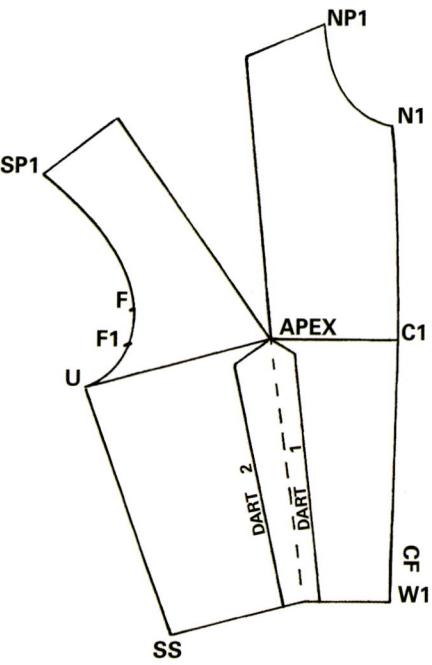

Figure 7.8 Close shoulder dart and mark waist darts.

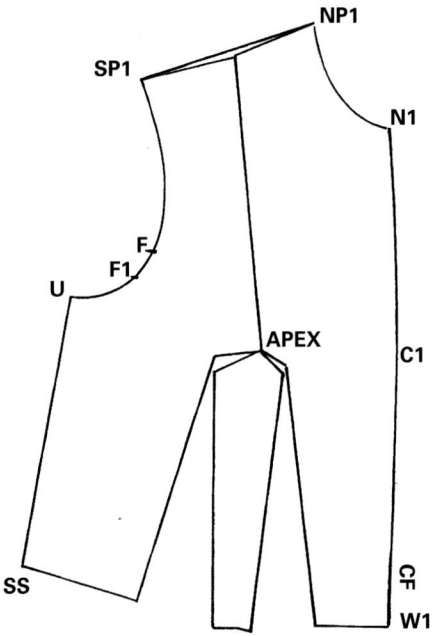

Figure 7.9 Close shoulder darts and open waist darts.

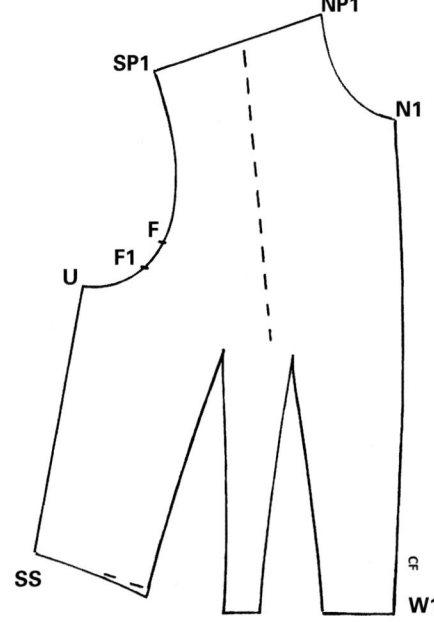

Figure 7.10 Shaped waist darts.

Shoulder and Neckline

Figure 7.11

1. The shoulder seam in this garment is very closely aligned with the modern shoulder seam.
2. Match front and back patterns at the shoulder from **NP** to **SP** and secure this with tape. Draw a new armhole going through a point approximately 3 cm (1⅛") away from **SP**.
3. Mark a point approximately 1.5 cm (⅝") below **SP** on the back pattern.
4. Draw a line from **NP** to this point. This is the new shoulder seam.

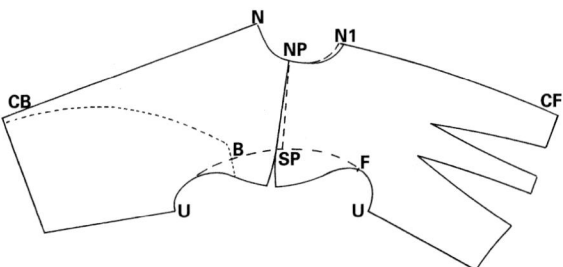

Figure 7.11 Shoulder and neck fringe placement.

5. Continue the new shoulder seam with a small curve into the armhole.
6. The small dotted line indicates the trim placement.

Finishing and Finessing the Pattern

Figure 7.12
1. True up the all seams.
2. Side seam placement was not standard in the nineteenth century. It was often further towards the back than it is today. This makes the back appear narrower. If you choose to move the **SS** from 2 cm–3 cm (¾"–1⅛") towards the back, retain **U** in the original position.

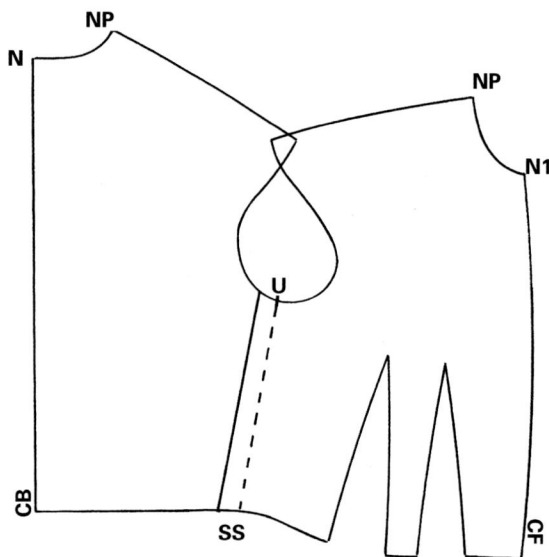

Figure 7.12 Alternative Side Seam.

Sleeve Adaptations

Figure 7.13, Figure 7.14 and Figure 7.15
Sleeves in the 1860s fit the armhole with little ease, had a full, rounded elbow and a fitted wrist.

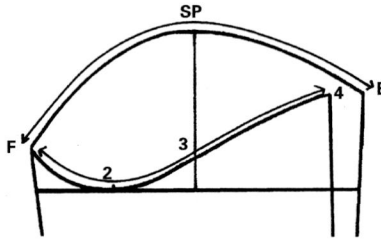

Figure 7.13 Measure sleeve cap.

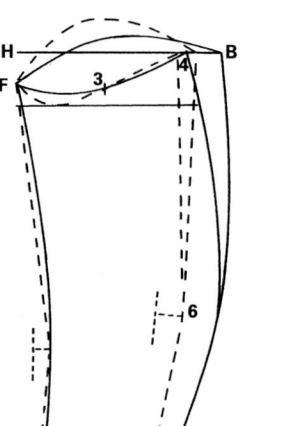

Figure 7.14 1860s sleeve adaptations.

19th-Century Patterns for the Modern Body

Use the Historical Two-piece Sleeve found in Chapter 1 for this draft. To achieve the correct look, the sleeve head is made wider and even shallower than it is in this block.

1. Measure the sleeve head from **F**, through **SP**, and to **B**. Record this measurement.
2. Measure the undersleeve head from **F**, through **2** and **3**, to **4**. Record this measurement.
3. Extend the line **H–B** to the right 2.5 cm (1"). Move **B** to this new position.
4. Redraw a shallow sleeve head from **F** to a new **B** using the upper sleeve head measurement.
5. Move **4** about 1.5 cm (⅝") to the right on the line **H–B**.
6. Redraw a shallow undersleeve head from **F** to the new **4**.
7. Draw the back seams from **B** and **4** with a wide rounded elbow 4 cm–6 cm (1⅝"–2½") to the right of **6** (see Figure 7.14).
8. Continue drawing the back seam to a fitted wrist.
9. Using the original front seam as a guideline, draw a new front seam with a gentle curve.

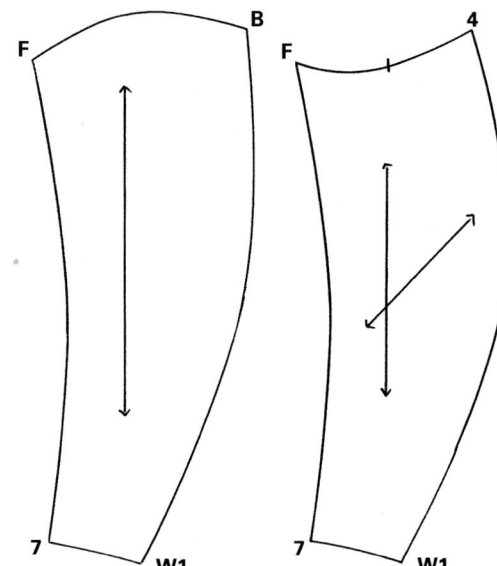

Figure 7.15 Topsleeve and undersleeve.

COLLAR

The primary collar is so narrow that it could be thought of as a binding. It is 1.5 cm (⅝") wide and cut on the straight of grain.

SKIRT DRAFT

The bell-shaped skirt of the 1850s gave way to a triangular silhouette in the 1860s. Early in the decade, dressmakers followed the long-established method of pleating a rectangle of fabric onto a straight waistband. As the decade progressed, and the fashion for wider hems took hold, dressmakers created skirts with a number of gored panels. Dividing the skirt into panels offered an almost limitless number of options for creating new and interesting silhouettes. As such, panel skirts became the most important skirt styling for the rest of the nineteenth century.

The primary dress in Figure 7.1 has no fullness at the front and minimal pleating around the sides, but has deep cartridge pleating at the back for 5 cm (2") on either side of the **CB** closure. The following is a draft for a simplified skirt, with seven, rather than nine, panels.

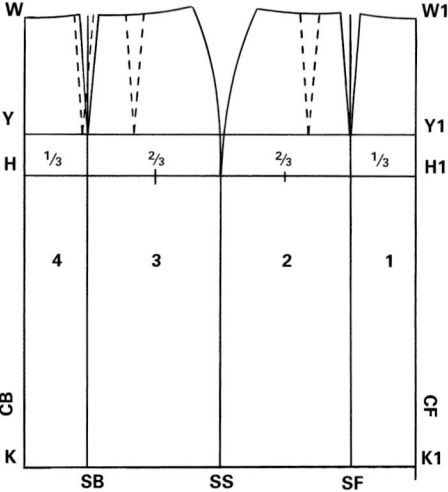

Figure 7.16 Modern six-panel skirt.

Six- or Seven-panel Skirt

Figure 7.16

1. Complete the Straight Skirt Block found in Chapter 1.
2. Divide **H–H1** into six equal portions; three on the back pattern and three on the front pattern.
3. On the front, use these divisions to form two panels. The area from **CF** to one-third is the first panel. The area from this division to the **SS** is the second panel. Draw a line parallel to the **CF** to distinguish the two front panels.
4. Transfer the front waist dart to the front division.
5. On the back, the area from **CB** to one-third is one panel. The area from this division to the **SS** is the second panel. Draw a line parallel to the **CB** to distinguish the two back panels.
6. Transfer one back waist dart to the back division. The second back waist dart will be gathered or pleated into the waistband during the construction stage.
7. Label the panels 1–4 from right to left.
8. Extend the draft to full length. In this case, the length is 109 cm (43").
9. Separate the panels.
10. If the **CB** is placed on a fold, the skirt pattern has six panels. If the **CB** is treated like a seam, the skirt pattern has seven panels.

SKIRT HEM FORMULA

Hems in the 1860s averaged 300 cm–510 cm (120"–200") in circumference. Chapter 2 has suggestions for choosing an appropriate hem diameter for a particular garment. The hem width of each panel can vary, as long they add up to your desired measurement. Because we are working with a lot of volume, there is no need to work with fractions. Round up measurements for easier calculations. The dress in Figure 7.1 has a full hem circumference of about 420 cm (165"). Therefore, the pattern hem is 210 cm (82"–83").

The following instructions use the cutting and spreading method of incorporating extra volume into the pattern. In practice, this can become cumbersome because the size of paper is quite large. With experience, you will be able to use the measurements alone, or visualize the shape for a good pattern. There is an important distinction from cut and spread examples in previous chapters, as the pattern pieces are spread unequally.

Panel 1

Figure 7.17

1. Place the **CF** on a vertical and horizontal grid.
2. The horizontal gridline corresponds to the waist. The vertical gridline corresponds to the **CF**.
3. Divide the panel in half, vertically.
4. Cut the pattern from the hem to the waist along this division.
5. Spread the pattern hem until it equals 30 cm (12").
6. Secure the pieces in place, or trace onto another piece of paper.

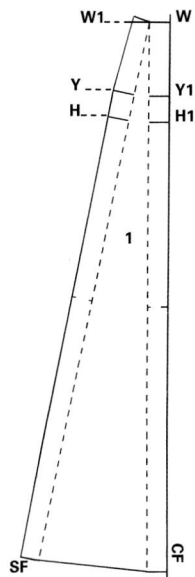

Figure 7.17 Skirt panel 1.

Panel 2

Figure 7.18

1. A horizontal gridline corresponds to the line **W–W1**.
2. Divide **panel 2** in half, vertically.
3. Cut up along this centre division.
4. Spread the pattern on the waist 5 cm (2") along the gridline, to account for one pleat.
5. Spread the pattern hem until it equals 60 cm (23½").
6. Do not alter the right edge of **panel 2**.
7. On the left edge of the panel, draw a straight line from the hem to the waist. This creates a wedge-shaped pattern. A small amount of hip curve is removed from the pattern, but this amount, and more, has been added to the pattern during the cut and spread process.
8. Blend a new waistline to smooth the angles created by the cut and spread process.

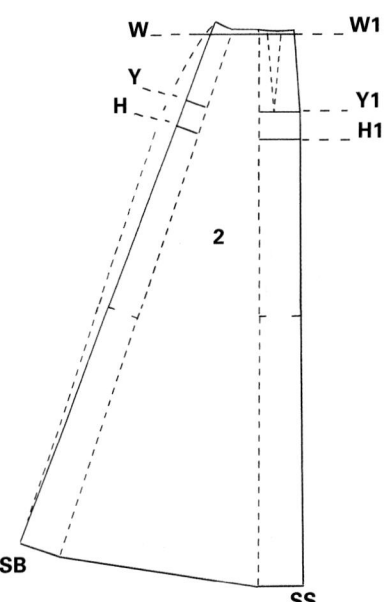

Figure 7.18 Skirt panel 2.

Panel 3

Figure 7.19

1. A horizontal gridline corresponds to the line **W–W1**.
2. Divide **panel 3** in half, vertically.
3. Cut up along the centre division.
4. Spread the waist 10 cm (4") along the gridline, to account for two pleats.
5. Spread the pattern hem until it equals 60 cm (23½").
6. On the right edge of **panel 3**, draw a straight line from the hem to the waist. A small amount of hip curve is removed from the pattern.
7. Blend a new waistline to smooth the angles created by the cut and spread process.

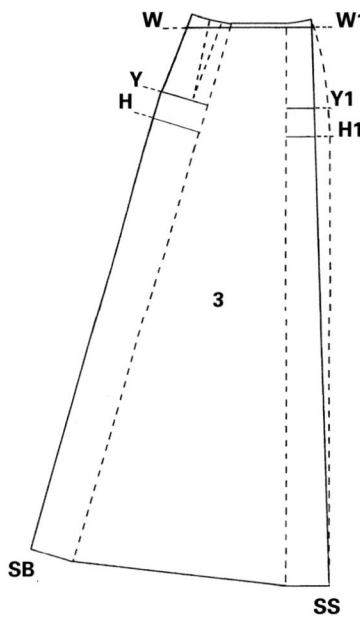

Figure 7.19 Skirt panel 3.

Panel 4

Figure 7.20

1. **Panel 4** is essentially a rectangle.
2. Move the **CB** to the left, for a rectangle 60 cm (23½") in width.
3. Extend the hem 12 cm (5") below the original hem length at the **CB**.
4. For a longer train, add more length.
5. In making up, **panel 4** is seamed along **CB**.

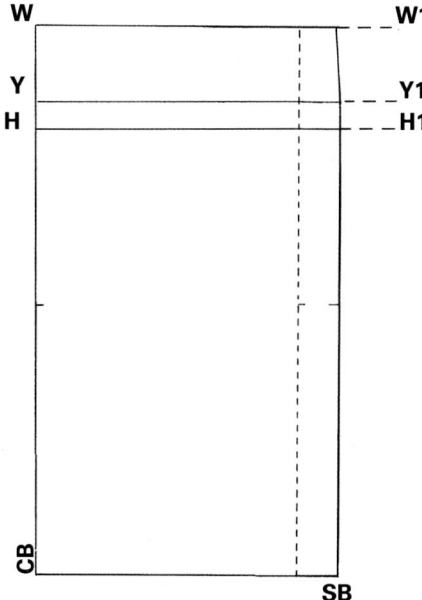

Figure 7.20 Skirt panel 4.

Completion

Figure 7.21, Figure 7.22 and Figure 7.23

1. Blend the waist with a smooth and continuous curve.
2. True up the hem. Draw the hem with a smooth and continuous curve.
3. Add straight-of-grain arrows. This may be the most important action in determining the shape and hang of the skirt:
   a. **Panel 1**, the **CF** is on a fold.
   b. **Panel 2**, the straight-of-grain is parallel to the front edge.
   c. **Panel 3**, the straight-of-grain is parallel to the front edge.
   d. **Panel 4**, the straight-of-grain is parallel to the **CB**.

The primary gown has a restrained bustle with bow that anticipates the larger bustle of the 1870s.

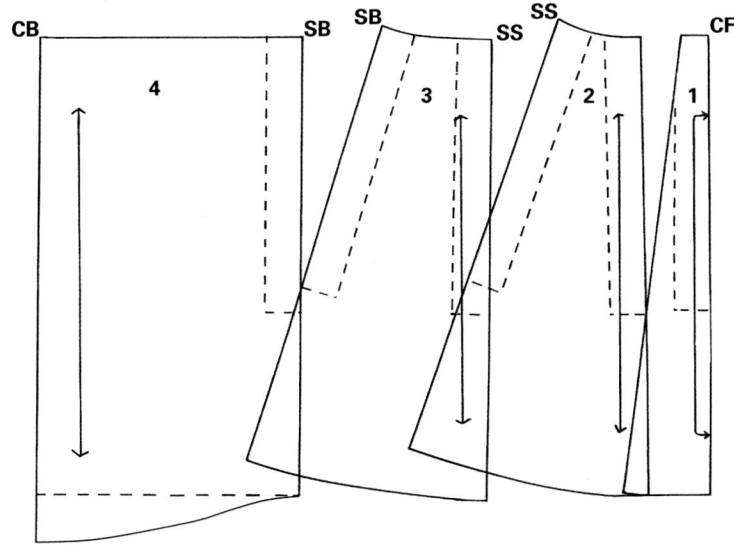

Figure 7.21 1860s skirt in panels.

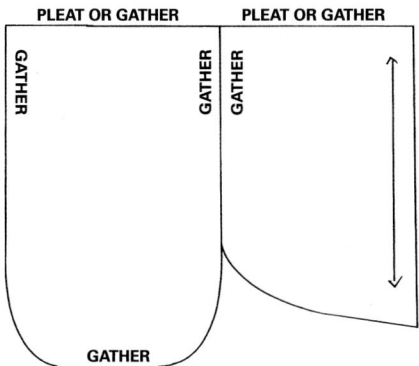

Figure 7.22 Petal-shaped bustle.

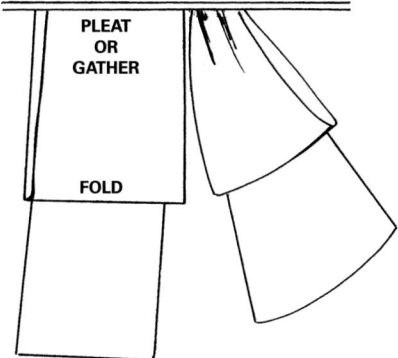

Figure 7.23 Bow.

Finessing the Pattern

Figure 7.24

The primary two-piece dress in Figures 7.1 and 7.2 has nine panels rather than the seven in the previous instructions. See Figure 7.24 for a nine-panel skirt pattern. The divisions produce an eight-panel skirt; a front, a back and six side panels. When width is added to panel 4, it becomes two panels rather than one.

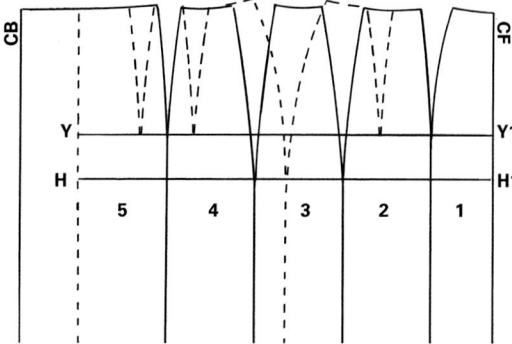

Figure 7.24 Nine-panel skirt divisions.

1. Start **panel 1** at the waist starting 11 cm–12 cm (4½") from the **CF**.
2. Draw a gentle curve from the waist to the line **Y–Y1** and then continue in a straight line to the hem.
3. Divide the area between **panel 1** and the **CB** into four equal panels.
4. Redistribute the waist suppression with deeper darts between **panels 2, 3** and **4**.
5. Add width to the back panel as needed.
6. Widen each panel hem to achieve the correct hem circumference.
7. Redraw the waist and hem to complete the pattern.

Figure 7.25 This fashion plate beautifully shows the silhouette of an elliptical hoop skirt.

Detailed Instructions for an Elliptical Hoop Skirt[2]

Rather than providing a pattern for the dresses illustrated in Figure 7.21, the alternative draft in this chapter is for a structure that provided the foundation for their shape; an elliptical-shaped hoop skirt. This shape is complicated. The front is relatively flat, the sides are closer to the body and are less curved than the bell shape of the 1850s, and the back projects at an acute angle from the waist. This following pattern produces a small hoop skirt. For a larger one, increase the measurements, but follow the shaping advice.

Instead of using the cutting and spreading technique described earlier in the chapter, each panel and seam in this draft is tackled individually. The right side of each panel remains relatively straight, while the left side adds volume and is drawn with a curve. Each curve starts progressively closer and closer to the waist from the front to the back.

Panel 1

Figure 7.26
Since a panel skirt provides an opportunity to create shape around the body, the 1860s hoop skirt starts with the same six-panel skirt that was used for the primary skirt.

1. Repeat the Skirt Draft instructions for the six-panel skirt.
2. Shorten the length. A good hoop skirt hem is about 15 cm (6") above the floor.

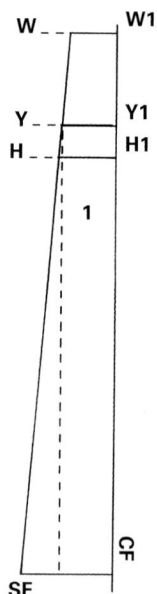

Figure 7.26 Hoop skirt panel 1.

Panel 2

Figure 7.27

1. On the right side of **panel 2**, trace the seam line from the waist to **Y–Y1**.
2. Draw a straight line from **Y–Y1** to a point about 6 cm (2½") to the right of the original hem.
3. On the left side of **panel 2**, draw a guideline from 4 cm (1⅝") below the waist to a point approximately 12.5 cm (5") to the left of the original hem.
4. Using the guideline, draw a smoothly curved line. Add about 4 cm (1⅝") of width through the thigh area, and gradually straighten the line from about the knee to the hem. This is the Side Seam (**SS**).

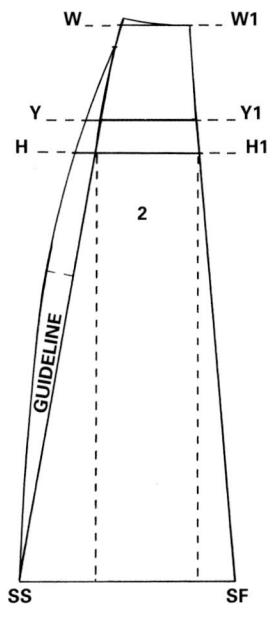

Figure 7.27 Hoop skirt panel 2.

Panel 3

Figure 7.28

1. On the right side of **panel 3**, draw a straight line from the **H–H1** to a point about 6 cm (2½") away from the hem base.
2. On the left side of **panel 3**, draw a guideline from 2 cm (¾") below the waist to about 16 cm (6⅜") from the hem base.
3. Draw a gently curving line from 2 cm (¾") below the waist to 5 cm (2") beyond the guideline through the thigh area, and gently straighten from the knee.

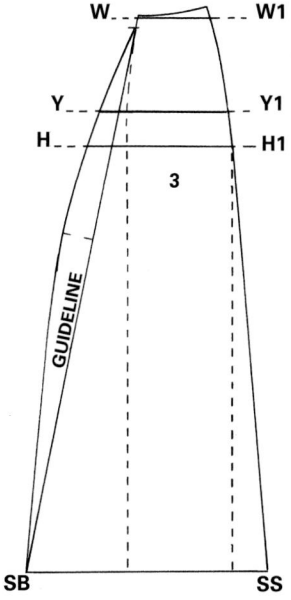

Figure 7.28 Hoop skirt panel 3.

Panel 4 (Back)

Figure 7.29

1. On the right side of **panel 4**, draw a straight line from **Y–Y1** to about 6 cm (2½") from the hem base.
2. On the left of **panel 4**, draw a guideline from the waist to 21 cm (8¼") from the hem base.
3. Draw a gently curving line from the waist to 6 cm (2½") beyond the guideline through the thigh area, and gently straighten from the knee. This is the Centre Back (**CB**) seam.
4. Cut along the seam lines, leaving excess at the waist and hem.

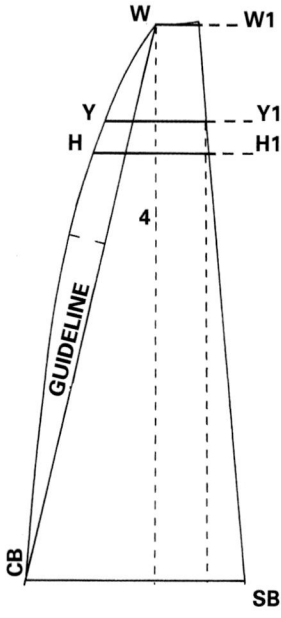

Figure 7.29 Hoop skirt panel 4.

Check Pattern

Figure 7.30

1. Lay pattern pieces so that they join from about the mid-thigh to the hem. At this stage, the hems and waists will not be true. Laying them thus will help you visualize how they will go together. The front has a small amount of shaping close to the waist. There is more shaping at the side and back.
2. If the seams appear too bulbous, reshape them now. If they appear too straight, redraw with a soft curve.
3. True up the seams from the waist to the hem.
4. Extend the **CB** 7 cm–13 cm (3"–5") below the hem and redraw the hem. This accounts for the extra length needed for the elliptical shape.

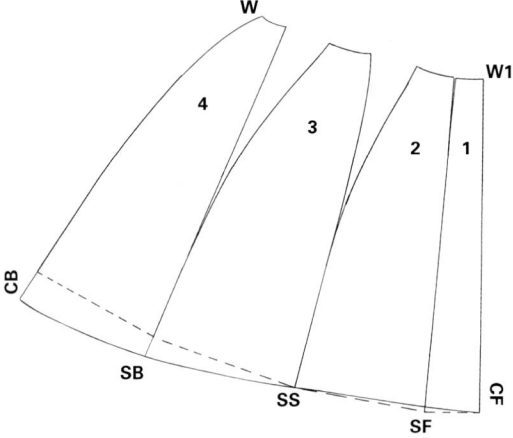

Figure 7.30 Hoop skirt pattern pieces laid out to show shapes.

Casings

Figure 7.31

Illustrations of period hoop skirts have up to twelve casings for hoop wires. As few as three wires will give an adequate shape for some applications. These instructions are for five hoops.

1. Place one casing along the hem.
2. Place the top casing at **H–H1**.
3. Place the others equally distanced apart.
4. Measure, but also eye, the curves. You may find this gives a smoother line. Make sure that each casing placement meets the **CB** at a right angle.
5. This hoop skirt will open on the left **SF** seam, so leave extra seam allowance for a placket.

Completion

Figure 7.31

1. Blend the waist with a smooth and continuous curve.
2. True up the hem. Draw the hem with a smooth and continuous curve.
3. Add straight-of-grain arrows, as illustrated in Figure 7.31.

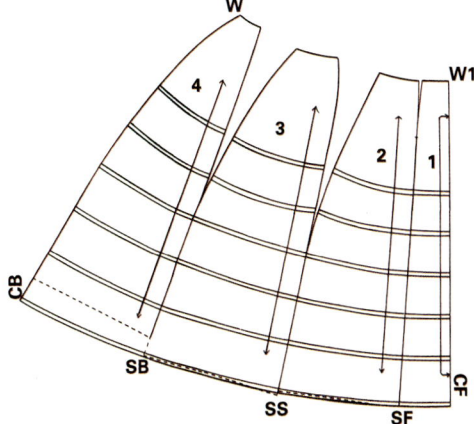

Figure 7.31 Hoop skirt with casings.

NOTES

1. Charles Dickens, *All the Year Round*, September 1859, quoted in S. Garfield (2001) *Mauve: How one Man Invented a Colour that Changed the World* (New York: W. W. Norton). See also Vettese-Foster, S. and Christie, R. M. (2013) 'The Significance of the Introduction of Synthetic Dyes in the Mid 19th Century on the Democratisation of Western Fashion', *Journal of the International Colour Association*, 11: 1–17.
2. I am grateful to Dr Lynn Sorge for introducing me to the idea of looking at each side of the seam independently. This adaptation enabled me to devise a dependable method of drafting an elliptical hoop skirt.

8

Development of Period Patterns, 1870–79

Period Dress in Historical Context

The woman whose daughter wore this three-piece wedding dress must have looked at it with amazement (Figures 8.1 and 8.2). Without the technological advances and dissemination of high fashion, which had been established in the years between her own marriage and her daughter's, it would have been beyond the realm of her imagination. The yards of silk making up this dress are adorned with gathered ruffles, giant bows, crocheted lace and hand-worked buttons. Together, all of the elements would have been draped over an extraordinarily shaped metal armature.

The sewing machine made the creation of this elaborate garment possible. While it did not eliminate the need for fine, hand-finishing stitches, the sewing machine gave the skilled technician a reprieve from the endless rows of straight stitching that were involved in bias binding and gathering ruffles. To those engaged in its manufacture, the sewing machine presented the potential for substantial wealth and success. The third quarter of the century witnessed the establishment of hundreds of factories throughout North America and worldwide.

The first machines scarcely resembled the ones we use today. In the United States, Elias Howe patented the first lock stitch machine in 1846. He sought to mimic the process of hand-stitching. With this machine, the fabric hung from sharp projections below the needle mechanism and inched forward with each stitch, in a manner not unlike the way fabric moves through the fingers as it is being hand-stitched. His key innovation was changing the needle

Figure 8.1 Side back view. This spectacular dress has many masculine features but is ultimately extremely feminine.

Figure 8.2 Front view detail of chestnut wedding dress.

to a curved one with the eye at the pointed end. It pierced the fabric and, on its return, threw out a thread loop. A second thread, carried by a reciprocating shuttle, moved through the loop, making an interlocking stitch.[1] Bostonian Isaac Singer countered with his Singer's Perpendicular Action Sewing Machine, patented in 1851. With this machine, the fabric rested on a table and the needle moved through it in an up and down motion, hence the perpendicular action. It had a presser foot that secured the fabric flat and in place while it was being stitched.[2] In 1854, Allen B. Wilson of Wheeler and Wilson added serrated metal teeth called 'feed dogs', which helped feed the fabric through the stitching process.[3] The Wheeler and Wilson Manufacturing Company sold more sewing machines in the United States than any other company during the 1850s and 1860s.[4] Newton Wilson of London introduced a machine in 1868 that could make buttonholes and satin stitch embroidery.[5] In the 1870s, Richard Wanzer, who owned a factory in Ontario, Canada, developed a machine with a reversible feed. This allowed the operator to sew both forwards and backwards without stopping.[6]

Manufacturers began adding useful features to their machines, making them more appealing to the sewer. The first thread cutter was patented in the United States in 1857. The first bobbin winder was patented in 1862. By 1865, companies had developed various attachments for their machines, including hemmers, binders, tuck makers, frillers and gatherers, as well as specialized feet for felling, braiding and binding.[7] With the skilful handling of these extras, any operator could elevate simple straight stitch to create beautiful decorative detailing and extravagant finishes. These steady improvements in the mechanization and usability of the machines prompted sales to soar. Between 1873 and 1876, a total of 2,303,941 sewing machines were sold in the United States alone.[8]

The increased speed of clothing production made possible by the sewing machine affected the individual sewer, small dressmaking establishments and large factories alike. It also sparked the rapid and continual changing of styles that has become a crucial defining element of modern fashion.[9]

DESCRIPTION

This jacket may have been drafted by a tailor rather than a dressmaker (see Figure 8.2). It has the appearance of a jacket worn over a light top, and the seaming is similar to a man's tailored jacket. The boned bodice has a sculpted waist and full peplum. Three large crochet buttons accentuate the asymmetric front closure. The back also has an asymmetric look, with a single swag draped from the left shoulder to a buttoned centre back waist. An elaborate triple shawl collar frames the face. Broad two-piece sleeves with decorative cuffs are set smoothly into a dropped shoulder. A brown satin inner chemisette with a small stand collar fills the corsage area.

The skirt is draped and gathered on to an underskirt with seven gored panels. The bustle is created by an extended back panel that is gathered into the side back seam. Below the bustle, three bias flounces sweep towards the hem and a small train. They are edged with the same rust crochet lace that backs the collar and bodice hem. The front panel is horizontally divided by two rows of gathered ruffles, a bias puff and a flounce.

Primary Step-by-Step Drafting Instructions

To start this draft, you will need a completed front and back Modern Basic Block pattern without the optional back shoulder dart. Because this jacket fits more loosely than other bodices in this book, removing ease from the pattern is optional. If you chose to remove ease, do so in the following manner.

Remove Excess Ease

Figure 8.3

1. Draw a new Centre Back by removing 0.5 cm–1.5 cm (³⁄₁₆"–⅝") at **W**.
2. Remove 1.5 cm (⅝") from each Side Seam from **U** to nothing at **W–W1**.

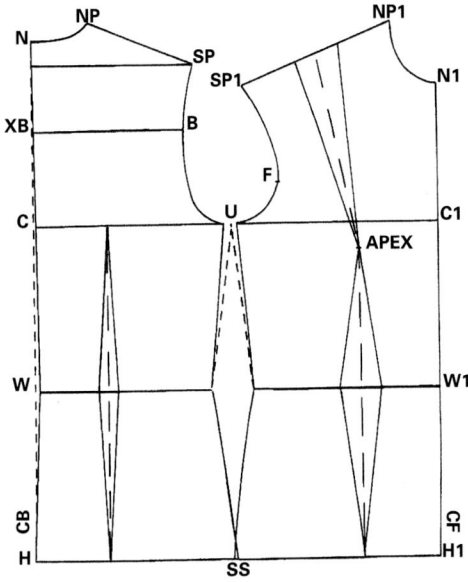

Figure 8.3 Remove excess ease.

BODICE BACK

The primary bodice back has six panels separated by a Centre Back (**CB**) seam, two Side Back (**SB**) seams, and two Side Side Back (**SSB**) seams. The side side back panel will join the side front panel to form an underarm panel.

Guideline 1

Figure 8.4

1. Draw a line from **B** to the point of the dart and continue to a point 3 cm–6 cm (1⅛"–2½") from **W**.
2. Complete the guideline with a perpendicular line from the waist to the hem.
3. This is the guideline for the **SB** seam.

Guideline 2

Figure 8.4

1. Draw a straight line from **X** to the right side of the dart at the waist.
2. Complete the guideline with a perpendicular line from the waist ending at the hem.
3. Extend the line from **X** to the armhole.
4. This is the guideline for the **SSB** seam.

Side Back (SB) Seam

Figure 8.5

1. Using guideline 1, draw a long, smoothly curved line from **B** to the waist, and continue in a straight line to the hem. This is one branch of the **SB** seam.
2. Cut along this line from the hem to the point of the dart.
3. Close the dart:
    a. Cut along one side of the dart.
    b. Close the dart above the waist. The second branch of the **SB** seam will automatically appear when the dart is closed.
    c. The dart will overlap below the waist.

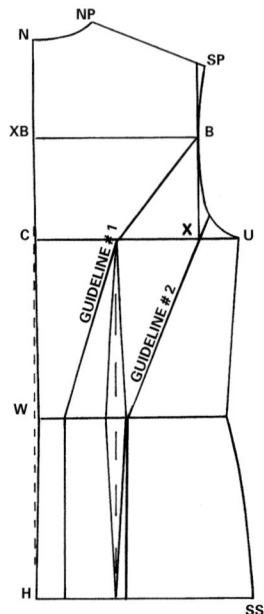

Figure 8.4 Back seam guidelines 1 and 2.

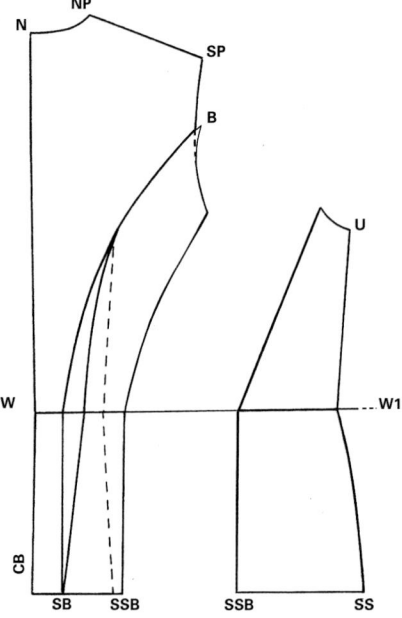

Figure 8.5 SB seam, SSB seam.

4. Draw the second branch of the **SB** seam from **B** to the waist, smoothing out any angles.
5. Continue drawing the **SB** seam from the waist to the hem, joining both branches at the hem. This creates a flare and accounts for the lower dart overlap (see Figure 8.5).

Side Side Back (SSB) Seam

Figure 8.5
1. Using guideline 2, draw a long, smoothly curved line from the armhole to the waist, and continue in a straight line to the hem. This is one branch of the **SSB** seam.
2. Cut along this branch of the **SSB**.
3. Set aside the side side back panel. This will become part of the underarm panel.

Bodice Front

Figure 8.6, Figure 8.7 and Figure 8.8
1. Draw a vertical line from **F** to the line **U–C1**.
2. Find the midpoint of this line and extend it to the armhole. This is **F1**. **F1** is the beginning of the Side Front (**SF**) seam as well as the front balance point for the two-piece sleeve.
3. Move the waist dart towards the **SS**.
    a. Reposition the area above the waist with the point meeting **F1**, as illustrated in Figure 8.7.
    b. Shift the waist area towards the **SS** by the full dart width.
    c. Continue the area below the waist with a centre line that is perpendicular to the waist.
    d. The dart is now labelled as the **SF** seam.

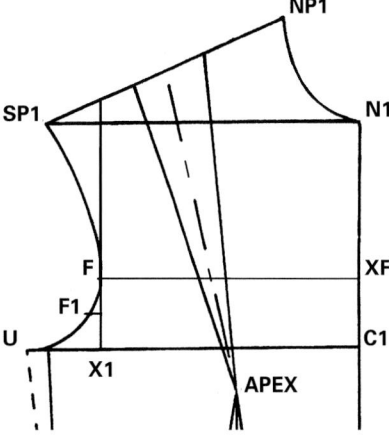

Figure 8.6 Find F1. This is the front balance point for the Historical Two-piece Sleeve.

4. Remove the shoulder dart and redraw the shoulder.
   a. Mark a point that is horizontally level with **NP1**, and about 1.5 cm (⅝") to the left of **NP1** (see Figure 8.7).
   b. Apply the shoulder measurement from this point to the line **SP1–N1**.
   c. By adjusting the shoulder in this manner, both **NP1** and **SP1** remain at the same horizontal level. Only the shoulder dart width is removed.
5. Relabel **NP1** and **SP1** in their new positions.
6. Blend the new armhole from **SP1**, through **F** and **F1** to **U**.
7. Draw the new front edge to mimic the front edge of the primary jacket front in Figure 8.1.
8. Shape the **SF** seam to take out the any sharp angles.
9. True up each branch of the **SF** seam from the waist to **F1**.
10. True up each branch from the waist to the hem.
11. Separate along the **SF** seam to create a front and side front pattern.

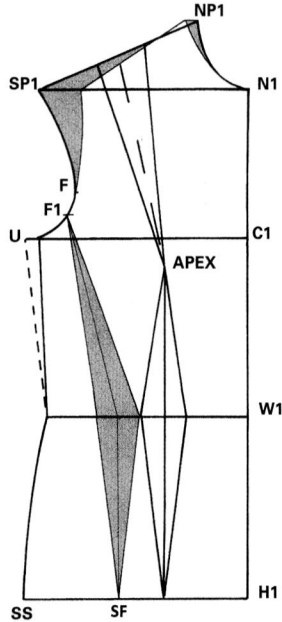

Figure 8.7 Transfer the shoulder and waist darts.

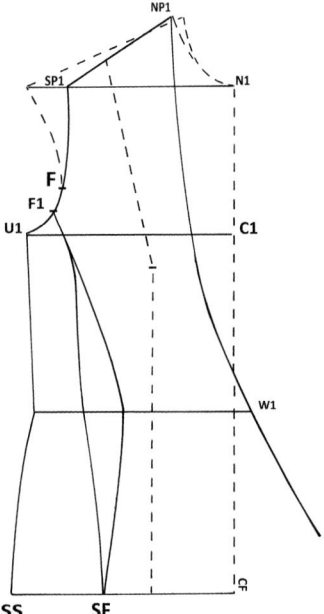

Figure 8.8 Shape the SF seam and separate the front and side front patterns.

19th-Century Patterns for the Modern Body

Side Panel with Peplum

Figure 8.9 and Figure 8.10

The underarm panel is formed by joining the **SSB** and the **SF** panels.

1. Separate the **SSB** and the **SF** panels along the waist (**W–W1**).
2. Being careful to keep the waists along a horizontal grid, join the two upper panels at **U**.
3. Measure the distance between the **SS** seams on the line **W–W1**.
4. Transfer this measurement from the **SS** to the right of **SSB**. This is one branch of the **SSB**.
5. Redraw the waist in a convex curve (see Figure 8.10).
6. Join the lower section of the two panels at the waist. They will naturally splay out with the hip curves.
7. Redraw the peplum waist in an opposing curve. Having opposing curves at the waist will create a sharper fit.

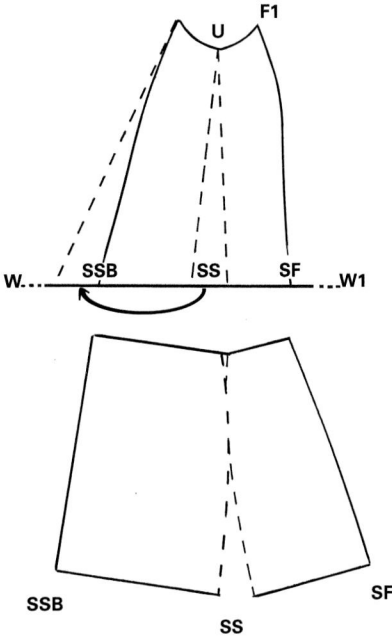

Figure 8.9 Side panel and side peplum.

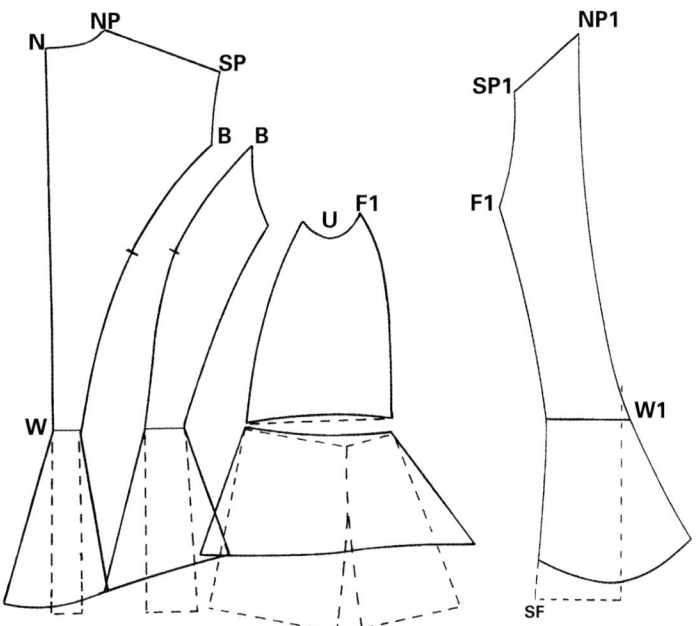

Figure 8.10 Adding flare and hem.

Chapter 8 Development of Period Patterns, 1870–79

Completion

Figure 8.10

1. Add flare to each panel below the waist. The amount of flare will depend on the fullness of the skirt and the desired effect.
2. In this case, approximately 1.5 cm (⅝") is added to the area over the side hip, and approximately 2.5 cm (1") flare over the seat area.
3. Draw the hem and true up the seams.

Shoulder and Neckline

Figure 8.11
The shoulder line on this dress sits a little to the back of a modern shoulder.

1. Match **NP** to **NP1**, and **SP** to **SP1**. Secure the front and back together along the shoulder line with tape. Call the points **NP** and **SP**.
2. Mark a point 1.5 cm (⅝") to the back of **NP**.
3. Mark a point approximately 3 cm (1⅛") to the back of **SP**.
4. Connect the points. This is the new shoulder seam.
5. Redraw the armhole from **B** to **F1** through a point 1.5 cm–2.5 cm (⅝"–1") beyond **SP**.

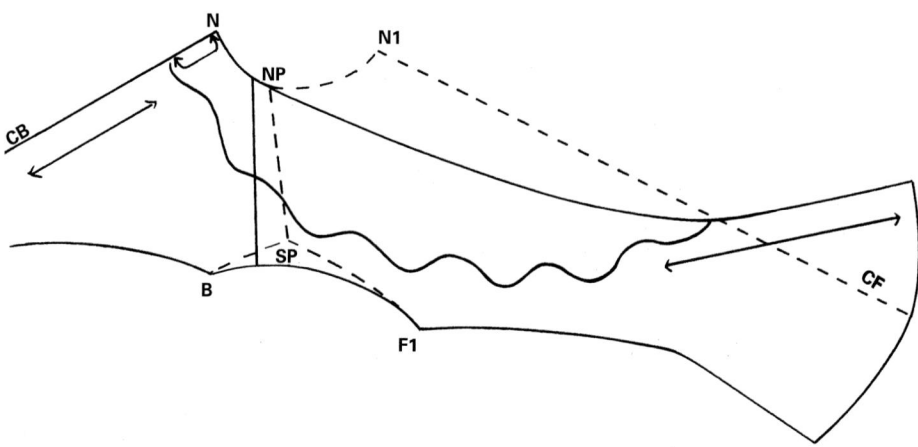

Figure 8.11 Shoulder and neckline with flat collar.

Collars

Figure 8.12 and Figure 8.13

There are three separate collars on the primary jacket; a scallop edged flat collar, a standing collar and a inner ruffle.

The **flat collar** pattern is traced from the joined front and back patterns along the neck edge.

1. The outer edge is free-hand scallops starting at approximately 5 cm (2") below **N** on the **CB**.
2. Add 0.5 cm (³⁄₁₆") at the neck edge and the **CB**. This will allow the collar to sit more comfortably onto the jacket. This minor change has not been included in the sketch.

The **stand collar** is developed from the flat collar.

1. Mark three lines approximately where the shoulder rounds (see Figure 8.12).
2. Cut along the lines.
3. Separate each about 0.5 cm (³⁄₁₆") along the neck edge and 2.5 cm (1") along the outer edge. During construction, the extra length will be eased into the neck.
4. Add 1 cm (³⁄₈") at the **CB**.
5. Blend the angles of the inner edge for a smooth neck.
6. Redraw the outer edge so that the collar is wider where it frames the face.

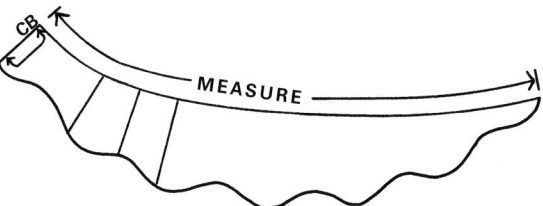

Figure 8.12 Flat collar.

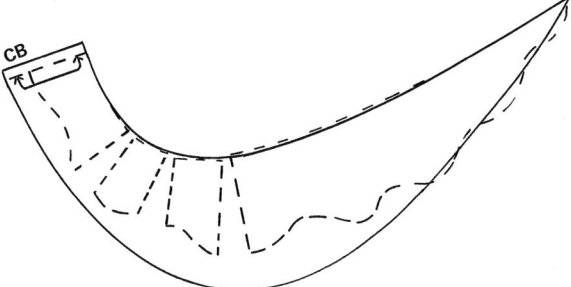

Figure 8.13 Stand collar.

The third collar is a **soft ruffle**. It is not drawn because it is essentially a rectangle.

1. Measure the neck edge.
2. The ruffle is two to three times the neck edge measurement, depending on the fabric used.
3. Cut this on the bias for more drama.

Sleeve

Figure 8.14

For this sleeve, use the Historical Two-piece Sleeve draft found in Chapter 1. Note that the arm of the 1870 sleeve is shorter and wider than in the historical draft.

1. Shorten the length about 6 cm (2½").
2. Redraw the front seam starting at **F**, straighten through the inner elbow and add 1 cm (⅜") at the hem.
3. Redraw the back seam. Start at **B** and add 1 cm (⅜") along the length of the seam.

Cuff

Figure 8.14

The cuff pattern is copied from the bottom 10 cm (4"). Add 0.5 cm (³⁄₁₆") at the front edge and place on a fold. Add a slight flare to the back.

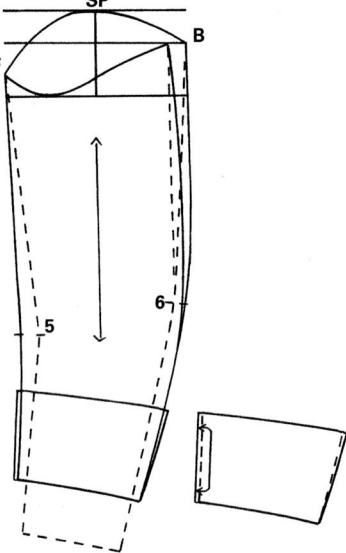

Figure 8.14 Period sleeve and cuff.

SKIRT

At first glance, it is almost impossible to interpret the primary skirt and translate it into a draft. Yards and yards of fabric, arranged in flounces, ruffles and an impressive bustle, obliterate almost all of the structural seaming. Only on further investigation of the extant garment does the structure become clearer. In fact, it is a seven-panel skirt. The panel skirt was popularly used in the second half of the nineteenth century. A number of seams placed strategically around the body provide numerous opportunities to increase or decrease volume wherever the designer deems it necessary.

To accommodate the 1870s aesthetic, a broad front base is important for the application of ruffles and flounces. The back base also needs to be wide enough to accommodate the bustle and still more rows of ruffles.

Foundation Skirt

Figure 8.15

1. Start with the Straight Skirt Block found in Chapter 1.
2. Divide **H–H1** into six equal portions; three on the back pattern and three on the front pattern.
3. On the back, use these divisions to form two panels. The area from **CB** to the ⅔ mark is one panel. The area from this division to the **SS** is the second panel. Draw a line parallel to the **CB** to distinguish the two back panels.
4. On the front, repeat the process. Use the divisions to form two panels. The area from **CF** to the ⅔ mark is one panel. The area from this division to the **SS** is the second panel. Draw a line parallel to the **CF** to distinguish the two front panels.
5. Transfer one back waist dart to the back division. The second back waist dart will be gathered, or pleated, into the waistband during the construction stage.
6. Transfer the front waist dart to the front division.
7. Label the panels 1–4 from front to back.
8. Extend the draft to full length; in this case, 100 cm (40").
9. Separate the panels.

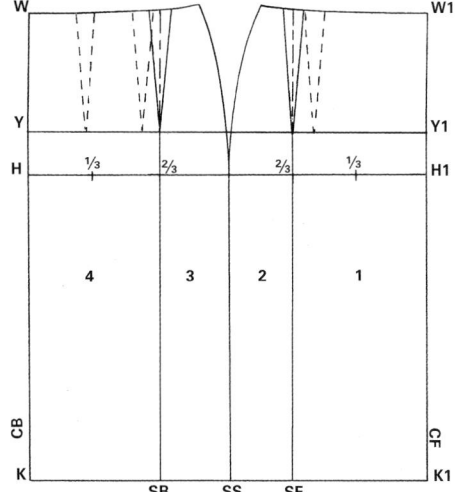

Figure 8.15 Six-panel skirt.

EXPANDING THE HEM

In Chapter 7, we used the cut and spread method of adding volume to the hem. In this chapter, we will add to the hem without cutting and spreading the pattern. On close inspection of the actual garment, the total hem circumference was found to be 336 cm (134"). Therefore, the pattern hem measurement is 168 cm (67"). The following instructions offer a reasonable distribution of this measurement.

However, we rarely have the actual measurements of a historical garment. When that is the case, the pattern maker must determine an appropriate hem width and gauge the angle of each pattern piece by eye, using Figures 8.16 and 8.17.

Panel 1

Figure 8.16

1. Place the **CF** on a vertical grid.
2. Add 7.5 cm (3") to the left of the panel on the line **W–W1**, for a small pleat.
3. Mark the hem width 35 cm (14") from the **CF**.
4. Draw a straight line from the hem to the new waist.

Panel 2

Figure 8.16

1. The front edge of **panel 2** is a straight line from the hem to the line **W–W1**.
2. Add 15 cm (6") to the measurement of the original waist for two small pleats.
3. The hem of **panel 2** is 38 cm (15") from the **SF**.
4. Mark this measurement at the hem.
5. Draw a straight line from the new hem to the new waist.

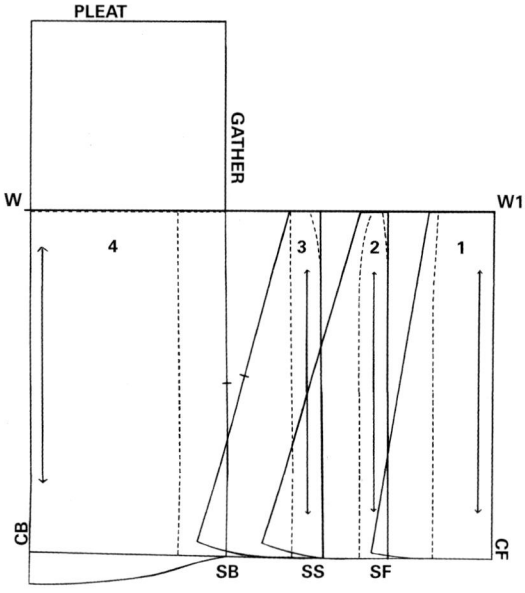

Figure 8.16 Altered skirt pattern.

Panel 3

Figure 8.16

1. The front edge of **panel 3** is a straight line from the hem to **W–W1**.
2. On the waist, determine how much pleating is needed. For two pleats, add 15 cm–20 cm (6"–8") to the measurement of the original waist width.
3. Mark the hem as 38 cm (15") from the **SS**.
4. Draw a straight line from the new hem to the waist.

Panel 4

Figure 8.16

Panel 4 is a large rectangle. The fabric from the top of this panel is incorporated into the bustle, so it is much higher than the other panels. The actual pattern height may depend on the type of fabric used.

1. The width of **panel 4** is 57 cm (23").
2. Extend the rectangle above **W–W1**. In this case, the rectangle height is about one and a half times times the original full length measurement.
3. Create a small train by lowering the hem 10 cm (4") at the **CB**.

Completion

Figure 8.17

1. True up the waist.
2. True up the hem.
3. Adding indications for pleats is optional, as it may be preferable to pleat during construction.
4. Add fabric grain indicators:
    a. **Panel 1**, the **CF** is on a fold.
    b. **Panel 2**, the straight-of-grain is parallel to the front edge.
    c. **Panel 3**, the straight-of-grain is parallel to the front edge.
    d. **Panel 4**, the straight-of-grain is parallel to the **CB**.

MAKING UP

Panels 1–4 are constructed from chestnut-coloured silk taffeta. Panel 4 is gathered along the **SB** seam from the notch to the top of the pattern and stitched to panel 3. Panel 3 has a decorative, triangular-shaped portion, which is included in the **SS**, and tacked into place on the scalloped edge. The gathered flounces are applied to this skirt base. The top is pleated into the waistband with deep pleats in the bustle area and smaller pleats at the seams. The waistband is a simple double layer of light cotton.

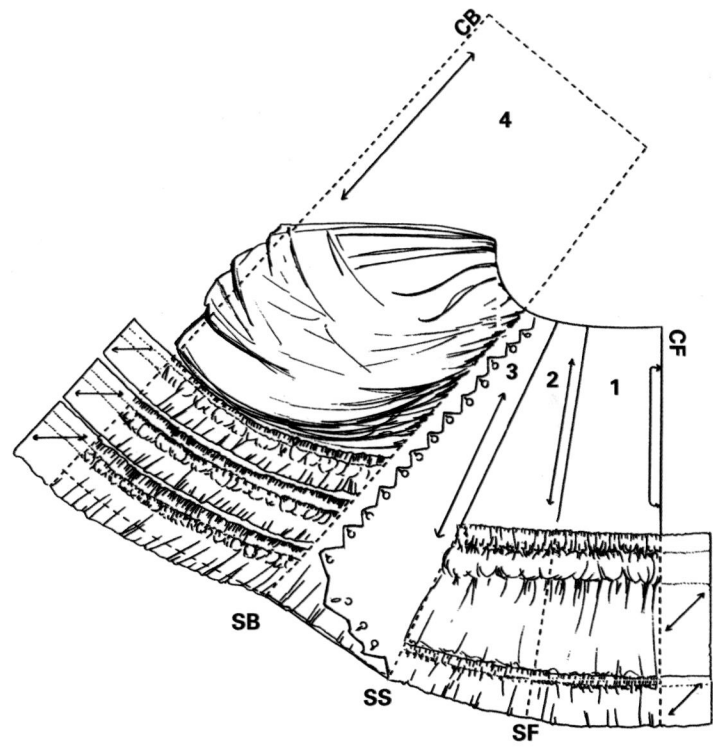

Figure 8.17 Flat rendering of the three-dimensional skirt.

Figure 8.18 Alternative dresses with two different back bustles.

Alternative Day Dress Draft Adaptations

The fashion plate in Figure 8.18 shows the slimmer line that became popular in the latter part of the 1870s. The primary bodice pattern can be used for the alternative dress bodices, with slightly different hems and slimmer sleeves. Note that the shoulders are much closer to the natural line of articulation. The skirt is cut narrower than in the early part of the decade. The following draft can be used as a foundation skirt for designs from 1875 through the 1880s.

Start by following the panel skirt instructions for the primary skirt.

IVORY DRESS

This dress has a graphic colour story with a solid black back panel. A large red bow is added to the lowest draped pick-up. Ivory, lace-edged draperies are set in the **SB** seam. The cut and spread technique that was used in Chapter 7 can be used to add volume. However, the amount needed for the correct period silhouette is relatively small. Therefore, apply volume to the hem in the following manner.

Expanding the Hem

Figure 8.19

1. On a clean piece of paper, draw a grid with a vertical line for the **CF**, and horizontal lines for **W–W1**, **Y–Y1**, **H–H1** and the full length.

Panel 1

1. Place the **CF** on the vertical grid line.
2. Mark a point 8 cm (3¼") to the left of the hem.
3. From this point, draw a straight line to **Y–Y1** and continue to the waist.

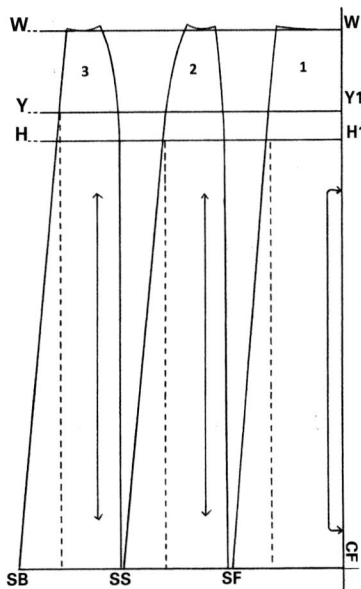

Figure 8.19 Expanded hem of panels 1–3.

Chapter 8 Development of Period Patterns, 1870–79

Panel 2

1. Mark a point 8 cm (3¼") to the left of the hem.
2. From this point, draw a straight line to the **H–H1** and, following the curve of the original, continue to the waist.

Panel 3

1. Mark a point 8 cm (3¼") to the left of the hem.
2. From this point, draw a straight line to the **H–H1** and, following the original curve, continue to the waist.

Panel 4

Figure 8.20

Panel 4 is a rectangle, and is the bustle of the skirt. Estimate the width and height needed with a measuring tape. Its width and height may depend on the fabric used.

1. Draw a line 10 cm (4") away from and parallel to the **CB**.
2. Extend the line above **W–W1** approximately 20 cm (8"). This accounts for about 5 cm (2") for each of the four draped pick-ups.
3. Create a train by adding about 25 cm–30 cm (10"–12") below the original hem.

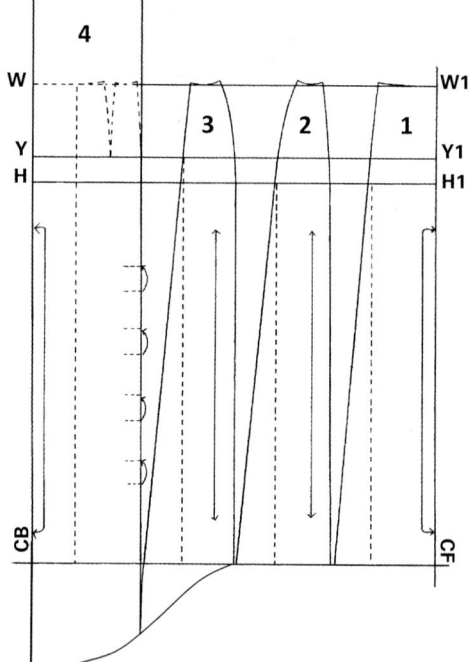

Figure 8.20 Back panel pattern for the ivory-coloured dress.

Completion

1. True up the waist.
2. True up the hem.
3. Add straight-of-grain indications:
    a. **Panel 1**, the **CF** is on a fold.
    b. **Panel 2**, the straight-of-grain is parallel to the front edge.
    c. **Panel 3**, the straight-of-grain is parallel to the front edge.
    d. **Panel 4**, the straight-of-grain is parallel to the **CB** or on the fold.

Blue Dress

Figure 8.21

Panel 4 is not draped with a bustle effect. Rather, back skirt emphasis is achieved with vertical pleating and bows.

1. Complete panels 1, 2 and 3, as outlined in the ivory dress instructions.
2. Panel 4 is made wider, according to the width of three box pleats.
3. The pleat closest to the body is the largest. Add 25 cm (10") beyond the **CB** for two folds of 12.5 cm (5").
4. For the middle pleat, add 20 cm (8") for two folds of 10 cm (4").
5. For the final pleat, add an additional 7.5 cm (3").
6. Mark a triple box pleat, or drape the pleats during the skirt's construction.
7. Add about 30 cm (12") of length for a train.
8. Add 5 cm (2") above **W–W1** at the new **CB** to nothing at the original **CB**.
9. The front draping may be an independent swag, or an apron.
10. For an apron, see the instructions in Chapter 9.

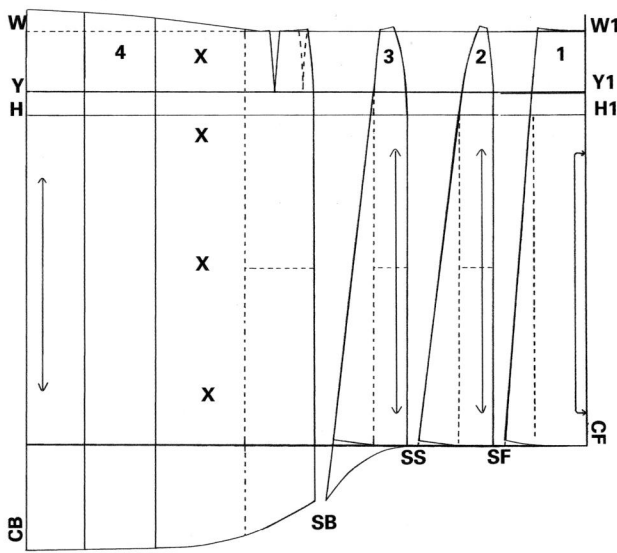

Figure 8.21 Skirt pattern for the blue dress.

Completion

1. True up the waist.
2. True up the hem.
3. Add fabric grain indications:
    a. **Panel 1**, the **CF** is on a fold.
    b. **Panel 2**, the straight-of-grain is parallel to the front edge.
    c. **Panel 3**, the straight-of-grain is parallel to the front edge.

NOTES

1. Carol Head (1983) *Old Sewing Machines* (Princes Risborough: Shire Publications), 6.
2. Ibid., 7.
3. Ibid., 11.
4. Ibid.
5. Janet Arnold (1972) *Patterns of Fashion 2: Englishwomen's Dresses and Their Construction c.1860–1940* (London: Macmillan/Drama Books), 4.
6. Martha Brent (1980) 'A Stitch Machine in Time: Sewing Machine Industry of Ontario, 1860–1897', *Material Culture Review*, 10: 14.
7. Head, *Old Sewing Machines*, 15, 16.
8. C. M. Depew (ed.) (1895) *One Hundred Years of American Commerce* (New York: Haynes & Co.), 534.
9. 'Fashion is dress in which the key feature is rapid and continual changing of styles. Fashion, in a sense, *is* change.' Elizabeth Wilson (1985) *Adorned in Dreams: Fashion and Modernity* (Oakland: University of California Press), 3.

9

Development of Period Patterns, 1880–89

Period Dress in Historical Context

The 1880s progressed with unprecedented forward momentum in industry and technology, which in turn steered the world of fashion. Clothing manufacturing expanded as specifically designed equipment revolutionized the industry in Europe and North America. Even the relatively small city of Halifax, Nova Scotia, Canada felt the increase in industrialization. Tailors and clothiers were second only to the boots and shoes industry as the largest employers in the port city. Almost 300 women and 50 men found work with a single local tailoring company, Clayton & Sons Tailors & Clothiers. The newly built brick and glass building boasted separate lavatories for men and women. It was equipped with steam-powered sewing machines. Women earned an average of $3.00 per week, while their male counterparts earned $10.00 per week.[1]

The mobilization of females in the workforce was a phenomenon of the last quarter of the nineteenth century. Most of these women were young, between the ages of seventeen and twenty-five. Possibly spurred on to add to the family coffers, they earned personal income and a new sense of independence unimaginable to their mothers. For the first time, women had the prospect of controlling their own future. They became part of the growing working class, with disposable income to spend on clothing.

Figure 9.1 Dress front. This two-piece dress is a wonderful example of the period silhouette. It has the most extreme silhouette of the century, with high rounded bust and tiny waist.

Figure 9.2 Sleeve detail

In 1889, the working class spent an average of 10 per cent of their income on clothing;[2] almost twice the amount often allotted in today's family budgets. Fashion's response was to provide more options for specific functions. These included ball gowns, reception dresses, afternoon dresses, dinner dresses and even carriage dresses. The period's silhouette was the most sculpted and unnatural of the century. The bust was high and rounded. Corsets were pulled much tighter than in earlier decades for an even tinier waist. Bodice backs emphasized a neat curvature, from which emerged draperies that shifted from low pick-ups to the gravity-defying bustle.

> The style of drapery varies so much that it is impossible to give anything like rules for its production. Sometimes it has been looped up at the right side and sometimes at the left. It is quite a matter of taste. … The variety is infinite. … Indeed, it is not too much to say that a really skilful operator can arrange as many good effects with his drapery as a musical composer can arrange from the musical scale.'[3]

Professional dressmakers needed immense skill to fit the complex patterns:

> Dressmaking is not what it was ten years ago, for within the last few years the tendency of the times has called forth the most artistic skill. The close-skin-fitting busts and sleeves of to-day require scientific cutting and fitting. A fault at once shows itself, and disfigures the wearer; consequently, it is more essential to ladies to have perfect-fitting garments now than it has been at any previous time.[4]

Figure 9.3 Advertisement in McDowell's Garment Drafting Machine instruction booklet.[5]

Entrepreneurs met the challenge to provide efficient drafting solutions. By the 1880s, the sewing machine was standard equipment. Paper patterns had been in circulation since the early 1870s. During the 1880s, pattern-cutting systems and mechanical devices took on a new prominence. The simplest form of these tools was based on the tailor's square. A tailor's square has incremental measurements on one side and fractional divisions of the most commonly used measurements on the other side. The square greatly reduced the need for calculating measurement by mathematical equations. Some companies added curves to the standard rule, which greatly aided pattern makers in the shaping of armholes and curved seams. In the United States, the Library of Congress registered 106 professional instructional booklets with mathematically derived cutting systems from 1880 to 1889, a jump from only 22 between 1870 and 1879.[6]

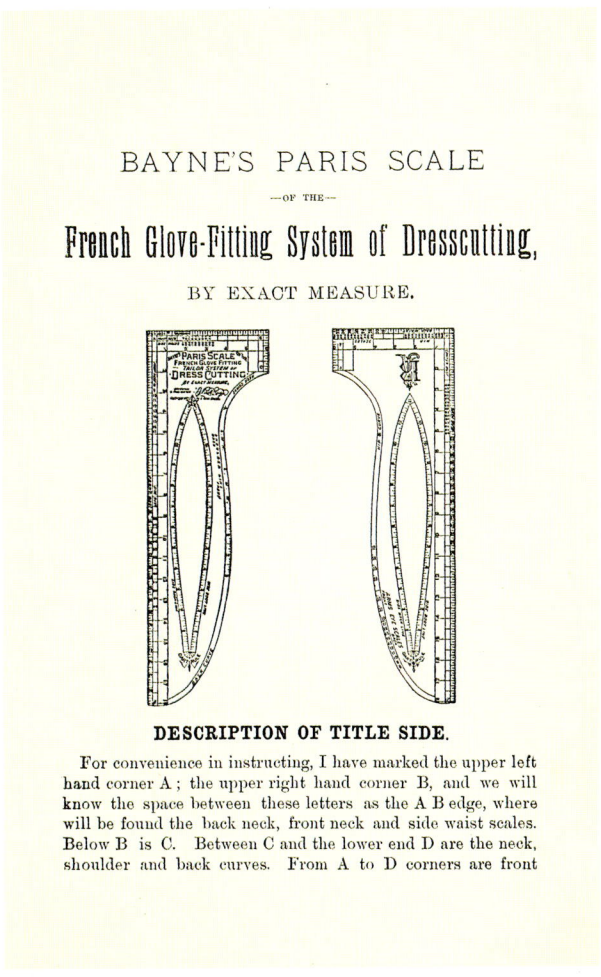

Figure 9.4 Example of cutting systems using a curved tailor's square.[7]

Some developers devised more complex tools for making patterns that might eliminate the need for any calculations. One of the most popular was designed by Albert McDowell of New York City. It had brass frameworks for three or four bodice panels, as well as a sleeve. They resembled a child's Meccano set, with adjustable sliders. This allowed them to reduce or expand to fit all measurements and body shapes. McDowell produced five different forms from 1879 to 1891, each reflecting the changes in fashion.[8] At one point, McDowell stopped altering his machine because fashion changed more quickly than his developments. He established a branch of schools, McDowell School of Fashion Design, which survived well into the twentieth century.

DESCRIPTION

The primary garment for this chapter is a beautiful mulberry coloured silk that exemplifies the complexity of cut and draperies of the period (see Figures 9.1 and 9.2). The front extends below the natural waist in a deep point, and angles up towards the waist at the side. Shaping is achieved with two darts on each side that almost reach the bust and armholes. The centre front curves over the bust, with a long line of pressed metal buttons. The back is cut in four panels, the centre of which ends with an elegant pleated swallow tail. The slim two-piece fitted sleeves, smoothly set into high armholes, contribute to the bodice's narrow shoulder line. The sleeve hem is edged with gathered bobbin lace.

Like many skirts of the period, its layering of textured applications make it look more complex than it actually is. It has three separate items. The underskirt is a relatively straight cotton skirt with a darted waist that is edged with a row of small pleats. These are just visible under the main skirt while stationary, but would have provided a lovely movement when in motion. The main skirt is pleated with wide box pleats. The overskirt has a draped front apron and moderately full back bustle that are gathered together and mounted on a waistband.

Primary Step-by-Step Drafting Instructions

Before beginning the 1880s block, it is a good idea to remeasure the client, especially if the garment is going to be worn over a corset. Take the measurements with the corset laced as tightly as it is expected to be worn. To start this draft, you will need a completed front and back Modern Basic Block pattern with the optional back shoulder dart found in Chapter 1. It begins with minor revisions to the block.

Adjust Side Seam, Remove Excess Ease

Figure 9.5

1. Redraw the **SS** to reduce the amount of ease at the underarm and redistribute the shaping at the waist:
   a. Mark a point 1 cm–1.5 cm (⅜"–⅝") on either side of **U**.
   b. On W–W1, mark a point 1 cm (⅜") to the right of the back **SS** and to the left of the front **SS**.
   c. Connect the points for new front and back **SS**.
   d. Continue to the hem.
2. Draw a new curved **CF** by shaping it 0.5 cm (³⁄₁₆") to the left of **N1** and **W1**. This shaping is often exaggerated in an 1880s bodice by rounding the bust area beyond the draft parameters.
3. Draw a new **CB** starting from nothing at **XB** and to the right of **W** 0.5 cm–1.5 cm (³⁄₁₆"–⅝").
4. Draw a new hem 10 cm (4") below **W–W1**. Cut off and discard the lower portion.
5. Adjust the back waist dart to end at the new hem. Do not adjust the front dart to the new hem.
6. To find **F1**, follow the directions in Chapter 8, Bodice Front, points 1 and 2 (page 143).

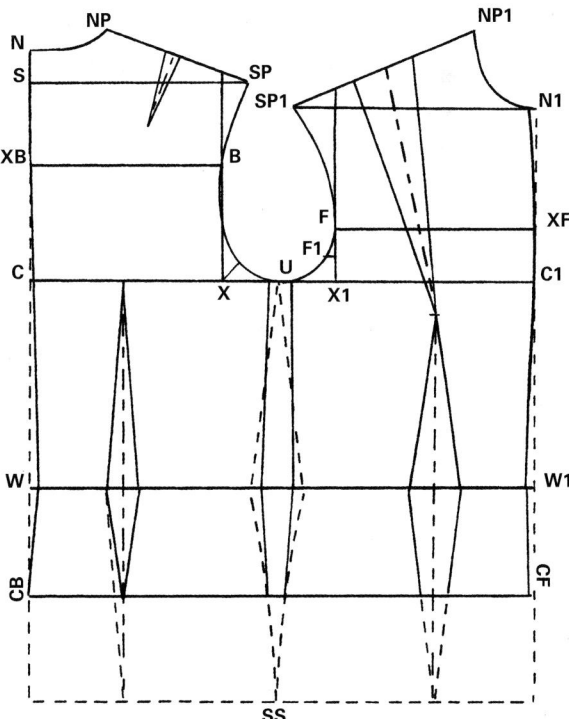

Figure 9.5 Removal of ease.

Bodice Back

Figure 9.6 and Figure 9.7

The back shoulder dart must be removed for an 1880s block. This actually improves the period silhouette as it helps give the garment a tighter armhole, rather than the more generous ones that are common in modern clothing. Remember that the seam lines are as much for an appealing line as they are for fit. Once you understand the mechanics of seam placement, you can adjust them for the greatest visual impact.

1. Extend the back shoulder dart in the Modern Basic Bodice Block to the line **XB–B**.
2. Cut from **B** to the extended dart.
3. Close the shoulder dart. This transfers the dart into the armhole.
4. Label the lower **B** as **B1**.

Guideline 1

1. Draw a line from **B** to the top point of the waist dart and continue to a point 3 cm–6 cm (1⅛"–2½") from **W**.
2. Complete the guideline with a perpendicular line ending at the new hem.
3. This is the guideline for the new **SB** seam.

Guideline 2

1. On the waist, find the midpoint between the left side of the dart and the **SS**.
2. Draw a straight line from this midpoint up to **X**, and continue with a slight angle to the armhole.
3. Complete the guideline with a straight perpendicular line from the waist ending at the new hem.
4. This is the guideline for the **SSB** seam.

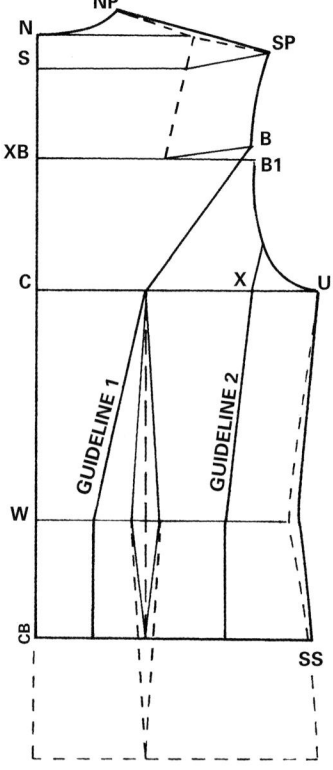

Figure 9.6 Seam guidelines 1 and 2.

Side Back Seam (SB)

Figure 9.7

1. Using guideline 1, draw a long, smoothly curved line from **B** to the waist. This is one branch of the **SB** seam.
2. Cut along this line from the hem to the point of the dart.
3. Close the waist dart:
   a. Cut along one side of the dart.
   b. Close the dart above the waist. The second branch of the **SB** seam will automatically appear when the dart is closed.
   c. The dart will overlap below the waist.
4. Draw the second branch of the **SB** seam from **B1** to the waist, smoothing out any angles.
5. Divide the dart overlap, and apply to both branches of the **SB** from the waist to the hem.
6. Using guideline 2, draw a long, smoothly curved line from the armhole to the waist, and continue to the hem. This is one branch of the **SSB** seam.
7. Draw the second branch of the **SSB** from the armhole to the waist, incorporating a small dart of 1.5 cm (⅝"), and continue to the hem.

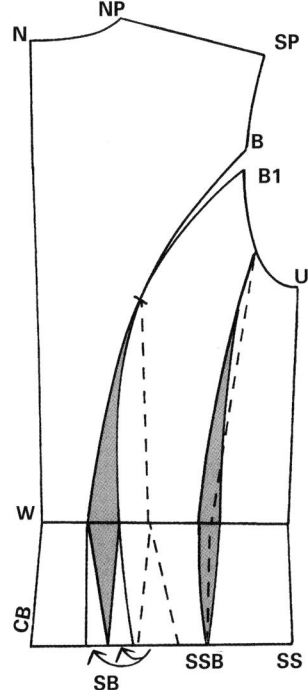

Figure 9.7 SB and SSB seams.

Finishing

Figure 9.8

1. Add pleats to the back panels as desired. This example has an inverted double box pleat at the **CB**.
2. Add a small flare 1 cm–2 cm (⅜"–¾") on the panels below the waist.
3. Draw the hem according to style.
4. True up all seams and darts.

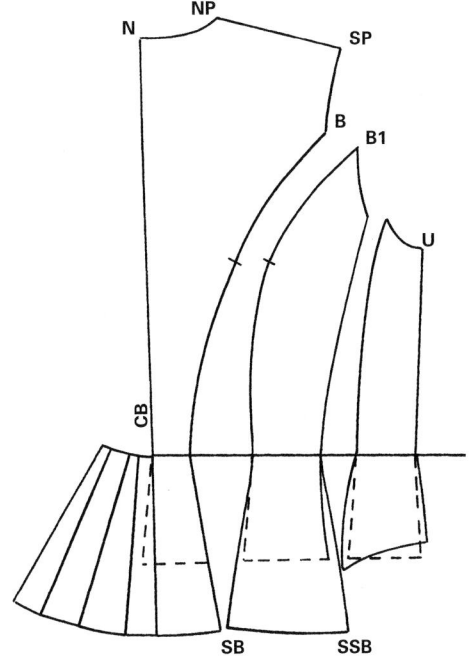

Figure 9.8 Back, side back and side side back panels with pleats and flare.

Bodice Front

Figure 9.9, Figure 9.10 and Figure 9.11

In the 1880s, two front waist darts per side helped produce the high rounded bust that was popular in the period.

1. Raise the **Apex** to the line **U–C1**.
2. Redraw the shoulder and waist darts to reflect the new **Apex** position.
3. Draw two waist darts:
   a. **Dart 1**. The positioning of the modern dart works well for most 1880s designs. However, you may find it is preferable to position the dart closer to the **CF**. In that case, move the **Apex** 1 cm (⅜"), or further, towards the **CF**. Redraw the shoulder and waist darts to reflect the new **Apex** position.
   b. **Dart 2**. Draw a line parallel to the centre of dart 1, 6 cm–7 cm (2½"–2¾") towards the **SS**. This line should start at the new hem and finish 4 cm–6 cm (1⅝"–2½") below the underarm line **U–C1**. This line is the centre of the new dart 2.
4. Cut up the centre of dart 1 to the **Apex**, leaving a small hinge.
5. Cut up dart 2 and continue on an angle to the **Apex**, leaving a small hinge.
6. Close the shoulder dart and equally open darts 1 and 2.
7. True up the shoulder.

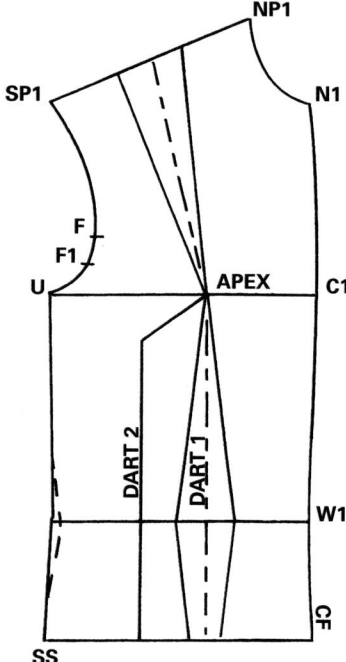

Figure 9.9 Front darts with raised Apex.

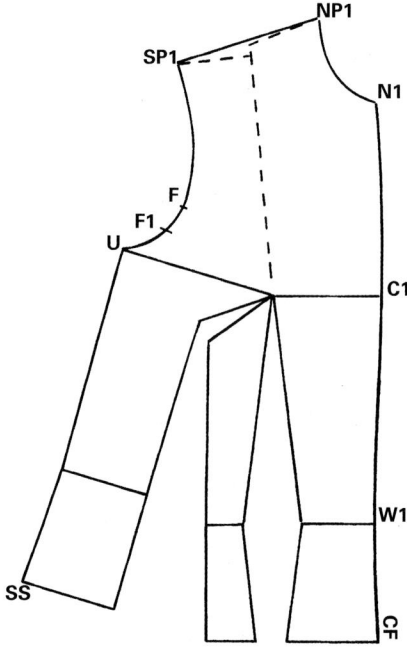

Figure 9.10 Shoulder dart transfer.

8. Complete dart 2 by adding some volume below the waist to the hem to mimic dart 1:
    a. Add 1 cm (⅜") to the hem on one branch.
    b. Shape the second branch to mimic the first.
9. Shape the darts, true up the darts, and draw the hem (see Figure 9.11).

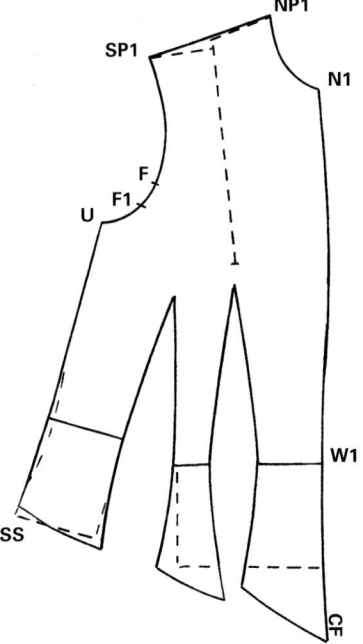

Figure 9.11 Shaped darts.

Shoulder and Neckline

Figure 9.12
The shoulder seam of the primary dress sits further towards the back than in the Modern Basic Block.

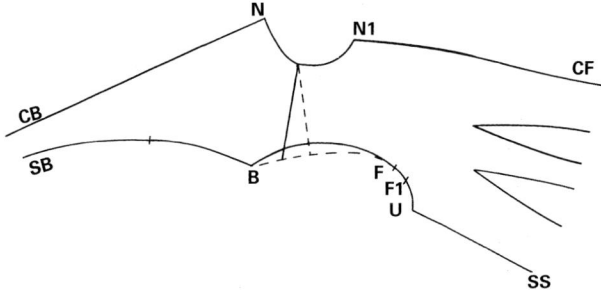

Figure 9.12 Shoulder and neckline.

1. Match front and back patterns at the shoulder from **NP** to **SP** and secure with tape.
2. Mark a point approximately 4 cm–6 cm (1⅝"–2½") below **SP** on the back pattern.
3. Connect this point with **NP**. This is the new shoulder seam.
4. Draw a new armhole from **F** to **B** approximately 1.5 cm (⅝") inside **SP**.

Collar

1. The collar pattern is a simple rectangle. The height is 2.5 cm–3.5 cm (1"–1½"). The width is the measurement from **N** to **N1** on the bodice. This creates a pattern that is half the neck. The **CB** is placed on the fold of the fabric.
2. **N** is at the **CB**.
3. **N1** is at the **CF**.
4. Mark the pattern to indicate that the **CB** should be placed on the fold of the fabric.

FINESSING THE PATTERN

Side Seam placement was not standard in the nineteenth century. In the primary dress, the **SS** appears to be slightly more forward than the modern **SS**. Check the waist measurement of the pattern, and adjust the seams and darts if necessary.

Sleeves

Figure 9.13
Sleeves in the 1880s fitted closely to the arm with little ease. Gathers at the elbow gave some flexibility for day-to-day activities. The following draft manipulation produces these gathers, and positions the lower part of the undersleeve on the fabric's bias. Both adaptations give the sleeve some flexibility for more comfortable movement.

Use the Historical Two-piece Sleeve found in Chapter 1 for this draft.

1. Complete the top and undersleeve patterns.
2. Scoop the front and back seams on both the top and the undersleeve by 1 cm–1.5 cm (⅜"–⅝"), as indicated.
3. Mark a point 1.5 cm (⅝") on either side of **6** on both the top and the undersleeve.
4. Cut the undersleeve sleeve pattern from **6** to **5**, leaving a small hinge.
5. Spread the cut 3 cm–6 cm (1⅛"–2½").
6. In making up, gather the undersleeve to match the notches on either side of **6** on the top-sleeve.
7. When setting the sleeve, the front seam matches **F1** on the bodice.

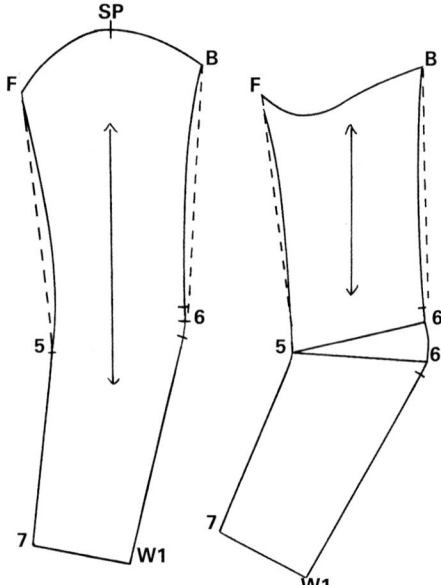

Figure 9.13 Sleeve.

Note, in extent garments, gathers are seen on the top or under sleeve at the elbow.

SKIRT

Examinations of period garments show that skirts often had casings for horizontal hoops. Presumably these were used in the absence of a bustle, or to increase the volume of the bustle. Sometimes, strips of cardboard were used in the casing, possibly a convenient alternative to steel hoops.

Foundation Skirt

Figure 9.14
This draft will produce a moderate foundation skirt without pleats. It has the placement for steel casings, and can be used as a draft for a separate tournure, or bustle.

Start with the Straight Skirt Block from Chapter 1. This draft has enough ease for an early 1880s skirt or petticoat. Divide the Straight Skirt Block in the same manner as the skirt in Chapter 8 (see Figure 8.15, page 149). Extend the pattern to the full length.

1. Cut a clean piece of paper that is at least the length of the full skirt. In this case, the skirt is 100 cm (39½").
2. Draw a grid with a vertical line parallel to the paper's right edge. This is the **CF**.
3. Draw perpendicular lines for **W–W1** and **H–H1**.

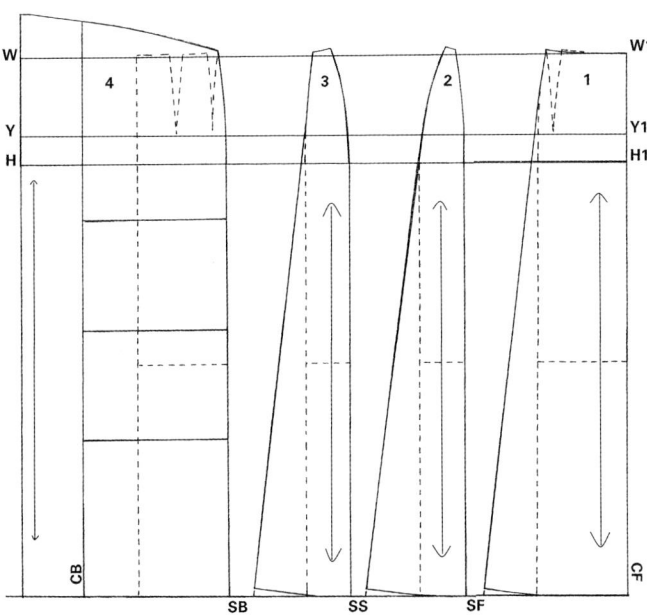

Figure 9.14 Foundation skirt.

Panel 1

1. Place the **CF** on the vertical gridline.
2. Mark a point 10 cm (4") to the left of the hem.
3. With a straight line, join this point to Panel 1 on the line **Y–Y1**.
4. Continue along pattern to the waist.

Panel 2

1. Place the pattern on the lines drawn out for **W–W1** and **H–H1**.
2. Mark a point 10 cm (4") to the left of the hem.
3. With a straight line, join this point to Panel 2 on the line **H–H1**.
4. Continue along the **SS** to the waist.

Panel 3

1. Place the pattern on the lines drawn out for **W–W1** and **H–H1**.
2. Mark a point 10 cm (4") to the left of the hem.
3. With a straight line, join this point to Panel 3 on the line **Y–Y1**.
4. Continue along the pattern to the waist.

Panel 4

1. Panel 4 will become the bustled part of the skirt so must be treated in a slightly different manner.
2. Place the pattern on the lines drawn out for **W–W1** and **H–H1**.
3. Draw a line 10 cm (4") to the left, and parallel, to the **CB**.
4. Extend this line 10 cm (4") above **W–W1**. This will account for the extra length needed to reach the waist from an extended bustle.
5. Mark the straight-of-grain parallel to the **CB**.

Casings

1. The top casing can be as high as the design needs. In this case, it is below the **H–H1**.
2. The following casings are about 10 cm–15 cm (4"–6") apart to reach a length of mid-calf.

Completion

1. True up the waist.
2. True up the hem.
3. Add straight-of-grain indications:
    a. **Panel 1**, the **CF** is on a fold.
    b. **Panel 2**, the straight-of-grain is parallel to the front edge.
    c. **Panel 3**, the straight-of-grain is parallel to the front edge.
    d. **Panel 4**, the straight-of-grain is parallel to the **CB**.

Making up

1. Use 2 cm (¾") wide twill tape for the casings. Finish each casing with a length of tape, which, when tied together, will hold the wires in place and produce a bowed shape.

Skirt Options

This pattern is for a foundation skirt. It can be altered for a bustle petticoat pattern by increasing the number of casings and adding ruffles to panel 4.

1. This pattern can be adapted for an overskirt by adding 2 cm (¾") to the width of each panel. This is easily done by adding 1 cm (⅜") to each seam.
2. Greater volume may be added to the back panel for a fuller bustled look. It can be tricky to estimate how much volume is needed. Chapters 2 and 4 describe methods of estimating the amount of volume needed using a measuring tape.
3. This foundation pattern has four panels, but one or more of these may be joined so the skirt has fewer seams.
4. Length may be added to panels 3 and 4 to form a train.

PLEATED OVERSKIRT

Figures 9.15 and 9.16

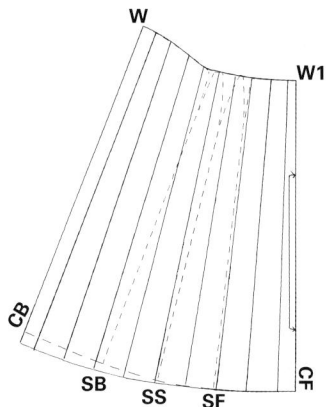

Figure 9.15 Lines for pleating.

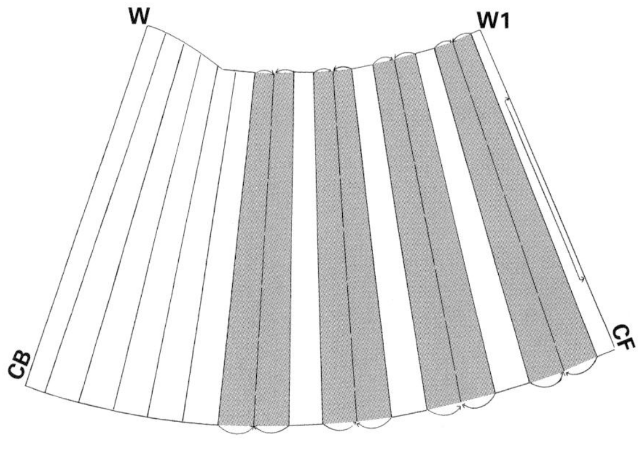

Figure 9.16 Partial pleating.

Pleated skirts like the one in the primary dress were very popular in the 1880s. The primary dress has box pleats that look to be 6.5 cm (2½"). To keep the pleats closed, they were stabilized with tapes on the underside.

To draft a skirt with pleats, draw lines in the foundation skirt pattern from the hem to the waist at 6.5 cm (2½") intervals. Cut along these lines and spread each to double the pleat width. The patterns will become very large, and the fabric will need to be pieced.

Alternatively, determine the skirt in the following manner.

Pleated Skirt Formula

1. Measure the hip over any undergarments that may affect the hip width, like a bustle or petticoat. In this case, the hip measurement is 127 cm (50").
2. Each pleat needs three times the visible width at the hip level. Therefore, a width of about 381 cm (150") of fabric is needed: 127 cm (50") × 3 = 381 cm (150").
3. To determine how many pleats are needed, divide the hip measurement by the pleat width: 127 cm (50") ÷ 6.5 (2.5) = 20.

Formula to Determine the Waist Pleat Underside

The standard waist measurement used in this book is 68 cm (27").

1. Determine the width of pleats in the design: 6.5 cm (2½").

2. How many pleats of this width are needed? 20.
3. Determine how much fabric is left over after the visible pleats are accounted for by subtracting the waist measurement from the width of fabric: 381 cm (150") − 68 cm (27") = 313 cm (123").
4. Divide the remaining fabric by the number of pleats: 313 cm (121") ÷ 20 = 15.65 cm (6").
5. Therefore, the amount of fabric at the back of each pleat is 15.5 cm (6") at the waist.

BUSTLE

The bustle is possibly the most distinguishing feature of the 1880s silhouette. Depending on the specific year, and the type of gown, these draperies shifted from low pick-ups to gravity-defying bustles. By the end of the decade, bustles were a thing of the past.

Flat Pattern Method of Drafting a Bustle and Apron

Figure 9.17
This is most successful for a separate bustle like the primary dress.

1. Trace the upper part of the skirt pattern that will become the bustle. Joining the patterns at the seams as well as possible, copy from the waist to the knee.
2. Draw a bustle outside the skirt parameters.
    a. The front is to be relatively smooth, so add 1 cm (⅜") beyond the **CF**.
    b. Add at least 5 cm (2") to the **CB**, as this is the area that will have most bustle.
3. This example shows the front drape and the back bustle overlapping. When it is drawn up, the front and back will no longer overlap.
4. Gather or pleat the fabric into a controlled area at the side or the side back.

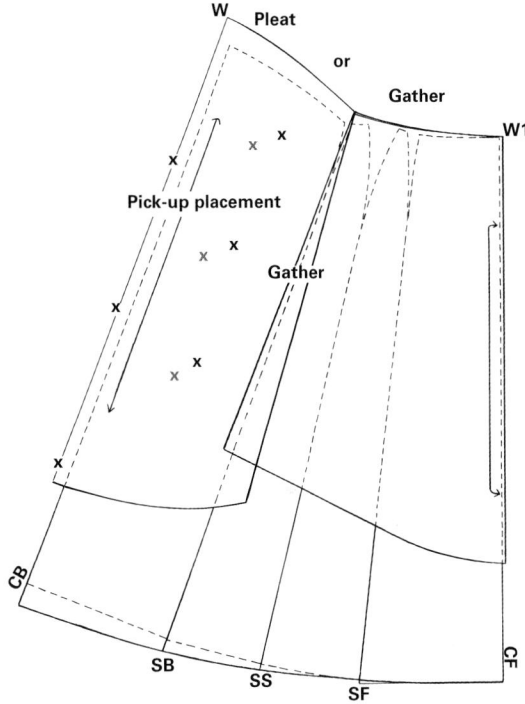

Figure 9.17 Bustle and apron patterns.

Draping a Bustle

Figure 9.18

This book provides instructions on flat pattern techniques. However, some instruction on draping techniques is useful. A draped bustle is most easily accomplished with a dress-form.

1. Mount the completed foundation skirt onto the dress-form.
2. Cut a length of flat tape and secure to the waist of the dress-form.
3. From this tape, secure three lengths of tape at the rear that hang over the shaped skirt.
4. Secure a length of fashion fabric at the waist.
5. Pull up the fashion fabric as desired and safety pin to the hanging tape.
6. Continue until the draping has the desired effect.
7. Replace the pins with permanent stitching.
8. Finish the bustle with the tape in place.

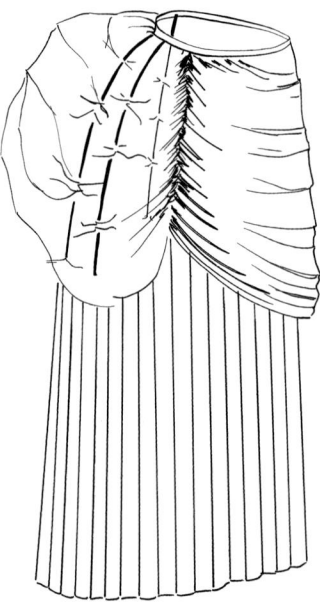

Figure 9.18 Bustle draping showing internal tapes.

La Mode Illustrée, 1880

Figure 9.19 Two alternative dresses with slimline skirts.

Alternative Day Dress Draft Adaptations

For a brief period in the continuum of fashion chronology, styles became completely divorced from the existing silhouette. At the end of the 1870s, and for a short period in the 1880s, the bustle and fully draped skirts were set aside and were replaced with a slim line that followed a woman's natural shape, albeit with the help of a corset. The style became known as the 'princess line', in honour of Princess Alexandra of Denmark. This long line was uninterrupted by a seam at the front or back waist. Almost all of the shaping was accomplished with seams that extended from the shoulder to well below the natural hip line. The concept of seams, which stem from the shoulder or armhole in lieu of darts, was introduced in the 1840s, and is covered in Chapter 5. But those seams stopped at the waist. The longer princess seams took on greater importance in shaping the garment.

The alternative dresses seen in the 1880 illustration from *La Mode* clearly show the princess seams (Figure 9.19). Extant dresses show that in some cases, the princess line is used for either the front or back, but not necessarily both. The blue dress has a princess seam line starting very close to the neck point. The tan dress in the same illustration has a princess seam which starts much closer to the shoulder point. The exact position is a style decision rather than a functional one, and depends entirely on the design. However, if the design calls for princess seams in the front and back, they should stem from the same position on the shoulder.

The two dresses are not a front and back view of the same dress, so assumptions must be made. For example, I assume that the front of the blue dress has a centre front closure with a row of buttons. It will be slim to the hip level. This front may be boned to keep the slim line. The bottom will have draping much like the back.

The following alternative draft is for the blue dress. Before starting the draft, determine how much hem circumference is needed for the design and the woman wearing the dress. In each of these alternative dresses, the bodice hem ends above the knees, so walking would be unencumbered. For this pattern, 125 cm (50") is a sufficient circumference to drape nicely around the bodice hem. The back will be slightly wider than the front because more draping occurs at the back.

Alternative Day Dress Draft

To start this draft, you will need a completed front and back Modern Basic Block with the optional shoulder dart found in Chapter 1.

1. Find and mark the point **F1** in the manner laid out in the instructions for the primary garment. (See page 143.)
2. Extend the length to knee level. Separate the front and back patterns at the **SS**.

Bodice Back

Figure 9.20 and Figure 9.21

Before starting the draft, determine a reasonable length. It may be useful to do a gathering sample of the fashion fabric to see how much gathering is needed. Another idea is to imagine what level on the body the fabric may reach without any gathering on the seams. In this case, it looks like the bodice's hem would reach close to the body's knees, so the waist to knee measurement is used for the length.

The back bodice has three panels. Two of these panels will merge together towards the end of the drafting process.

For a garment that has multiple seams, it is often simpler to remove the dart, and redistribute the waist reduction throughout the seams.

1. Mark a point about 2 cm (¾") from the **CB** to the right of **W**.
2. Draw a line from **XB** to this point. Continue the line to **H**. Continue in a straight line to the line **K–K1**. This is the new **CB**.
3. Shift the shoulder dart to a position 3 cm (1⅛") from **NP**.
4. Mark a point about 5 cm (2") to the right of the new **W**.
5. Connect the left branch of the shoulder dart to this point and continue this line to **H** with a small flare. Continue in a straight line to the line **K–K1**. This is one branch of the **SB** seam.
6. Starting on the right side of the shoulder dart, draw another line through the line **W–W1** about three quarters of the original waist dart from the first line. Continue with a flare to the line **K–K1**. This is the other branch of the **SB** seam.
7. On the line **W–W1**, mark the midpoint between the **SB** seam and the **SS**.
8. Mark a point about 2.5 cm (1") below **B** on the armhole.
9. Connect the two points, and continue this line through **H–H1**. Continue to **K–K1** with a flare.
10. This is one branch of the **SSB** seam.
11. Draw the second branch of the **SSB** seam incorporating the remainder of the original dart plus 1 cm (⅜").
12. Continue through **H–H1**. Add a flare to **K–K1**.
13. Continue the **SS** from the line **H–H1** to **K–K1** with a small flare.
14. Separate the three back panels.

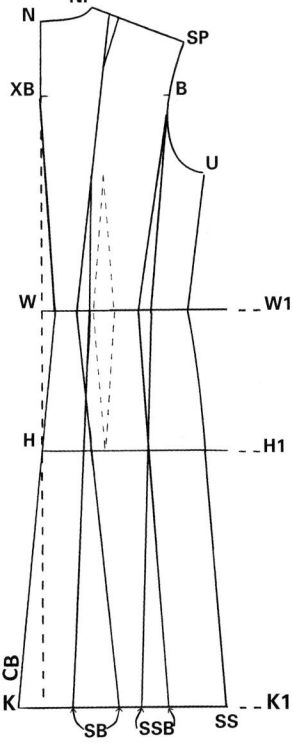

Figure 9.20 Back bodice and development of the princess line.

The back patterns could be finished at this stage. However, instructions 16–18 will give the pattern a more period feel.

15. Separate the three back panels and place them on a clean sheet of paper, keeping the waist, hip and hem along horizontal grids.
16. Place the three panels so that the hems equal about 38 cm (15"). The panels may overlap. If so, overlap the **SB** seam rather than the **SSB** seam.
17. Pivot the side back panel so that the **SSB** seam is almost perpendicular to the hem. It is not entirely clear why garments of this period were joined at the hem and splayed out towards the shoulder. It changes the grain to a partial bias so it may result in a smoother fit.
18. True up the **SB** seam.
19. True up the **SSB** seam.
20. Redraw the hem.

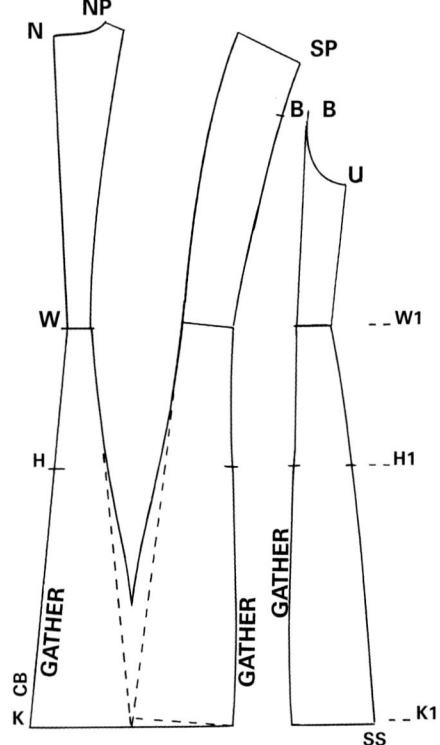

Figure 9.21 Princess line back panels.

Bodice Front

Figure 9.22

1. Extend the front pattern to the full length of the back.
2. Mark a point 3 cm (1⅛") from **NP1** on the line **NP1–SP1**.
3. From this point, draw both sides of a new **SF** seam, incorporating the shoulder dart and half the depth of the waist dart.
4. Continue both branches of the **SF** seam line to the full length, adding 2.5 cm–3 cm (1"–1⅛") to each at the hem.
5. Add a second parallel dart to the left of the first dart, incorporating the remaining part of the first dart and any remaining ease.
6. Add a small flare to the **SS** below the waist to mimic the back **SS**.
7. For a better fit, add a small waist dart between the second dart and the **SS**.
8. Add a distance equal to the depth of the dart above **U**, and redraw the armhole.
9. Draw a new **CF** with a greater curve over the bust area, and a small flare below the waist.

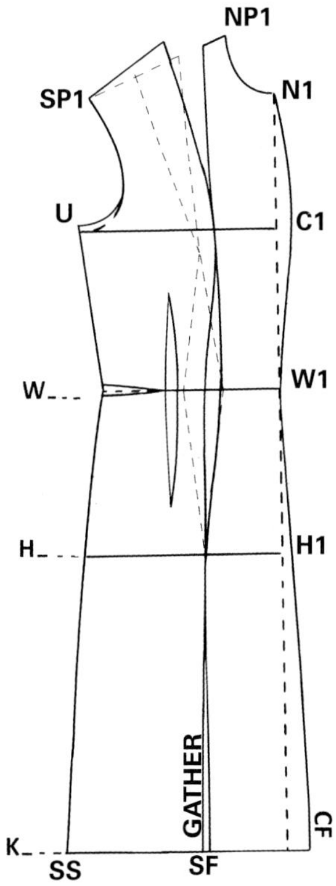

Figure 9.22 Princess line front pattern.

Shoulder

1. Complete the shoulders in the same manner as the primary dress.

Finishing

1. True up all seams.
2. Gather from the hem to the hip line on the **CB**, and **SSB** seams, and on the **CF** (see Figure 9.21).

Skirt

1. The foundation skirt is the panel skirt full length, with no added fullness at the hem.
2. For the blue dress, the overskirt is the same pattern, with an added 5 cm (2") per panel for draping.
3. Instructions for pleating the tan overskirt are the same as for the primary dress.

Sleeves

1. Sleeves are the same as with the primary dress.

Chapter 9 Development of Period Patterns, 1880–89

NOTES

1. M. E. MacKay (2004) 'Three Thousand Stitches: The Development of the Clothing Industry in Nineteenth-Century Halifax', in A. Palmer (ed.) *Fashion: A Canadian Perspective* (Toronto: University of Toronto Press), 170.
2. Ibid., 171.
3. Quote from J. P. Thornton (1901) *The Sectional System of Ladies' Garment Cutting Compromising Bodices, Jackets, Ulsters, Skirts, Habits, Etc.* (London: Thornton Institute), 239.
4. Quote from Elizabeth Gartland (1884) *The American Lady-tailor Glove-fitting System*, 12. Available at https://archive.org/details/americanladytail00gart. Accessed 2 December 2024.
5. This image is from an instruction booklet for 'Practical Lessons on How to Cut and Finish Garments' by A. McDowell & Co., 4 West 14th Street, New York. Author's collection.
6. C. B. Kidwell (1979) *Cutting a Fashionable Fit: Dressmakers' Drafting Systems in the United States* (Washington: Smithsonian Institution Press).
7. Reid J. Bayne (1883) *Bayne's Self-instruction Book for Dress Cutting by the French Glove-fitting Tailor System*. Available at https://archive.org/details/baynesself-instru00bayn. Accessed 2 December 2024.
8. Ibid., 54.

10

Development of Period Patterns, 1890–1900

Period Dress in Historical Context

This charming outfit embraces a major period aesthetic that significantly altered the fashion industry throughout the 1890s, which continued well into the twentieth century. A two-piece outfit comprising a decorative blouse matched with a darkly coloured skirt provided innumerable options for mixing and matching clothing items. The addition of a few simple blouses could expand an average woman's wardrobe with outfits that could take her from a casual game, to the classroom, or to an event where smart dress was required.

Most women's wear in 1890 was still the product of the custom dressmaking trade, or was made at home. Only a few items, such as easy to fit mantles and cloaks, had been available in shops since early in the century. In the 1880s, some manufacturers began producing women's suits, and larger department stores offered them in relatively small quantities. For example, Altman & Co., the luxury department store and chain based in New York City, showed seven ready-made walking suits in its 1882–83 catalogue.[1] Other New York companies, Bloomingdales and Lorde & Taylor, also advertised 'Popular Walking Costumes'.[2] The suit jacket could be donned and doffed at the convenance of the wearer, so most women wore a full blouse under the jacket. As the suit became more popular, the need for a variety of inexpensive, readily available blouses increased.

Figure 10.1 In the 1890s, the blouse and skirt combination was at the height of fashion.

Figure 10.2 Tracing seams and darts is important to understand the bodice draft.

Illustrator Charles Dana Gibson caught the zeitgeist of the day with sketches of a beautiful young woman actively engaged in leisure activities such as golf, motoring, bicycling or reading. With hair piled high on her head, she was often shown wearing a blouse and skirt very much like the primary outfit of this chapter. She became immortalized as the 'Gibson Girl'. The Gibson Girl represented the ideal woman of the era; independent, athletic, elegant and blessed with a natural casual beauty. She was physically curvaceous, with an ample bosom and tiny waist. She was decidedly feminine, and often shown wearing finely woven cottons and silks with inserted lace, pintucks, ruffles and bows. Yet she carried the self-assured stance of a man with her head held high. Her blouse, which became commonly known as a 'waist' or 'shirtwaist', was a direct descendant of a loose-fitting man's shirt. Men's furnishings, including detachable high starched collars and cuffs, boater hat, tie and cufflinks, completed the Gibson Girl look. It was a fashionable styling that blurred the strictly gendered division of clothing, which had been sacrosanct throughout the century.

As outlined in previous chapters, the huge variations in women's bodies did not lend themselves to the mass production of fitted garments. However, boy's and men's shirts, which were a mainstay of the ready-to-wear industry, needed very few adaptations to produce modern waists for women who were captivated by the latest fashion. What started as a costume worn for sporting activities, or as an accessory to a suit in the late 1880s, became the staple of every woman's wardrobe. By 1895, 'almost every leading shirt-maker had taken up production of women's waists.'[3]

> In 1899, the trade journal *The Cutter-Up* proclaimed 'Day by day the waist intrenches itself more deeply in the esteem of women. It is so easily managed and so much is possible with it that its permanency seems assured. It is worn by rich and poor alike, is ornate or simple, and lends itself to fashionable use, no matter what the occasion.'[4]

Companies that manufactured shirtwaists in the United States more than doubled their output from 1890 to 1900.[5]

Retailers claimed that the shirtwaist's decorative details put them beyond the skills of the home sewer. This did not deter pattern companies from including many in their repertoire. *The Delineator* noted their advantages of versatility: 'The shirt-waist is promised an extended vogue for house wear during Autumn and Winter', and added a stylish twist. A 'girdle gives a finished air to a toilette composed of a shirtwaist and a plainly draped skirt'.[6] In a recurring feature called 'The Dressmaker at Home' or 'The Dressmaker', *The Delineator* included sewing tips for lined and unlined shirtwaists, methods of applying boning to darts and seams, and even the instructions to build a custom dress-form.

While recognizing the shirtwaist's value, they were but a small portion of the patterns *The Delineator* made available to the home sewer. Within its pages were sketches and descriptions of all types of dress, from children's wear and simple dresses to ball gowns. Outdoor clothing with muffs and fur collarettes were featured in the winter months; spring's fashions in May. There was always a section for menswear, accessories and even dresses for dolls. *The Delineator* gave women the competence to become as knowledgeable in sewing as the custom dressmaker. While the home dressmaker could not have the depth of experience of her custom counterpart, she now had the information and materials needed to produce fine clothing.

DESCRIPTION

This blouse, believed to have been remade from an 1880s dress, encompasses the Art Nouveau aesthetic, which found a foothold in the 1890s (see Figures 10.1 and 10.2). It is a lovely wool challis with a botanical print of purple flowers on a yellow background. Its sculptural seaming references organic tall grasses with long curving darts and seam lines, which seem to splay open for the wearer's face. In terms of cut, the long line is exaggerated with a built-up neckline that hugs the neck and adds length to the torso.

Like many bodices of the period, the sculptural details hide the more functional details of hook and eye closures. This can make for complicated drafting and dress construction as closures are hidden beneath layers of gathered fabric. This blouse can be seen as having two layers. The inner layer has a front jabot that covers the neck area and fits snugly against the corset. Its closure takes any donning stress so the outer blouse can be closed without any tension on the hooks and bars. The second, outer layer covers these closures and invisibly closes at the lower centre front.

The skirt, which was originally worn with the blouse, has a very full hem made possible with gored seams. Skirts of the era were often cut as a portion of a circle. This appears to be a full quarter circle from the centre front to the centre back, making it a full half-circle shape.

Primary Step-by-Step Drafting Instructions

We need to look very carefully at this bodice before attempting its pattern. It may also be necessary to study dress history of the period to understand exactly what is happening in terms of seaming and darting. Before starting this draft, carefully determine the seaming, dart and tuck placement. Mark their placement on the image (Figure 10.2).

To start this draft, complete a front and back Modern Basic Block pattern. Some of the ease that is incorporated in the Modern Basic Block draft will be removed in developing a historical pattern. The first step in creating this draft is converting the two patterns into three; a back, a front and an underarm panel.

Development of the Underarm Panel

Figure 10.3

1. Cut off and discard the section below the waist from the front and back patterns.
2. Draw a horizontal gridline on a clean piece of paper.
3. Place the front and back patterns on the gridline along **W–W1** and join the patterns at **U**.
4. Measure and record the **SS** waist reduction on the line **W–W1**.
5. Draw a vertical line from **X** to **W–W1**.
6. Mark a point on either side of this line on **W–W1** to equal one half of the waist reduction.
7. Connect these points to **X** and continue a line with a slight angle into the armhole. This is the **SSB** seam.
8. Mark a point 2.5 cm (1") to the right of **U** on the line **C–C1**.
9. Draw a vertical line from this point to **W–W1**.
10. Mark a point on either side of this line on **W–W1** to equal one half of the waist reduction and connect all points. This is the new **SF** seam.
11. Extend the **SF** seam into the armhole if needed.

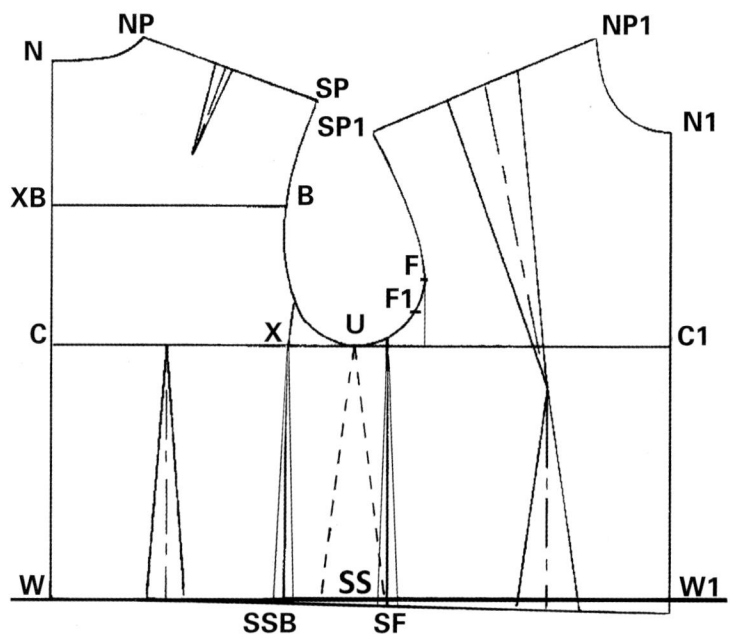

Figure 10.3 Development of side panel.

Bodice Back/Underarm Overblouse and Lining

Figure 10.4

The back shoulder dart must be removed for the 1890s draft.

1. Draw a horizontal line from the end point of the shoulder dart to the armhole.
2. Cut along this line.
3. Half-close the shoulder dart. This transfers half of the dart into the armhole.
4. Call the openings created in the armhole, **1** and **2**.
5. Draw **NP**–**SP** to equal the shoulder measurement. This removes the second half of the shoulder dart at **SP**.

Side Back (SB) Seam

Figure 10.4 and Figure 10.5

1. Draw a guideline from **1** to the waist dart point on the line **C–C1**.
2. Continue the line to approximately 6 cm (2½") to the right of **W** on the line **W–W1**. This point can vary, depending on the best visual placement (see Figure 10.4).
3. Draw a new **CB** from **XB** to the waist. (see Figure 10.5)
4. Using the guideline, draw a long, smoothly curved line. This is one branch of the **SB** seam.
5. Cut along this branch to the waist dart point.
6. Close the waist dart.
7. Draw the second branch of the **SB** seam from **2** to the waist, smoothing out any angles.
8. True up the seam.

Shaping/Reducing Ease

Figure 10.5

All seams must be nipped in to reduce the ease in the draft, and perfect the bodice shape.

1. Shape both sides of the **SSB** seam 0.5 cm (³⁄₁₆").
2. Shape the **SF** seam 0.5 cm (³⁄₁₆").

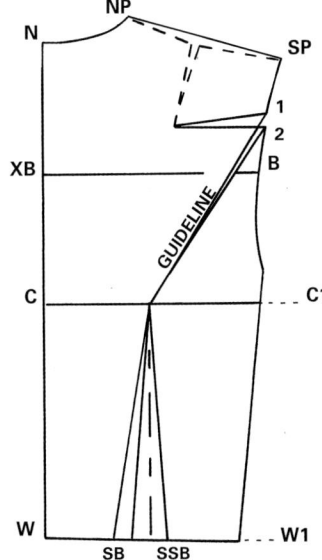

Figure 10.4 Underbodice, guideline for **SB** seam.

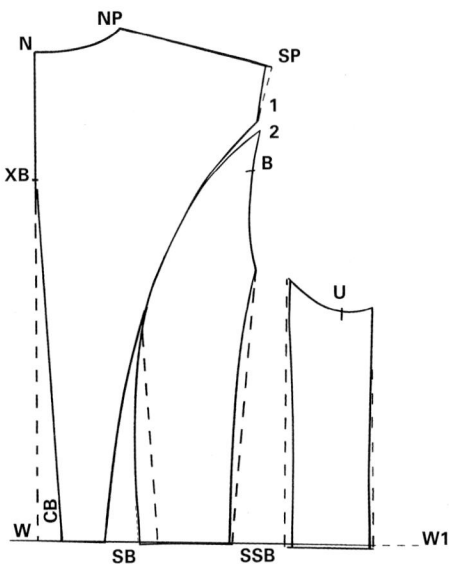

Figure 10.5 Underbodice removal of ease.

Neckline Build-up

Figure 10.6

1. Draw a vertical line from **NP**.
2. Mark a point about 1.75 cm (⅝") above **NP** on this line.
3. On the line **NP–SP**, mark a point 2 cm (¾") from **NP**.
4. Draw a curved line connecting the two points.
5. Measure and record the measurement of this curved, built-up neck line.

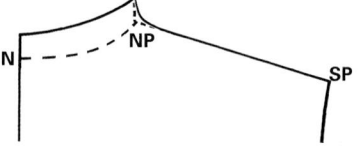

Figure 10.6 Back neck build-up.

BODICE FRONT LINING

Figure 10.7, Figure 10.8, Figure 10.9

The bodice front lining uses the same instructions as found in Chapter 9. Recognizing that there are some differences in length and width of the bodice front mentioned earlier in this chapter, follow the instructions for the Bodice Front 1–9 in Chapter 9 (please see pp. 166–7). Then proceed with instructions for bib placement.

1. Draw a section for a bib.
2. Remove this section.
3. Cut and spread the bib.
4. Redraw the bib neck and bottom.
5. In making up, gather the top edge to match the original **NP1–N1** measurement. Firmly attach one side of the bib onto the lining and prepare the other side with hook and eye attachments.

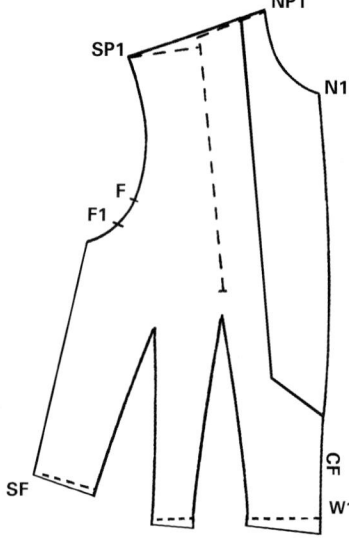

Figure 10.7 Bodice front lining showing bib placement.

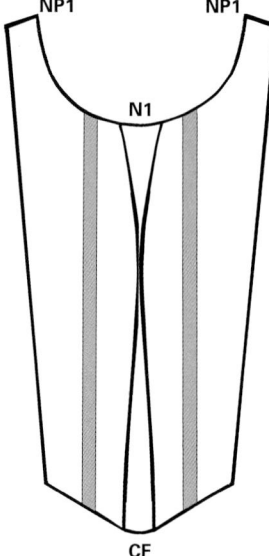

Figure 10.8 Extended bodice front bib.

Figure 10.9 Illustration of underbodice closures.

Overblouse Front Neckline Build-up

Figure 10.10

1. On the line **NP1–SP1**, mark a point 2 cm (¾") from **NP1**.
2. From this point, apply the back build-up measurement, and raise it 1 cm (⅜") from **NP1**.

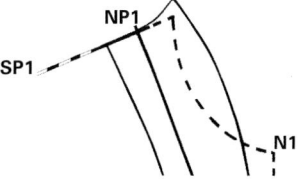

Figure 10.10 Overblouse front neckline build-up.

Front Decorative Seaming

Figure 10.11, Figure 10.12, Figure 10.13 and Figure 10.14

1. Draw a new front neckline. Start with a outward curve at the neck and modify it to a straight line. Stop the line about half way between **CI** and **W1**.
2. Draw a second line following this new neckline.
3. Draw a third line about 2 cm (¾") from the second.
4. Cut along the third line and set aside. In making up, there are two sections that are seamed together.
5. Close the waist dart and open the shoulder dart.
6. Draw two new front darts.
7. Partially close the shoulder dart and open the waist darts.
8. Draw two or more lines for tucks.

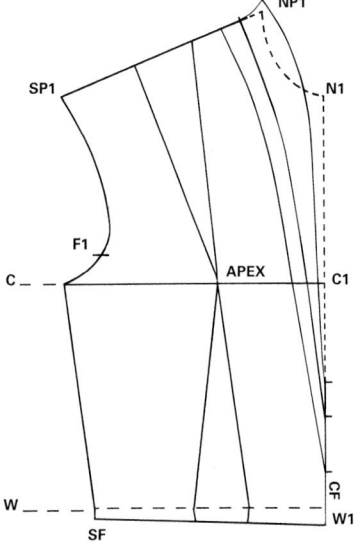

Figure 10.11 Front neckline and seaming.

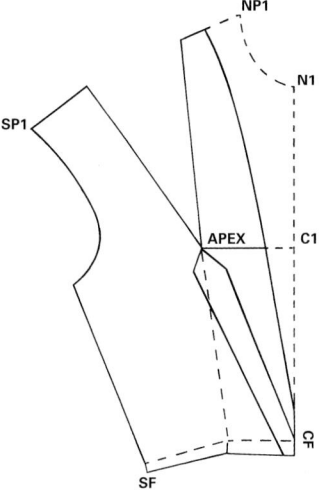

Figure 10.12 Draw front darts.

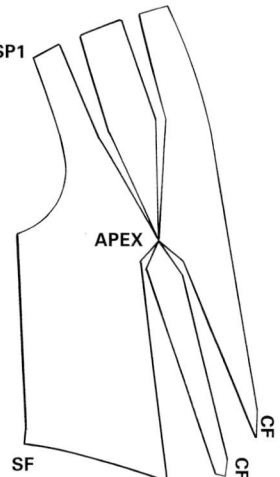

Figure 10.13 Waist darts and tucks opened.

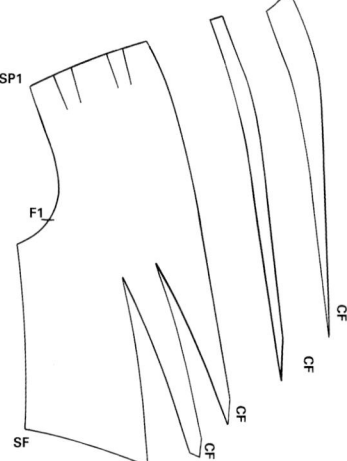

Figure 10.14 Pattern showing waist darts, shoulder tucks and front edge seaming.

SLEEVES

Complete the Historical Two-piece Sleeve found in Chapter 1 for this draft.

Undersleeve

Figure 10.15
1. Mark a point 1.5 cm (⅝") on either side of **6**.
2. Cut from **6** to **5**, leaving a small paper hinge.
3. Spread the cut 6 cm (2½").
4. Draw a curved elbow line connecting the two positions of **6**.
5. Measure the length of the back seam from **4** to the top notch.

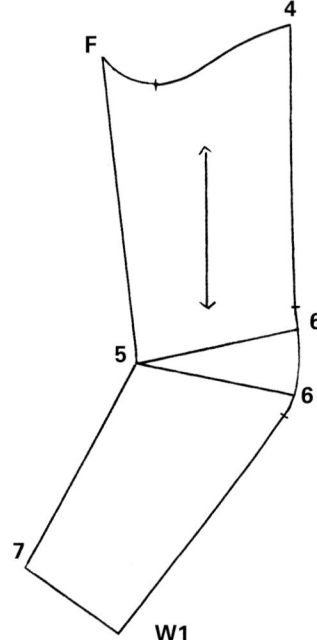

Figure 10.15 Undersleeve draft.

Topsleeve

Figure 10.16
1. Mark a point 1.5 cm (⅝") on either side of **6**.
2. Cut from **6** to **5**, leaving a small hinge.
3. Spread open the cut 6 cm (2½").
4. Draw the back seam line by connecting **W1** to **6**, and continuing in a straight line.
5. The length of this line is the length of the undersleeve back seam plus 3 cm (1⅛"). Call the end point **B**.
6. Apply the undersleeve measurement from **6** to **4** to the topsleeve from **B**. Mark this point with a notch.
7. In making up, gather the topsleeve to match the notches on either side of **6**.
8. In making up, the sleeve head is pleated into the armhole.
9. When setting the sleeve, **F** on the sleeve matches meets **F1** on the bodice.

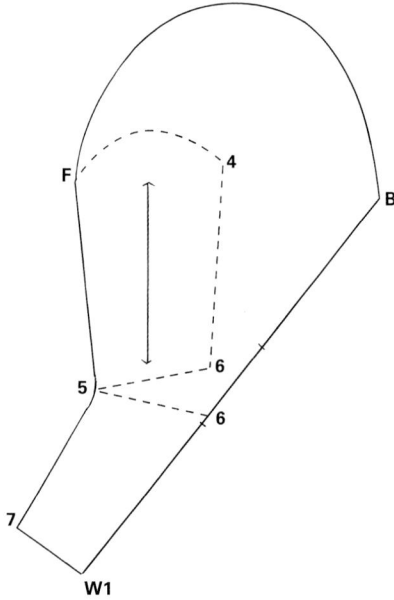

Figure 10.16 Topsleeve draft.

SKIRT

The primary skirt has a triangular shape with a wide hem and narrow waist. Skirts in this period were often made with a number of panels that are fitted into the waist with seams or tucks. Pleats or gathers were concentrated at the **CB**. The following draft shows a method of dividing the modern skirt into panels, which is slightly different from the previous drafts in this book. It produces a skirt that has a wide flare at the back and enough ease along the waist for a small pleat at the **CB**.

Creating Panel Skirt

Figure 10.17 and Figure 10.18
1. Join front and back patterns.
2. On the front pattern, extend a line from the dart point to the hem. This divides the panel.
3. Label the panels **1** and **2**.
4. On the back, draw a line from the dart point closest to the **SS**, to the hem.
5. Label the panels **3** and **4**.
6. Separate front and back at the **SS**.
7. Cut along these lines from the hem to **Y–Y1**, and from the waist to **Y–Y1**, leaving a small hinge.
8. Close the darts at the waist. The hem automatically opens.
9. Cut the skirt into four panels.
10. Extend each panel to the full length.

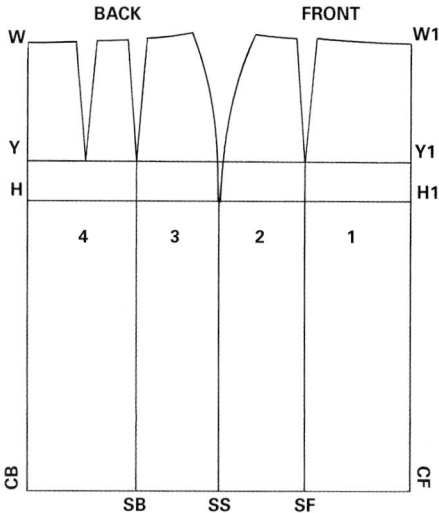

Figure 10.17 Panel skirt.

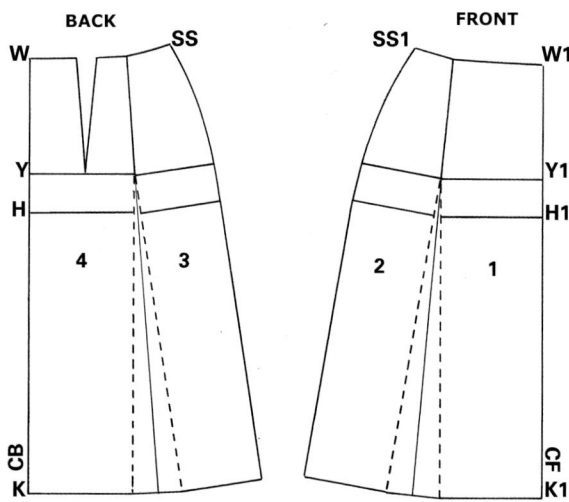

Figure 10.18 Modern skirt divided into two panels.

Chapter 10 Development of Period Patterns, 1890–1900   **191**

Panel 1

Figure 10.19
1. Mark a point about 8 cm (3⅛") to the left of the hem.
2. Join this point to the waist.

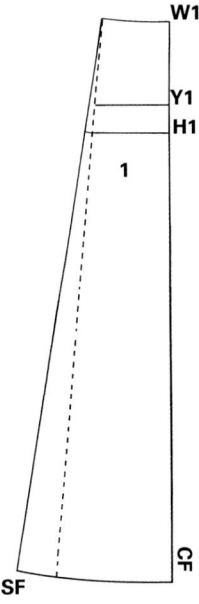

Figure 10.19 Panel 1.

Panel 2

Figure 10.20
1. Mark a point 8 cm (3⅛") to the right of the hem.
2. Join this point to the waist.
3. Mark a point 8 cm (3⅛") to the left of the hem.
4. Join this point to **H–H1** and continue to the waist.

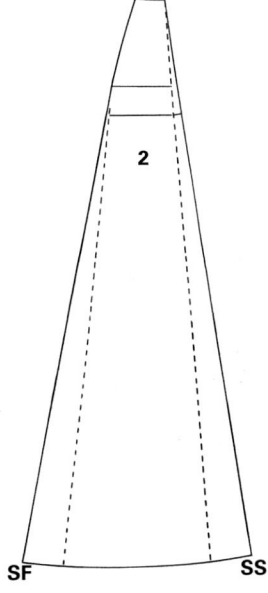

Figure 10.20 Panel 2.

Panel 3

Figure 10.21

1. Mark a point 8 cm (3⅛") to the right of the hem.
2. Join this point to **Y–Y1** and continue to the waist.
3. Mark a point 8 cm (3⅛") to the left of the hem.
4. Join this point to the waist.

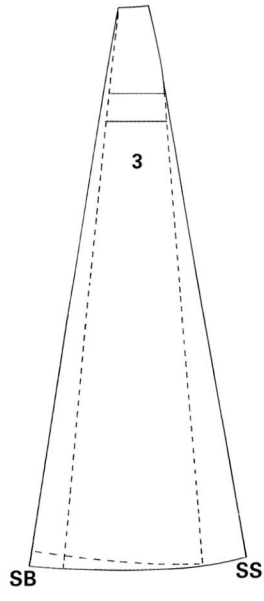

Figure 10.21 Panel 3.

Panel 4

Figure 10.22

1. Mark a point 8 cm (3 1/4") to the right of the hem.
2. Join this point to the waist.
3. Mark a point 4 cm (1 5/8") to the left of the hem.
4. From this point, draw a line parallel the **CB**, to the waist. and continue above the waist line approximately 2.5 cm (1"). This is the new **W**.
6. From **W**, draw an angled line the full skirt length plus about 6.5 cm (2 1/2"). This is the new **CB**.
7. Draw a more angled line for a greater flare.
8. Redraw the waist in a smooth curve.

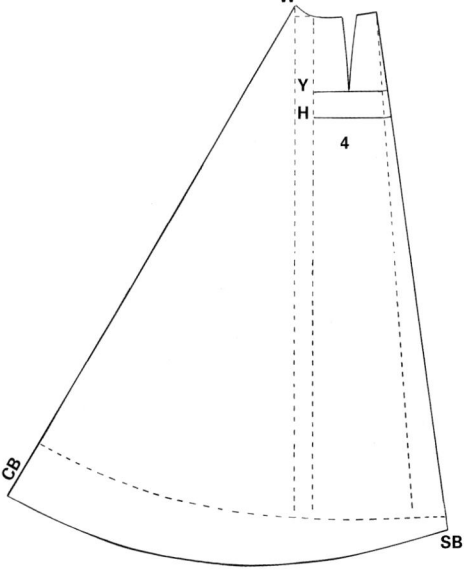

Figure 10.22 Panel 4.

Chapter 10 Development of Period Patterns, 1890–1900

Completion

Figure 10.23
1. True up the waist.
2. True up the hem.
3. Add straight-of-grain indications:
    a. **Panel 1**, the **CF** is on a fold.
    b. **Panel 2**, the straight-of-grain is parallel to the front edge.
    c. **Panel 3**, the straight-of-grain is parallel to the front edge.
    d. **Panel 4**, the straight-of-grain is parallel to the front edge.

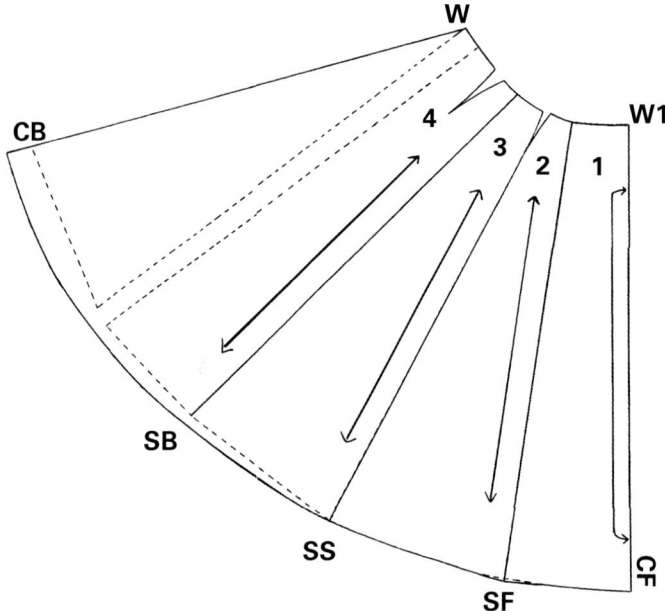

Figure 10.23 Panels joined with straight-of-grain marked.

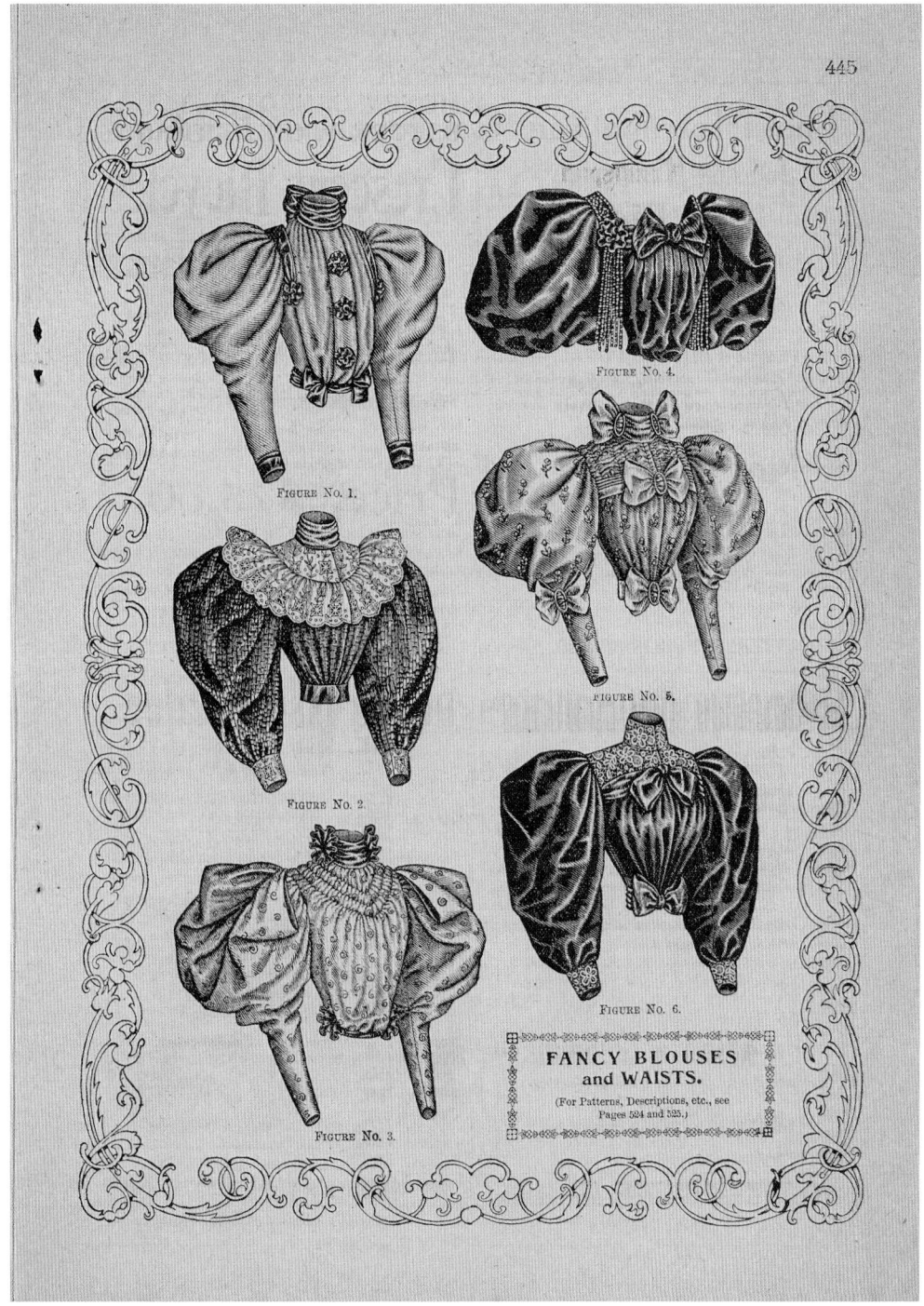

Figure 10.24 Various sleeve designs from *The Delineator*, April 1895.[7]

Alternative Period Sleeve Draft Adaptations

The two-piece sleeve was a common style throughout much of the nineteenth century. The sleeves followed the natural curve of the arm. They were often pitched to join the bodice low on the armhole at the balance point **F1**. This places the front seam in line with the thumb; a lovely placement for decorative openings. The tailor T. H. Holding suggested one reason for a very curved arm in his booklet *Ladies' Cutting Made Easy*, published in 1885: 'A lady in wearing a dress is mostly sitting, the arms are curved or forward, and the bent sleeve best fits the arm under such condition.'[8] For this reason, even though many of these sleeves can be developed from the Historical One-piece or Modern One-piece Sleeve draft, they will sit more convincingly if developed from the Historical Two-piece Sleeve in Chapter 1.

The two-piece sleeves in this book are developed from the tailored British half and half sleeve. In the tailoring tradition, the sleeve front is always placed to the left of the page and the sleeve back is placed on the right. This is in contrast to many women's drafts, which place the sleeve in the opposite direction. Texts that show patterns taken directly from clothing often vary their positioning. To help the student feel comfortable with both orientations, the following pages show sleeve drafts in both.

Sleeves Number 1 and 5

Figure 10.25

1. Start with the Historical Two-piece Sleeve in Chapter 1.
2. Draw a line from **6** to **5** in both the top and undersleeve.
3. Cut from **6** to **5**, leaving a small hinges.
4. Open the cut 3 cm (1⅛").
5. Join the topsleeve and undersleeve patterns from **6** to **W1**.
6. For a sleeve with greater curve at the elbow, cut from **W1** to **6** and spread 6 cm (2½").
7. Draw a new sleeve head adding height and width.

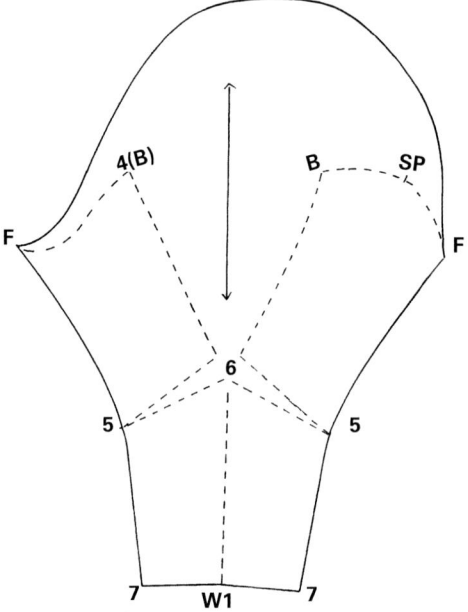

Figure 10.25 Pattern for styles 1 and 5.

Sleeve Number 3

Figure 10.26

This sleeve has two cowls that meet at the **SP**. A cowl is an open drape that is cut on a true bias. Because the cowl is open, the lining will be visible. Therefore, the top part of the sleeve lining should be constructed with the fashion fabric.

1. Start with the Historical Two-piece Sleeve and a large piece of paper,
2. In the centre of the paper, draw a line three times the length of **W1** to **6**. Label the top of this line, **SP**. This is the top of the draft.
3. Match the topsleeve and bottom sleeve along the back seams from **W1** to **6** and place on the bottom of this line.
4. Cut the top and bottom sleeves from **6** to **5** and open 10 cm (4").
5. Draw two 45° angled lines from **SP** to **W1** approximately 25.5 cm–30.5 cm (10"–12") long to form a right angle at **SP**. Label the ends of the straight lines **SP**. These will become the cowls.
6. In a sweeping curve, join the straight lines to the top and bottom sleeve head at **F**. Setting this sleeve will be easier if you follow the original underarm for part of the new sleeve head.
7. Add a 5 cm (2") extension from **SP** to **SP** to **SP**. This becomes a facing to the cowl area, as illustrated in Figure 10.26.
8. In making up, fold along the cowl, join the three **SP**s together.
9. Gather the rest of the sleeve head.
10. Stitch the seam through **F**, **5** and **7**.
11. This illustration has three small tucks above the elbow; however, this draft will produce an attractive sleeve without the tucks.
12. It may be beneficial to gather below the **SP** and attach the outer sleeve to the lining at this point.

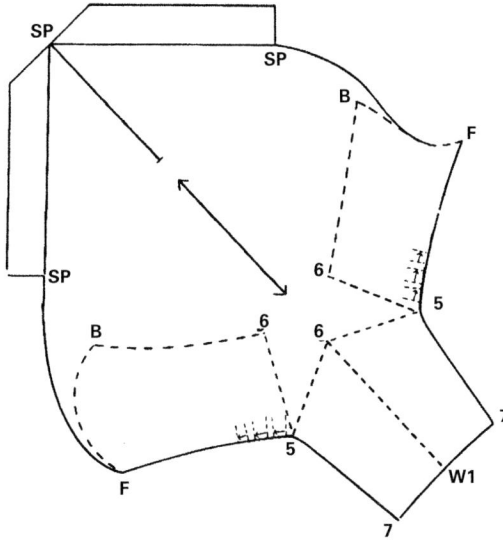

Figure 10.26 Style 3, cowl sleeve.

Sleeve Number 4

Figure 10.27, Figure 10.28 and Figure 10.29
This pattern is used for both the lining and outer sleeves. Figures 10.27, 10.28 and 10.29 show the pattern with different levels of fullness.

1. Start with the Historical Two-piece Sleeve.
2. Remove the section below the elbow.
3. Join the top and bottom sleeve from **6** to **B**.
4. This pattern can be used for a sleeve lining without added fullness.
5. For added fullness, draw divisions and cut and spread as desired.
6. Add height from **F** through **SP**, to **B**.

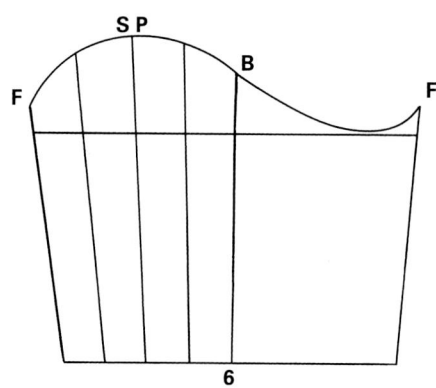

Figure 10.27 Elbow-length sleeve.

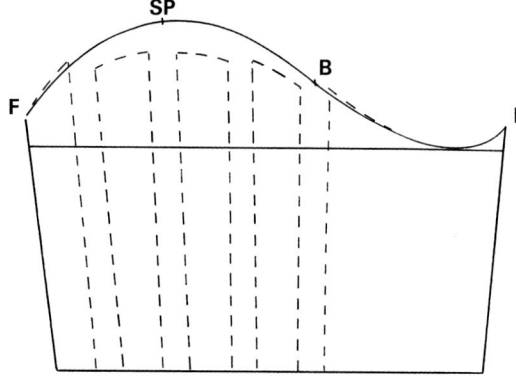

Figure 10.28 Sleeve lining.

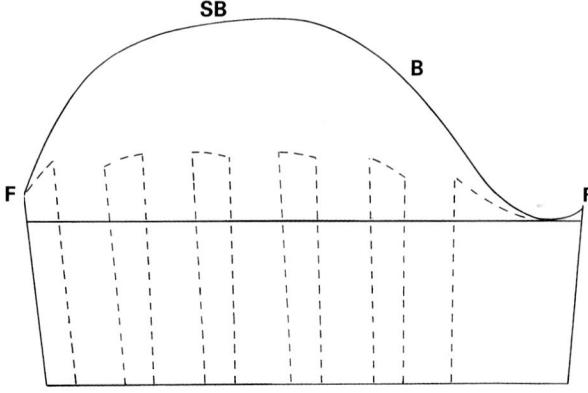

Figure 10.29 Full short sleeve.

Sleeves Number 2 and 6

Figure 10.30

Because this sleeve is so full, and is not shaped to follow the curve of the arm, it is possible to use either the Modern or Historical One-piece Sleeve draft. The underarm seam at **U** will match **U (U1)** on the bodice.

1. Remove 5 cm (2") above **W–W1**. This is the cuff pattern.
2. Draw cutting lines the full length of the sleeve.
3. Spread sleeve pieces, as illustrated in Figure 10.30.
4. Draw a new sleeve head, adding as much height as is needed.

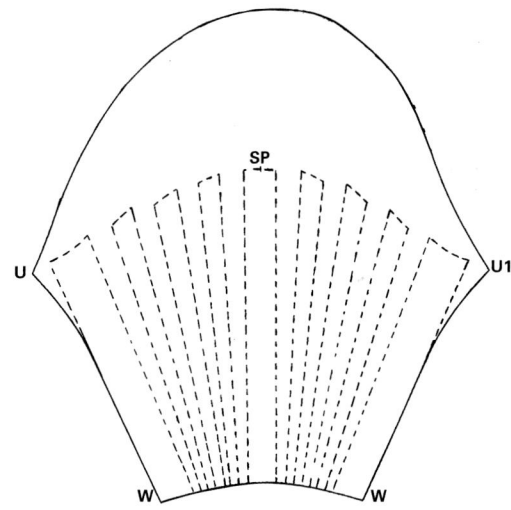

Figure 10.30 Spread pattern and add height for styles 2 and 6.

NOTES

1. Claudia Kidwell and Margaret Christman (1974) *Suiting Everyone: The Democratization of Clothing in America* (Washington: Smithsonian Institution Press), 139.
2. Ibid., 139.
3. Jean L. Parsons (2018) 'The Shirtwaist: Changing the Commerce of Fashion', *Fashion, Style & Popular Culture*, 5(1): 7–23.
4. Quoted in Kidwell and Christman, *Suiting Everyone*, 145.
5. Parsons, 'The Shirtwaist', 11, 20.
6. *The Delineator: A Journal of Fashion Culture and Fine Arts*, 1890, 36(4): 290. https://archive.org/details/ybxc6wq23g0c/page/n63/mode/2up?view=theater.
7. *The Delineator: A Journal of Fashion Culture and Fine Arts*, April 1895, 13. https://reader.library.cornell.edu/docviewer/digital-?id=hearth1891092_45_4#page/13/mode/1up.
8. T. H. Holding (2018) *Ladies' Cutting Made Easy* (Franklin Classics Trade Press), 7.

REFLECTIONS

In terms of complexity, nineteenth-century styles and the paper patterns needed to achieve that style developed in tandem throughout the century. They start, as explained in Chapter 3, with the relatively simple, but graceful, silhouette of c. 1815. This minimalist design is a perfect canvas to practise the modern basic block formulas, to begin an understanding of the intimate relationship between body and pattern, and to learn the transformative qualities of the preliminary pattern adaptations. Subsequent chapters tackle the extraordinary variations in shapes and fabric manipulations that are key to nineteenth-century fashion, with more advanced drafting techniques and alterations to the modern blocks. The book ends with the highly complex styles of the 1890s, including a jigsaw puzzled bodice pattern, and half a dozen sleeve variations.

With each chapter, the book builds on levels of difficulty, allowing students to hone their skills with orderly progression. As students proceed through the book and become more skilful, they will realize that the paper pattern has a beauty of its own. The sensuous curves, perfected proportions and mechanics of a precisely fitted pattern have their appeal. However, the pattern maker must move from paper to fabric as quickly as possible. All of the patterns in the proceeding chapters were initially drawn by hand, with a half-scale gauge. Each pattern was then tested with a cotton mock-up mounted on a half-scale, size 12 dress-form. This is a key step in the pattern-making process. It shows, in a tangible way, the relationship between the measurements on paper and the resulting shape in fabric. Mock-ups are usually made in inexpensive plain-weave fabric, but I chose printed quilting cotton to evoke a sense of the period aesthetic.

While mock-ups helped to ensure that the patterns reflected the correct silhouette and fabric volume that was needed, they do not assess the fit on a body. As all bodies are unique, fitting a full-size mock-up on an individual is a separate, and very important, step, which is not addressed in this book. Nonetheless, the skills acquired through adherence to the steps laid out here will put the student in good stead to address that challenge as well.

Chapter 3 Evaluation

Figure C.1 Side view of Chapter 3 primary dress mock-up.

Figure C.2 Detail showing pleated back of Chapter 3 mock-up.

In constructing this mock-up, I chose to test the short sleeve depicted in the alternative Figure 3.14, at the same time as the longer one in Figure 3.1 and 3.2. The manipulations to the Modern Basic Block found in Chapter 3 produced an excellent early eighteenth-century silhouette. The quilting cotton I used drapes much like the stiff silk of the primary garment. If one is using a lighter fabric, more fabric is needed and the pattern must reflect that added volume.

The only way to determine the correct amount of fabric is through sampling with different fabric widths and gathering density. For example, if, after sampling, it is decided that an attractive gather is three times the original width, then cut and spread the pattern section to reflect this proportion. The waist height, while correct for the period, is difficult for most people in terms of fit and attractiveness. Pattern makers may choose to lower the waist for more comfort.

Chapter 4 Evaluation

Figure C.3 Front view of Chapter 4 primary dress.

Figure C.4 Detail showing the piped, side back seam of the same dress.

Figure C.5 Detail showing the vandyked edging of the upper skirt and bias flounce.

I am very pleased with this mock-up. The silhouette is very good for a mid-to later 1820s dress. Quilting cotton is heavier than the original fabric and pattern makers may need to experiment with an additional skirt length if a lighter weight fabric is used.

    To my critical eye, the mock-up sleeve is slightly too top-heavy for the period. It reflects a pattern in which the individual sections were spread more at the top than at the bottom. To correct this, I spread the sleeve pattern sections equally. This is reflected in the pattern in the Chapter 4 instructions (see Figure 4.18).

Chapter 6 Evaluation

Figure C.6 Side back view of the primary dress mock-up in Chapter 6.

Figure C.7 Side front view of the same dress.

This pattern for the primary garment in Chapter 6 created a striking mock-up. It is mounted over a crinoline that enhances the silhouette, but even without an understructure, the skirt volume produced a good silhouette. While it is not necessary to add trim to most mock-ups, the fringe helps to identify the decorative band and the sleeve flounces seen in the photograph. Figure C.7 also shows that making a completed mock-up is not always necessary. All the information needed was achieved by completing one half of the dress.

Chapter 8 Evaluation

Figure C.8 The mock-up of the primary dress in Chapter 8 showing a bustle silhouette.

Figure C.9 The front view of the same dress.

Figure C.10 The side back view of the same dress.

This mock-up shows a spectacular silhouette. Even so, there is room for improvement. The high collar, while lovely, does not have the flouting of the original, as seen in Figures 8.1 and 8.2. I corrected this in the pattern by making the collar a little longer than the neck measurement (see Figures 8.12 and 8.13).

For the construction of this mock-up, I combined the bustle-making techniques of the chapter's primary garment, and the 'draping a bustle' technique, shown in Figure 9.18. Had the mock-up fabric been crisp silk taffeta, gathering along the side back seam would have created a bustle. The cotton does not have the same quality of loft, so, in addition, I used the draping technique explained in Chapter 9.

Chapter 10 Evaluation

Figure C.11 Front view of Chapter 10 primary outfit mock-up.

Figure C.12 Front detail showing the complicated seaming of the blouse.

This mock-up shows a very good silhouette in the skirt and the blouse. The sleeve volume looks almost demure when compared to other sleeves of the period. It is possible that the neckline of the mock-up is slightly higher than in the original, but it is correct for the period and also very attractive.

MEASUREMENT SHEET

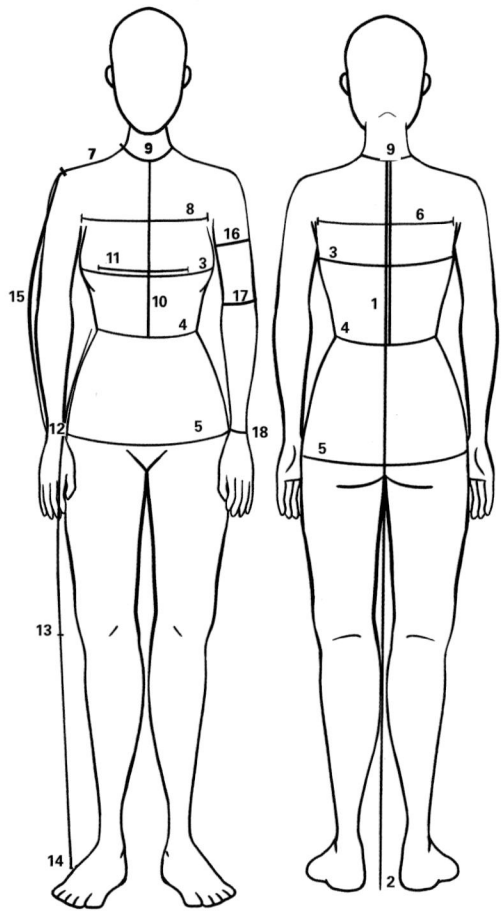

1. Nape to Waist
2. Nape to Floor
3. Chest (Bust)
4. Waist
5. Hip
6. Back Width
7. Shoulder
8. Front Chest Width
9. Neck
10. Neck to Waist Front
11. Bust Point to Bust Point
12. Waist to Hip (Side)
13. Waist to Knee (Side)
14. Waist to Floor
15. Sleeve Length
16. Bicep
17. Elbow
18. Wrist

BIBLIOGRAPHY

A Lady (2018) *The Workwoman's Guide by A Lady: A Guide to 19th Century Decorative Arts, Fashion and Practical Crafts* (Boston: Opus Publications). First published 1838. Available at https://books.google.com. Accessed 2 December 2024.

Anon (1825) *The Duties of a Lady's Maid: With Directions for Conduct and Numerous Receipts for the Toilette*. Available at https://books.google.com. Accessed 2 December 2024.

Anon (1843) *The Ladies Hand-book of Millinery, Dressmaking and Tatting*. Available at https://books.google.com. Accessed 2 December 2024.

Arnold, J. (1972) *Patterns of Fashion 2: Englishwomen's Dresses and Their Construction c. 1860–1940*. London: Macmillan/Drama Books.

Arnold, J. (1982) *Patterns of Fashion 1: Englishwomen's Dresses and Their Construction c. 1660–1860*. London: Macmillan/Drama Books.

Arnold, J. (2021) *Patterns of Fashion 1: The Content, Cut, Construction and Context of Englishwomen's Dress c. 1720–1860*. London: School of Historical Dress.

Baumgarten, L. (1998) 'Altered Historical Clothing', *Dress* (Journal of the Costume Society of America), 25(1): 42–57.

Bayne, J. R. (1883) *Bayne's Self-instruction Book for Dress Cutting by the French Glove-fitting Tailor System*. Available at https://archive.org/details/baynesselfinstru00bayn. Accessed 2 December 2024.

Bradfield, N. (2008) *Costume in Detail: 1730–1930* (new edn). Eric Dobby Publishing.

Bray, N. (1974) *Dress Pattern Designing: The Basic Principles of Cut and Fit*. London: Granada.

Brent, M. E. (1980) 'A Stitch in Time: Sewing Machine Industry of Ontario, 1860–1897', *Material Culture Review*, 10: 1–30.

Burman, B. (ed.) (1999) *The Culture of Sewing, Gender, Consumption and Home Dressmaking*. Oxford: Berg.

Cory, E. A. (Mrs) (1849) *The Art of Dressmaking, containing Plain Directions in Simple Language from the Fitting of the Pattern to the Finish of the Dress*. Available at https://books.google.co.uk/books/about/The_Art_of_Dressmaking_Containing_Plain.html. Accessed 2 December 2024.

Davidson, H. (2019) *Dress in the Age of Jane Austen: Regency Fashion*. New Haven: Yale University Press.

Depew, C. M. (ed.) (1895) *One Hundred of Years of American Commerce*. New York: Haynes & Co.

Emery, J. (1999) 'Dreams on Paper: A Story of the Commercial Pattern Industry', in B. Burman (ed.) *The Culture of Sewing: Gender, Consumption and Home Dressmaking*, 235–55. Oxford: Berg.

Errington, J. (1995) *Wives and Mothers, Schoolmistresses and Scullery Maids: Working Women in Upper Canada, 1790–1840*. Montreal: McGill-Queen's University Press.

Garfield, S. (2001) *Mauve: How one Man Invented a Colour that Changed the World*. New York: W. W. Norton.

Gartland, E. (1884) *The American Lady-tailor Glove-fitting System* (Philadelphia). Available at https://archive.org/details/americanladytail00gart. Accessed 2 December 2024.

Haggar, A. (1990) *Pattern Cutting for Lingerie, Beachwear and Leisurewear*. London: BSP Professional Books.

Hanssen, E. F. (2009) 'Symptoms of Desire: Colour, Costume, and Commodities in Fashion Newsreels of the 1910s and 1920s', *Film History: An International Journal*, 21(2): 107–21.

Head, C. (1983) *Old Sewing Machines*. Princes Risborough: Shire Publications.

Holding, T. H. (2018) *Ladies' Cutting Made Easy*. Franklin Classics Trade Press.

Holford, M. (1983) 'Dress and Society in Upper Canada, 1791–1841', *Costume* (The Costume Society), 17(1): 78–88.

Howell, M. J. (1845) *The Hand-Book of Dress-Making*. Available at https://archive.org/details/TheHandBookOfDressMaking. Accessed 2 December 2024.

Hunnisett, J. (1991) *Period Costume for Stage & Screen: Patterns for Women's Dress 1800–1909*. Studio City: Players Press.

Kidwell, C. B. (1979) *Cutting a Fashionable Fit: Dressmakers' Drafting Systems in the United States*. Washington: Smithsonian Institution Press.

Kidwell, C. B. and Christman, M. C. (1974) *Suiting Everyone: The Democratization of Clothing in America*. Washington: Smithsonian Institution Press.

Kingston Chronicle & Gazette (1834) 'The Subscriber Has For Sale', 3 February, p. 3, col. 3.

MacKay, M. E. (2004) 'Three Thousand Stitches: The Development of the Clothing Industry in Nineteenth-Century Halifax', in A. Palmer (ed.) *Fashion: A Canadian Perspective*, 166–82. Toronto: University of Toronto Press.

MacKay, M. E. (2007) *Beyond the Silhouette: Fashion and the Women of Historic Kingston*. Kingston: Queen's University.

MacKay, M. E. (2012) 'Through the Lens of Fashion: An Analysis of the Clothing of Women in Early Victorian Ontario', Master's Thesis. Toronto: Toronto Metropolitan University.

Mida, I. (2020) *Reading Fashion in Art*. London: Bloomsbury.

Mida, I. and Kim, A. (2015) *The Dress Detective: A Practical Guide to Object-based Research in Fashion*. London: Bloomsbury.

Palmer, A. (ed.) (2004) *Fashion: A Canadian Perspective*. Toronto: University of Toronto Press.

Parsons, J. L. (2018) 'The Shirtwaist: Changing the Commerce of Fashion', *Fashion, Style & Popular Culture*, 5(1): 7–23.

Schmiechen, J. A. (1984) *Sweated Industries and Sweated Labor: The London Clothing Trades, 1860–1914*. Chicago: University of Illinois Press.

Seligman, K. L. (2003) 'Dressmakers' Patterns: The English Commercial Paper Pattern Industry, 1878–1950', *Costume*, 37(1): 95–113.

Sykas, P. (2014) 'Investigative Methodologies: Understanding the Fabric of Fashion', in S. Black, A. de la Haye, J. Entwhistle, R. Root et al. (eds) *The Handbook of Fashion Studies*. London: Bloomsbury, 236.

The Delineator: A Journal of Fashion Culture and Fine Arts (1890), 36(4). https://archive.org/details/ybxc6wq23g0c/page/n63/mode/2up?view=theater.

The Delineator: A Journal of Fashion Culture and Fine Arts (1895) April, 13. https://reader.library.cornell.edu/docviewer/digital?id=hearth1891092_45_4#page/13/mode/1up.

Thornton, J. P. (1901) *The Sectional System of Ladies' Garment Cutting Comprising Bodies, Jackets, Ulsters, Skirts, Habits, Etc*. London: Thornton Institute.

Urquhart, J. W. (1881) *Sewing Machinery, Being a Practical Manual of the Sewing Machine …* . London: Crosby Lockwood, 17, 18.

Vettese-Foster, S. and Christie, R. M. (2013) 'The Significance of the Introduction of Synthetic Dyes in the Mid 19th Century on the Democratisation of Western Fashion', *Journal of the International Colour Association*, 11: 1–17.

Walker, G. (1835) *The Art of Cutting Ladies' Riding Habits, Pelisses, Gowns, Frocks, &c. Fifth Edition*. Available at https://books.google.com.

Waugh, N. (1968) *The Cut of Women's Clothes 1600–1930*. New York: Routledge.

Wilson, E. (1985) *Adorned in Dreams: Fashion and Modernity*. Oakland: University of California Press.

INDEX

Ackermann's Repository of the Arts 64
Allen B. Wilson 140
Altman & Co. 183
aniline dye 119–20, 137
apex 2, 12, 42, 52, 70, 87–8, 95–6, 105–6, 124, 166
armhole 13, 16–17, 24, 26, 27, 30, 33, 43, 49, 122, 161, 162, 163, 176, 196
Art Nouveau 185

balance points 21, 124, 143, 196
basque 3, 105
    see also peplum
Batt, Zelicia 83
Baumgarten, Linda 48
Bayne's Paris Scale 161
bias 64, 65, 67
    double-folder 121–2
    flounce 140, 202
    puff 140
    straight-of-grain movement 43
    trim 121
blending 3
    waist 51, 52, 69
    neckline 56, 57, 76, 77
block pattern measurements 6
Bloomingdales 183
bobbin lace 162
bobbin winder 140

bodice
    fan-shaped 114
    jigsaw puzzled 200
    modern basic 6–8
box pleats 44, 103, 109, 110, 115, 155, 162, 165, 172
bust point–bust point 7, 12
bust shape 2
bustle 173–4
    draping 174, 204
Butterick 120, 121
Butterick, Ebenezer 120–1
    Delineator, The 121
buttons 176
    crochet 140
    embroidered 47, 49
    half ball-shaped 121
    hand-worked 139
    machine made 140
    metal 162
    plum pudding 103

cage crinoline 102
cartridge pleats 3, 44, 92, 97, 103, 109, 122, 128
changeable silk 119
circle skirt 4
Clayton & Sons Tailors & Clothiers 159
closing the dart 51, 52, 69
collar band 97, 107, 111
collarettes 185

collars 168, 204
    detachable 184
    flat 146, 147
    primary 127
    soft ruffle 148
    stand 121, 140, 147
Cory, Mrs: *Art of Dressmaking, containing Plain Directions in Simple Language from the Fitting of the Pattern to the Finish of the Dress, The* 84
Costume Parisien 64
Cox & Minton 121
crinoline 101, 102, 109, 203
cross-grain 4
Cutter-Up, The 184
cutting and spreading (slashing and spreading) 3–4, 56, 57, 58, 76, 108, 129, 134, 149

Daguerre, Louis 102
dart transfer 4, 17, 52, 70, 87, 89, 166
darts
    closing 51, 52, 69
    drafting method 15
    fitting 16, 17, 64, 84
    folding method 15
    pivoting 5, 96, 178
    placement 11–14, 40, 121, 186
    shaping 1–2, 9, 15, 37, 38, 39
    terminology 4, 5

Delineator, The 121, 184–5, 195
Dickens, Charles 120
draft, defined 4
draping 84, 110, 111
    bustle 174, 204
    skirt 93
dressmakers 34, 48, 63, 64, 80, 83, 84, 114, 121, 127, 140, 160, 180, 184, 185

ease 7, 14, 17, 34, 42
    excess removal 67, 86, 104, 123, 141, 163, 187
engageante 108
Etherington, Agnes 47

fan-shaped bodice 114
feed dogs 140
flared skirt 4

gathering 4, 44, 49, 56, 76, 92, 139–40, 177
Gibson Girl 184
Gibson, Charles Dana 184
gigot sleeves 102
Godey's Lady's Book 84
Gordon, Mrs Eliza 119

half and half sleeve, *see* modern two-piece sleeve block
hem measurement 44
historical one-piece sleeve block 27–30
    completion 30
    frame 29
    instructions 28–30
    measurements 27–8
    sleeve divisions and arm shaping 29
    sleeve head shaping 30
historical two-piece sleeve block
    completion 33
    instructions 31–3
    modifying sleeve cap 32
    sleeve head shaping 32–3
Holding, T.H. 196

hourglass shape 63, 70, 71, 102, 103, 114
Howe, Elias 139
Hunnisett, Jean 109

jigsaw puzzled bodice pattern 200

Kingston Russel, Elizabeth 48
knife pleats 44, 47, 49, 53, 60, 97, 103, 109, 110, 115, 122

La Belle Assemblé 64
La Mode 176
Ladies' Cutting Made Easy 196
Ladies' Pocket Magazine, The 84
Lady, A: *Workwoman's Guide, The* 64, 65
Lady's Magazine, The 84
Lady's World of Fashion, The 84
Lorde & Taylor 183

mancheron 116
master pattern 4
Mauvine 120
McDowell, Albert 160, 162
McDowell School of Fashion Design 162
measurements
    accuracy of 2–3
    block pattern 6
    bodice block 7
    historical one-piece sleeve block 27
    horizontal 7
    modern one-piece sleeve block 17
    modern two-piece sleeve block 22
    straight skirt block 34
    vertical 7
measurement sheet 206
Millet, R.C. 102
mock-up, *see* toile
modern basic bodice block 7–8
    back body 11
    back horizontal lines 10

cutting out pattern 14
draft frame 9
finessing the pattern 14
fitting 16
front body 12
measurement chart 7
pattern 104
shaping side seam below waist 14
side seam and armhole 13
sleeve introduction 16–17
waist reduction and shaping with darts 14
modern one-piece sleeve block 17–18
    completion 21
    measurements for 17
    sleeve divisions and arm shaping 20
    sleeve frame 19
    sleeve head shaping 21
modern two-piece sleeve block 22–3
    completion 26
    measurements 22
    sleeve divisions 24
    sleeve frame 24
    sleeve head shaping 25
    wrist and arm shaping 25
Mowat, Helen 63. 64
Mowat, John B. 63

Niépce, Joseph 102
notches 4, 21, 26, 30, 33, 38, 91, 95, 96, 121, 151, 168, 190

organ pleats, *see* cartridge pleats
overskirt, pleated 172–3
oversleeve 78–9

Pagoda sleeves 103, 108
panel skirt 4, 127, 128, 132, 134, 148, 149, 153, 179, 191–4
pattern, defined 4
pattern making
    (1800–15) 50
    (1820–35) 63–5

(1840–49) 83–5
(1850–59) 101–3
(1860–69) 119
(1870–79) 139–40
(1880–89) 159–62
(1890–1900) 183–5
pattern making instructions
  alternative drafting
    (1800–15) 56–60
    (1820–35) 76–9
    (1840–49) 95–7
    (1850–59) 114–16
    (1870–79) 153–6
    (1880–89) 176–9
    (1890–1900) 196–9
  primary drafting
    (1800–15) 50–5
    (1820–35) 67–75
    (1840–49) 86–94
    (1850–59) 104–11
    (1860–69) 123–33
    (1870–79) 141–51
    (1880–89) 163–74
    (1890–1900) 186–95
peplum 5, 105, 106, 145
Perkins, William Henry 119–20
Peterson's Magazine 84
photography 41, 44, 102–3, 203
pin-to-the-form 64, 84, 114
pivoting the dart 5, 96, 178
pleats 5
  box 44, 103, 109, 110, 115, 155, 162, 165, 172
  calculation 110, 172
  overskirt 172–3
  cartridge (organ) 3, 44, 60, 92, 97, 103, 109, 122, 128
  knife 44, 47, 49, 53, 60, 97, 103, 109, 110, 115, 122
plum pudding buttons 103
Princess line 176, 177, 178, 179
Princess seam 94, 176

recycling 48
Rothwell, Hugh Cope 83
ruffle 74

selvage 4, 5, 109
sewing machine, 117, 156, 159
  development 101, 139–40, 161
  lock stitch machine 139–40
  relative value 83, 101, 102, 139
  Singer's Perpendicular Action Sewing Machine 140
silhouette 2, 34, 42, 48, 63, 85, 101, 102, 103, 114, 127, 133, 153, 159, 160, 164, 173, 176
Singer, Isaac 140
skirt
  basic pattern 74, 79, 92, 109, 127
  circle 4
  elliptical hoop 134–7
  flared 4
  panel 4, 127, 128, 132, 134, 148, 149, 153, 179, 191–4
  straight 34
  volume 109, 128, 174.
slashing and spreading, *see* cutting and spreading
sleeve body 116
sleeve cap 5, 20, 24, 25, 27, 59, 85, 115–16
  historical 29, 30, 32, 33
  measuring 126
  modifying 32
sleeve cuff 79
sleeve head 5, 21, 25, 26, 27, 30, 32–3, 53, 59, 73, 79, 90–1, 108, 115–16, 127, 190, 196, 197, 199
sleeves
  bell 85, 114, 115
  beret 78
  cap 91
  compound 78–9
  cowl 197
  elbow-length 198
  engageante 108
  gigot 102

  long 72
  mancheron 114, 115, 116
  pagoda 103, 108
  puff 73, 74
sloper 1, 5
standard skirt block 39
straight of grain 5, 20, 29, 43, 51, 53, 68, 72, 73, 74, 95, 127, 131, 137, 151, 154, 156, 170, 171, 194
straight skirt block 34–8, 39, 128, 149, 169

Tailor & Cutter, The 101
Talbot, W. Henry Fox 102
Thomson, W. S. and C. H., Skirt Factory 102, 103
toile (mock-up) 4, 5, 16, 17, 44, 73, 89, 93, 200–5
topsleeve 190
tracing 5
truing up 5, 38, 51, 69

undersleeve 108, 190
United Empire Loyalists 47
Urquart, John W. 101

Van Dyke, Sir Anthony 65
vandy-king 65, 74, 75, 79, 202
Vionnet, Madeleine 43
volume estimation 3, 44, 60, 73, 74, 78, 92, 148, 169, 200, 201, 203, 205

waist pleat underside formula 172–3
waist reduction 5
Walker, George: *Tailor's Masterpiece, The* 64, 65
Wanzer, Richard 140
Wheeler and Wilson Manufacturing Company 140
Whitney, Eli 48
Wilson, Newton 140
World of Fashion and Continental Feuilletons, The 84

FIGURE CREDITS

1.1 Rack of dresses. Agnes Etherington Art Centre, Queen's University, Kingston, Ontario, Canada xii

2.1 Unknown Maker, Wedding Dress, 1872–76, silk taffeta and satin. Agnes Etherington Art Centre, Queen's University, Kingston. Gift to Queen's Drama Club from an unknown donor, before 1948 (C48-471.1a-c). Photo: Paul Litherland 40

3.1 Unknown Maker, Day Dress, *c.* 1795 and reconstructed *c.* 1815, silk. Agnes Etherington Art Centre, Queen's University, Kingston, Ontario, Canada. Gift of Kathleen M. Richardson, 1988 (C91-719.01). Photo: Paul Litherland 46

3.2 Unknown Maker, Day Dress, *c.* 1795 and reconstructed *c.* 1815, silk. Agnes Etherington Art Centre, Queen's University, Kingston. Gift of Kathleen M. Richardson, 1988 (C91-719.01). Photo: Paul Litherland 46

3.13 Un justificatif supplémentaire est à envoyer au musée. Photo © RMN-Grand Palais (musée des châteaux de Malmaison et de Bois-Préau)/Gérard Blot 06-514575 1806 54

3.14 © Museum of London 55

4.1 Unknown Maker, Day Dress, *c.* 1825, lawn and cotton. Agnes Etherington Art Centre, Queen's University, Kingston. Gift of the Macdonald Family, 1948 (C48-469.1). Photo: Paul Litherland 62

4.2 Unknown Maker, Day Dress, *c.* 1825, lawn and cotton. Agnes Etherington Art Centre, Queen's University, Kingston. Gift of the Macdonald Family, 1948 (C48-469.1). Photo: Paul Litherland 62

4.3 *The Book of Trades*, 23 October 1804: Ladies Dress Maker. Rijksmuseum, Amsterdam 64

4.4 Walker, G. Detail of Plate 18, *The Art of Cutting Ladies' Riding Habits, Pelisses, Gowns, Frocks, & c.* Fifth Edition. London: Google Books 65

4.5 A Lady ed., Creative Media Partners. www.google.ca/books/edition/The_Workwoman_s_Guide/7I67wgEACAAJ?hl=en A Lady (1986) *The Workwoman's Guide by A Lady: A Guide to 19th Century Decorative Arts, Fashion and Practical Crafts.* Boston: Opus Publications 66

4.22 Mode de Paris 1828, The Metropolitan Museum of Art, Women 1827–29, Plate 047, public domain 75

5.1 Unknown Maker, Wedding Dress, 1848–52, silk taffeta. Agnes Etherington Art Centre, Queen's University, Kingston. Gift of Frederica Burna, 1948 (C48-470.1). Photo: Paul Litherland 82

5.2 Unknown Maker, Wedding Dress, 1848–52, silk taffeta. Agnes Etherington Art Centre, Queen's University, Kingston. Gift of Frederica Burna, 1948 (C48-470.1). Photo: Paul Litherland 82

5.3 *Petit Courrier des Dames*, 20 April 1846 84

5.4 M. J. Howell (1845) *The Hand-Book of Dress-Making*, Plate 3, https://archive.org/details/TheHandBookOfDressMaking 85

5.20 Mode de Paris 1828, The Metropolitan Museum of Art, Women 1827–29, Plate 047, Public Domain 94

6.1 Unknown Maker, Day Dress, 1857–59, silk. Agnes Etherington Art Centre, Queen's University, Kingston. Gift of Reginald Garrett, 1973 (C73-622.14a-b). Photo: Paul Litherland 100

6.2 Unknown Maker, Day Dress, 1857–59, silk. Agnes Etherington Art Centre, Queen's University, Kingston. Gift of Reginald Garrett, 1973 (C73-622.14a-b). Photo: Paul Litherland 100

6.3 Library of Congress Prints and Photographs Division, Washington, D.C. 20540 USA, https:hdl.loc.gov/loc.pnp/pp.print 103

6.19 Courtesy of the Louisiana State Museum, Gift of the Fashion Group of New Orleans, 1967.059.151 112

6.20 'Le Bon Ton', *Journal de modes*, February, 1859. Plate Number, v. 40, plate 51, https://tessa2.lapl.org/digital/collection/fashion/id/4304/rec/11 113

7.1 Unknown Maker, Day Dress, 1869, silk, satin, boning, and cotton. Agnes Etherington Art Centre, Queen's University, Kingston. Gift of the estate of Wilhelmina Gordon, 1968 (C68-590.14a-e). Photo: Bernard Clark 118

7.2 Unknown Maker, Day Dress, 1869, silk, satin, boning, and cotton. Agnes Etherington Art Centre, Queen's University, Kingston. Gift of the estate of Wilhelmina Gordon, 1968 (C68-590.14a-e). Photo: Bernard Clark 118

7.3 Silk swatch dyed in mauvine. Division of Home and Community Life, National Museum of American History, Smithsonian Institution. File/Slide N0: RWS2015-06374 id number CH318499 NMAH/H&C, https://americanhistory.si.edu/collections/search/object/nmah_2344 120

7.4 American Dress Chart, Front of Lady's Dress, *c.* 1868 [Danville, Indiana: publisher not transcribed]. Photograph. http://loc.gov/item/2018695346/. Cox and Minton graded bodice hybrid system 121

7.25 Metropolitan Museum of Art Digital Collections, https://libmma.contentdm.oclc.org/digital/collection/p15324coll12/id/5165/rec/82 133

8.1 Unknown Maker, Wedding Dress, 1872–76, silk taffeta and satin. Agnes Etherington Art Centre, Queen's University, Kingston. Gift to Queen's Drama Club from an unknown donor,

	before 1948 (C48-471.1a-c). Photo: Paul Litherland 138	10.25	*Delineator*, April 1895, www.historymuseum.ca/confederationdress/include/modalDelineator.php?lang=en&section=womens_wear&code=16 196
8.2	Unknown Maker, Wedding Dress, 1872–76, silk taffeta and satin. Agnes Etherington Art Centre, Queen's University, Kingston. Gift to Queen's Drama Club from an unknown donor, before 1948 (C48-471.1a-c). Photo: Paul Litherland 138	C1–C12	© M. Elaine MacKay, Photos: Jessie Redmond 201–5
8.18	*Journal Des Demoiselles*, 1875, Courtesy of the Libraries of Metropolitan Museum of Art, b17509853. Women 1875-1876, Plate 046 152		Measurements Designer: Hannah McDonald 206
9.1	Image courtesy of Toronto and Region Conservation Authority. Photo: Leslie Cook 158		
9.2	Image courtesy of Toronto and Region Conservation Authority. Photo: Leslie Cook 158		
9.3	Private collection of author 160		
9.4	Bayne, J. Reid, 1883, *Bayne's self-instruction book for dress cutting by the French-glove system*, Library of Congress 4 161		
9.19	Public domain, https://commons.wikimedia.org/wiki/File:Fashion_Plate_1880_Outdoors.jpg 175		
10.1	Courtesy of The Fashion History Museum, Cambridge, Ontario, Founder's Collection FC345 182		
10.2	Courtesy of The Fashion History Museum, Cambridge, Ontario, Founder's Collection FC345 182		
10.24	*Delineator*, April 1895, page 13, Canadian History Museum 195